DATING IN ARCHAEOLOGY

DATING
IN
ARCHAEOLOGY

A Guide to Scientific Techniques

Stuart Fleming

J. M. DENT & SONS LTD   LONDON

Made in Great Britain
for
J. M. DENT & SONS LTD
Aldine House, Albemarle Street, London

This book is set in 11 on 12 pt. Old Style No. 2

ISBN 0 460 04241 6

Contents

List of Figures

List of Plates

9.3 Fossil post-cranial bones of Galley Hill man, found in the Swanscombe Gravels in 1888

9.4 The Piltdown Skull, *Eoanthropus Dawsoni*

10.1 *Jesus in the midst of the Scribes*, attributed to the Antwerp master (c. 1510)

10.2 Macedonian silver tetrabols of the fifth millennium BC

10.3 X-ray fluorescence equipment designed in the 'non-dispersive' mode, known as the Isoprobe

10.4 The fall in fineness of Merovingian gold coinage during the century AD 580–680, in the Provençal mints

10.5a Jewelled bracteate set with garnets and blue glass and filigree of beaded wire with pseudo-plaitwork
   b Jewelled composite brooch with bronze cell walls and a gilt bronze rim

A.1 Fossil pollen remains:
   a. Hazel
   b. Oak
   c. Elm
   d. Common Bent

A.2 Important index species of land and freshwater mollusca:
   a. *Pupilla muscorum*
   b. *Cochlicopa*
   c. *Carychium tridentata*
   d. *Vallonia costata* and *Vallonia excentrica*

A.3 Foraminifera collected in plankton tows in the isothermal layer of the Indian Ocean:
   a. *Globigerinoides ruber*
   b. *Globigerinoides sacculifer*
   c. *Pulleniatina Obliquiloculata*

B.1 *The Penelli Sarcophagus*, in the Etruscan style

B.2 *Crowned Buddha*, seated with his hands in Dhyanamudra (Khmer, c. twelfth century AD)

TABLES

Abbreviations

EM = Early Minoan
MM = Middle Minoan
EH = Early Helladic
EB = Early Bronze

Preface

Scientific studies in archaeology now cover such a wide spectrum of techniques that, even excluding the *where?*, *how?* and *why?* in the background of an artefact's manufacture, there is still plenty to be said about *when?* The age of an archaeological object seems to hold the greatest fascination amongst these queries (though *why?* for Stonehenge and pyramid building must be high-ranking exceptions), perhaps because the sheer scale of man's past helps us to adjust to the reality of our own lifespan. However, that is a question for a philosopher to answer rather than me. As a scientist I have sought to direct the general reader's attention to the pith of each dating technique and then make him aware of the complications and limitations researchers in each field have encountered. Beyond general dating applications the publishers have allowed me a personal indulgence: to highlight some particularly fine case histories that have impressed me in their coherence of research and ingenuity. Still top of my list is the UCLA radiocarbon analysis for fossil sabre-tooth tiger bones from the Rancho La Brea seepage pits, despite their thorough tar impregnation.

I have paid particular attention to the bibliography, adding a special list to try and keep the text as up to date as possible. However, I am very conscious of how rapidly archaeological chronology is developing. Nowhere is this more true than in the definition of directions of past hominid evolution. At this very time fresh fossil finds at Laetolil (Tanzania) and Afar (Ethiopia) are laying the basis of a *Homo* lineage dating back four million years. Such antiquity for our origins, if confirmed, is capable of turning the conventional notions I describe in this book quite topsy-turvy in the coming decade. Only time will tell.

I cannot attempt to list all those who, through their generosity in supplying illustrative material, have given this book its breadth of coverage. I have only specially mentioned those who patiently responded to my battery of questions as I came to closer and closer grips with the task: Professor G. W. Dimbleby, Dr J. G. Evans, Professor R. L. Fleischer, Dr B. Grauert, Dr V. Giertz, Professor S. Hood, Dr C. M. Kraay, Dr P. R. S. Moorey, Dr K. P. Oakley and Professor M. Suzuki. I only hope the end-product does justice to their efforts.

May, 1976   STUART FLEMING

Chapter 1

Aspects of Archaeological Chronology

1 INTRODUCTION

The history of archaeological method as we understand it today is less than a century old. Site excavation around the Mediterranean earlier in the nineteenth century tended to resemble treasure hunts, particularly the stripping of Etruscan and Greek necropoli. Though the 'finds' were awe-inspiring (like Schliemann's gold Agamemnon death-mask), those artefacts that now tell us so much about the quality of life of ancient peoples, such as pottery sherds, bone fragments and vegetable remains, were largely discarded. Gradually, however, the number and quality of excavation reports increased, albeit with presumptive interpretations of low statistical merit and ignoring external evidence. Perhaps the major change of attitude was the appreciation that each civilization did not stand *in vacuo* either in everyday life or in its highly prized art works. Trade links and transmission of technology, even at an elementary level, fostered 'stylistic influences' while broader concepts like the Copper, Bronze and Iron ages and the Neolithic era gained meaning across continents.

Systematic attempts to construct links between early civilizations began with the work of Oskar Montelius in 1903, whose typological method sought to define tool and weapon development in one area and then compare that sequence with those of surrounding regions. Gradually, like a spider's web, the linkages spread out across Europe, Mesopotamia and Egypt, following a principle of 'diffusionism' whereby those regions most remote from the web's centre learnt of innovations only some centuries after their conception. At the heart of this system lay the genius of the Near East which had long been recognized in the hieroglyphic scripts of Egypt (first unravelled by Champollion in 1822) and in the Mesopotamian cuneiform writings deciphered around 1850. Some extreme diffusionist scholars, notably Grafton Smith in the 1920s, envisaged Egyptian influences on a world-wide scale, with 'civilization' being exported to South America in papyrus crafts.

In contrast, several authors of that period created an impression of multiple discoveries and advances simultaneously in many areas, though many of these notions owed as much to ultranationalism as to evidence of reliable chronology. But, in compromise, 1925 saw the publication of Gordon Childe's *The Dawn of European Civilization* which offered two routes of chronological linkage between the Near East and Europe. First, by colonization, traders from the Aegean carried knowledge of their metallurgical skill to Iberia. Strong similarities in funeral customs are clear in the early Minoan tombs in the Mesara Plain of Crete and the late Neolithic tombs of Spain. Second, by similar trading, the Balkan dwellers learnt of new skills and changes in religion via the Danube waterways. Of course this was also the time of fresh stimulus in Egyptology with Howard Carter's meticulous recording of the intact Tutankhamun tomb, carried out in the face of heavy pressures to bring forth all the treasures post-haste for the public to see.

For sheer foresight, Childe's book still stands as a remarkably accurate account of this cultural-linkage mechanism, though now much expanded in time scale and detail in books like *Ancient Europe* by Stuart Piggott,[1] and Childe himself in several later publications.[2] Only recently has the direction of linkage build up been questioned and much stronger evidence been presented for some independent invention in various parts of Europe (see Chapter 3.1*h*).[3]

Though our views of man's past must now have global horizons, the pattern of archaeological logic and interpretation has not changed over the past few decades. However, many new parameters besides artefact linkage are looked at in much greater detail and a large number of them relate to climate. The modification of man's life-style that poor weather can cause has long been recognized: the axeing of good farming land by rising shorelines,[4] the transformation of forests into rotting marshland[5] and a shortening of the crop-growing season are just a few examples. Fossil remains of foodstuffs [6] may reflect adaptation of farmers to new local conditions or to new contacts with their counterparts in neighbouring lands.

Two of the more important climate-related indicators of chronology, analysis of pollen distribution [7] and oxygen isotope ratio analysis,[8] are discussed only in Appendix A, as the main theme of this book is the direct methods of age determination. The notion of varve chronology [9] is also set aside in Appendix A as its major value lies in supplying an absolute time scale for many horizons of pollen distribution change. Some consideration is also given to dating information that can occasionally be gleaned from insect [10] and mollusca [11] remains in burial contexts.

2 CONTEXT STRATIGRAPHY TO ABSOLUTE DATING

To return to the archaeologist's viewpoint of chronology we must consider first the fundamental unit of context stratigraphy, i.e. the steady build up, layer by layer, of soil that carries in it the artefacts (often no more than debris) of the current site occupants. Layer super-position immediately provides a localized relative chronology and a progressive one unless some portions of the vertical sequence have been artificially removed. The cutting of rubbish pits, new house foundations and irrigation trenches can create major upheavals in the general context pattern. Nevertheless, a series of trenches linked together by their artefacts (or by soil type and small flora and fauna content in many instances) usually serves to indicate a general ground plan for each period of occupation and anomalies can be pinpointed and taken into account. (For example, the Tartara tablets, once a corner-stone of dating, are now recognized as misattributed.)

Then the pattern of artefact distribution for one site can be matched to a neighbouring one and eventually a complete regional picture emerges. For recent archaeology this distribution is often expressed in terms of pottery and metal-work style development, but in the more distant past (amongst fossil hominid sites, for example) evolutionary features of fauna are diagnostic.

The next step, region-to-region linkage, is a major one as it usually involves some assumptions about artefact or 'fashion' importation. Regional relative chronologies become tied together by equations like 'Troy building phase II b' = 'Phaistos Palace (Crete) level, Middle Minoan II A', which simplifies to Troy II b = MM II A. (In this example the import is a fashionable seal motif—Fig. 1.1a-d.)

The final stage is to translate all these ties into an absolute chronology and here we must look to some of the few historical docu-ments that offer us fixed dating points in the past. For example, we may suggest a date of c. 1850 BC for Troy II b on the basis of a similarly decorated seal found there and in the tomb of Sesostris III who reigned in Egypt between 1887 and 1850 BC.

This process of final date attribution is only applicable over the past 5,000 years within the eastern Mediterranean region, as the next section attempts to illustrate. It is worth noting here how very limited such a chronological web is within the overall framework of man's development with which later chapters deal. In time, our interest ranges back to the first evidence of hominoids from which we are derived, *Aegyptopithecus zeuxis* (Plate 4.1), of some twenty-eight million years antiquity. In space, our interest is worldwide and seeks to encompass many large regions of sub-Saharan Africa and South-East Asia that carry no more than tentative conventional dating until the past few centuries. It is the huge gaps in documentary knowledge of our past that supply the breeding ground for scientific chronological research.

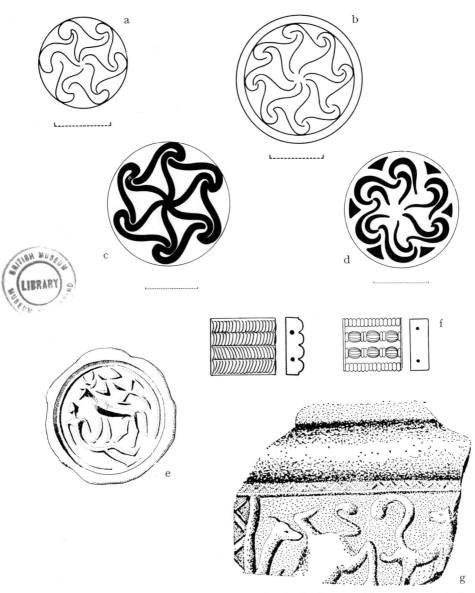

Fig. 1.1   a. Seal impression from Troy, level iib. Comparable motifs are to be found on Egyptian seals produced in the reign of Sesostris iii (1887–1850 BC) (impression b), on Cretan seals from Phaistos from a deposit of the first Palace there (phase MM iiA) (impression c) and at the central Anatolian site of Karahöyuk (level i) (impression d). (Marked scale all equal to one centimetre.) e. Line drawing of an Egyptian glazed steatite seal (Dynasty v) found at Tarsus (Turkey) in late EB ii levels. f. Line drawing of two types of faience bead found at Nuzi in Iraq. g. Impressed plaque from Tordos on the Danube tributary, the Maros (H. 75 mm). (Material drawn from references 14, 16, 26 and 27.)

Some of the hazards of 'single artefact' chronology should also be noted. An Iron Age farmer might well transfer some soil containing a Stone Age microlithic obsidian tool and dig it in with contemporary debris amongst his crops. Heirlooms can appear in contexts that date well after their time of manufacture and treasured goods may be totally out of place. Surely the most salutory illustration of this latter point is the Silurian trilobite fossil, more than 400 million years old, carried by Stone Age man from its natural source only to find a new resting place in a grotto at Arcy-sur-Cure, in France.

3   AN OUTLINE OF MEDITERRANEAN CHRONOLOGY (c. 3000–1500 BC)

Conventional archaeological dating principles are best illustrated by the way in which a 'web' can be constructed around the Egyptian Dynastic records that cover the period 3100 to 1100 BC (Fig. 1.2). The mainspring amongst these records is the so-called 'civil calendar' which was used for administrative and economic purposes, with a supplement that noted the passage of time within a king's reign.[12] Fortunately, the Roman writer Censorinus noted a coincidence in AD 139 of the first day in the Egyptian calendar and the day upon which the 'dog-star', Sirius rose heliacally. This same astronomical event became displaced by about a single day in each of the Egyptian's 'Sothic' year so that the matching occurred only every 1,456 years. Thus a statement like 'Year 7 in the reign of King Sesostris III: Sirius rose heliacally on month 4 of winter, day 16' can be translated to 1872 BC. Indeed this is the earliest date provided by this means.

The extent of the later Dynasties XII–XX which concern us here can therefore be fixed with great precision.[13] For the earlier Dynasties the main resources available to us are the royal annals, which name the kings in order of succession and indicate their reign duration. Foremost amongst these is the Palermo Stone of Dynasty V, a fragment of a large slab bearing a matrix of inscribed compartments. Under the heading of each king, each year is noted in terms of an important event at that time, plus the height of the Nile at the year's beginning. This is the only major document that itself originates from the period under discussion. It is now ascribed a date of about 2400 BC.

However, a papyrus of Dynasty XIX (c. 1300 BC) known as the Turin Royal Canon, though fragmented, gives a complete kings' list of some 955 years covering Dynasties I–VIII in its surviving portions. Now the beginning of Dynasty XII can be fixed close to 1991 BC, that of Dynasty XI to 2134 BC. Dynasties XI and X were contemporaneous while Dynasty IX lasted no more than thirty years (i.e. back to 2164 BC). Thereafter the Turin Royal Canon's span carries us through to the beginning of Dynasty I (3119 BC) with little room for more than 100 years uncertainty.

Fig. 1.2 Stylistic and chronological links between Egypt, Crete and southern Greece during the second and third millennia BC (reference 13).

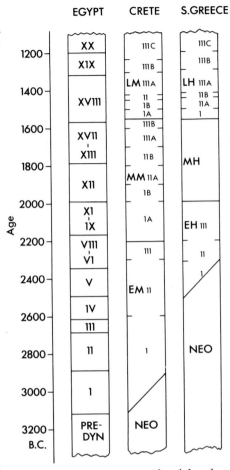

The web-threads out of Egypt are strong across to the island of Crete and onwards to the Greek mainland. The major artefact evidence, in imports, can be summarized as follows : [14]

(i) *Egypt to Crete*: Scarab from Dynasty XII excavated in the MM I B/MM II A transition levels of the Minoan Palace site of Knossos (Plate 1.1a).

Crete to Egypt: A characteristic MM II spouted jar found in a Dynasty XII tomb at Abydos in the lower Kingdom region of the Nile (Plate 1.1b). These links are further substantiated by finds of 'Kamares' ware pottery (MM I B/MM II A) at Kahun where the pyramid of Sesostris II (1906–1888 BC) is situated and by an ivory sphinx found at Mallia (further east along the Cretan coast than Knossos).

The final stages of the Neolithic phase at Knossos contained a fragment of an Egyptian stone vase which would date no earlier than Dynasty I. This gives a broad indication of the beginnings of the earliest Minoan phase (EM I) and serves to define the Cretan style changes through the third millennium BC (Fig. 1.2).

a

c

d

b

1.1   a. Egyptian scarab (Dynasty XII) excavated at Knossos (level MM I B–
MM II A) in Crete. (Reference number RR.58.378.) (Photograph: courtesy
of The British School at Athens.)
b. Cretan spouted jar (MM II style) found at Abydos in a Dynasty XII
Egyptian tomb. (Photograph: courtesy of the Ashmolean Museum, Oxford;
catalogue number. E.3295.)
c. Mesopotamian square seal from Kish. (Photograph: courtesy of the
Ashmolean Museum, Oxford; catalogue number 1931.119.)
d. Indus square seal from Harappa. (Photograph: courtesy of the Ashmolean Museum, Oxford; catalogue number 1956.1001.)

(ii) *Crete to southern Greece*: A goblet-shaped vessel that is character-istic of MM I A was excavated at Lerna in an early Helladic level, EH III. (c. 2050 BC) [15].

Southern Greece to Crete: EH III grey burnished bowl in MM I A levels of Knossos. There are several fashion links between Minoan and Helladic wares, notably the development of neat antisplash bowl rims and a decoration of red crosses that allows an equation, early EH II = EM II E (c. 2500 BC). The transition of Neolithic to EH phases remains ill-defined due to a paucity of wares surely attributable to the latter.

(iii) *Egypt to Anatolia*: A stamp seal of glazed steatite (Dynasty V) found in Early Bronze Age (late EB II) levels of Tarsus in the Cilicia region on the southern coast of Turkey (c. 2450 BC) [16] (Fig. 1.1e). Wooden cylinders were used extensively in the subsequent EB III phase to add decoration to Cilician pottery and over some 400 years this fashion spread into the Aegean to influence pottery styles, EH II and Troy I.

At this juncture Egyptian documentation can be supplemented by cuneiform writing from Mesopotamia.[17] For Sumer, to the south, a king list is preserved on a tablet known as the Weld-Blundell Prism (Ashmolean Museum, acc. 1923.444) that originates from the time of Sinmagir.[18] His reign is believed to lie in the nineteenth century BC and this document, supported by other fragmented similar finds, runs back to around 2900 BC. Unfortunately this very detailed chronology 'floats' in that there is no overlap with any other scripts of the second millennium BC. So we come forward, via an unspecified time gap, to a controversial time marker with the reign of Hammurabi who promulgated a law code that was to control trading activities in the region for many centuries to follow. The usual reign limits quoted are 1792–1750 BC, but an uncertainty of around seventy years has been mooted.

Part of the significance of Hammurabi's dating lies in its tie up to the contemporary ruler of Assyria to the north, Šamši-Adad I, who heads a fragmented record of kings of that region that brings us forward to around 1350 BC. The Babylonian record continues during this interval with some reliability, aided by some astronomical information such as The Venus Tablets of Ammizaduqa's reign (1646–1626 BC).[19] The First Dynasty ends shortly after, in 1595 BC.

Thereafter international correspondence between both these empires and those of the Hittites in Anatolia and the pharaohs of Egypt give the Assyrian king list a high dating precision well into the first millennium BC. After this the Assyrian calendar is marked by a list of 'limmus' (the name of an eponym drawn from an elite group of state administrators) which would be difficult to date but for the fact that some names also appear in the Babylonian calendar, which is still a reign list. Fortunately the latter was preserved in the writings of Theon of Alexandria (fourth century AD), linking his time to that of Nabonas-sar back in 747 BC in a detailed record of lunar eclipses.

Some early import links can be forged within this Mesopotamian chronology:

(iv) *Mesopotamia to Crete*: A First Dynasty cylinder seal from Babylon was excavated in a tholos tomb on the Mesara plains of Crete, at Platanos, and linked to pottery styles MM II A and MM II B at the Palace sites of Knossos and Phaistos.[20]
Platanos links to Egypt are in evidence with three scarabs, dating as early Dynasty XIII pieces, and to Syria through tanged daggers of around 1800 BC. The Babylonian seal probably dates to around 1850 BC.

(v) *Indus Valley to Mesopotamia*: A Babylonian tablet, probably from Ur, bears a mercantile agreement in its main text together with a well-preserved seal impression on one end.[21] The statement 'in the month Aiaru, the 20th day, the year Gungunum (of Larsa) brought the two great emblems into the temple of Nanna' provides an accurate date for the tablet of 1923 BC. The end decoration matches closely to a circular seal of a type commonly found on the Persian Gulf islands of Bahrein and Failaka.[22] The motif originates, however, in the Indus Valley (though the seals there are characteristically square) so that this Babylonian piece provides a vital time marker for the archaeology of that region.

This evidence also points to a primary trading route by sea on a scale quite competitive with the well-established overland routes by which lapis lazuli was carried from Badakhshan in Afghanistan to Tell Asmar on the Diyala tributary of the Tigris and thence to Kish, Nippur and Ur. The importance of the sea trade link has been underlined by recent excavations at Tepe Yahya in South-East Iran.[23]
Mesopotamia also provides another time marker for the Indus civilization, albeit rather less precisely, through the correspondence of seal decorations from the Kish area and from Harappa (Plates 1.1c, d) [24] and of etched cornelian beads found in the Royal Cemetery at Ur and those produced at Lothal, Harappa, Mohenjodaro and Chanhu-daro.[25] Textual evidence indicates that sea trade flourished around 2370 BC. Equation here of contexts Ur III to Lothal III would set a preliminary date for the Indus bead industry of 2350 BC, though similar finds in deeper contexts indicate the export market had been active for some 150 years before.

As the distance from Egypt and Mesopotamia is stretched, so the import evidence, though still available, becomes scarcer and tends to carry slightly greater margins of error in dating.

(vi) *The Balkans to southern Greece*: Imported flasks, burnished and incised or grooved with a decoration of spiral whirls, appear in early middle Helladic (MH) levels at Lerna (c. 1950 BC). They are thought to originate from Bubanj in southern Yugoslavia and fit into the so-called Vinca D period of the Balkans.

Amber beads from the Balkans are to be found in the Late Helladic shaft graves of Mycenae (LH I, LH II A) as are *nuzi* faience beads of northern Mesopotamian origin (c. 1550–1500 BC) [26] (Fig. 1.1f).

(vii) *Egypt to Britain*: Faience beads, particularly of the 'segmented' type, are found in the Middle Bronze Age contexts in Britain. In Egypt these beads date to Dynasty XVIII/XIX, i.e. c. 1300 BC.

(viii) *Mesopotamia to Romania*: A clay plaque found at Tordos on the Danube tributary, Maros, bears an impression of a cylinder seal, possibly of the carved wood type described earlier, though from Byblos on the coast of Syria (Fig. 1.1g).[27] The origins of this kind of seal lie in Mesopotamia in the fertile lands bounded by the rivers, Euphrates and Tigris, controlled by the city of Ur around this time, c. 2400 BC.

4 IMPORTANT DATING LINKS OF THE PRE-CHRISTIAN ERA

The last section outlined the basic principle of artefact linkage in chronology building. After 1500 BC, examples quotable for this proliferate to an extent that is impracticable to detail here, but some deserve brief attention.

A long link is forged between the Aegean and south-east Jutland by a sword unearthed from a stone-covered board coffin which was the primary interment in a burial mound.[28] This allows early bronze development of northern Europe to be pinned to around 1400 BC.

On mainland Greece the beginning of the first millennium BC heralds a rather nebulous era, known in pottery terms as the Protogeometric period.[29] Details of the eventual Dorian invasion of Mycenaean territory are uncertain, yet subsequent Greek styles are quite in contrast to the Late Helladic wares of the previous culture. Isolated wares are to be found abroad, like the cup with pendent semicircles excavated at Tell Abu Hawam, Palestine, (c. 900 BC) and Late Attic material found in the destruction layers of Hama, Syria (c. 720 BC).

Then Greek colonization to the west is matched by the fresh availability of literary evidence, notably in the writings of Thucydides and Eusebius. The establishment of the port of Syracuse in eastern Sicily in AD 733 is recorded in this way. At the same time initial settlement on mainland Italy can be evidenced by a scarab with the cartouche of Bocchoris (who ruled Egypt between 718 and 712 BC) found in a grave at Ischia.

Movement to the east brings in Tarsus once more as a key site with pottery wares, stylistically termed Protocorinthian and East Greek 'Bird' bowls, found there in layers associated with the sacking of the city by Sennacherib in 696 BC.

Thereafter the Attic wares of 570–470 BC rely for their dating on the signatures on the vase decoration (either the potter or the artist, sometimes both),[30] while eventually the documentary evidence of the Classical period (fourth to fifth century BC) takes stronger hold and allows some very accurate dating of ceramics by their pictorial detail. For example, several 'Apulian' vessels show a Persian king under attack from a bearded Greek who could be identified as Alexander. These scenes must date to within a couple of years of 334 BC, before the vase painters became aware that Alexander had no beard.

Greek import wares at this stage provide us with one particularly important dating link, as they are found in abundance in necropoli of Etruria where a strangely sombre and mystical civilization is now known to have flourished from the seventh century BC onwards. Etruscan ancestry and script remain amongst archaeology's great unknowns, but at least from the fifth century BC onwards a reasonable chronicle of their life style can be made.

The post-1500 BC period also sees the emergence of the first concrete written records of China, in the form of inscribed oracle bones. Their so-called *chia ku wen* scripts were the principal records of divination during the Shang Dynasty and indeed much of the Chou Dynasty that followed.[31] Each would carry a series of three date identifying characters (aside from the main text) as follows: (i) a 'Sothic cycle' indicator where two characters define a specific sixty-year period, (ii) the current ruler's name and (iii) a number matching the year of reign.

The Chinese scholar, Tung Tso-pin, recently undertook the task of interpretation of the vast number of bones found at Anyang, the capital of the later Shang rulers, on the basis that two oracle bones sharing the same ruler's name but different Sothic cycle characters could be used to define the time sequence of those cycles.[32] Other features, like mention of a ruler's father already in the chronological chain, allowed the details within each sixty-year period to be completed. Thus the foundation of the Shang Dynasty by ruler T'ang could be fixed as 1766 BC, P'an-keng's move of capital to Anyang set at 1384 BC, and the overthrow of Ti-hsin by the invading Chou dated to 1111 BC.

Scripts on bronzes (marking possession or reason of offering) become an increasingly important source of dating evidence during the Chou Dynasty, but by the third century BC rigorous documentation on bamboo slips removes any need for any such indirect evidence and brings us into the Chinese historical era proper.

At this stage, and indeed for some centuries to follow, areas that were to yield mighty civilizations, like the Gupta Empire in India (fourth to sixth century AD), the Aztec rule of Mexico (thirteenth to fifteenth century AD) and the Benin Empire in Nigeria (c. fifteenth to seventeenth century AD), lie dormant in our chronologial record. These regions are as much at the focal point of scientific attention as the early phases of man's development considered below.

5. CONVENTIONAL TIME ZONES OF EARLIER TIMES

Clearly the construction of the chronological web from excavated material, as presented in skeletal form above, has demanded great ingenuity and skill on the part of many archaeologists. Yet it is reasonable to reiterate a point made earlier that this web is extremely limited in scope both in time and space when put within the perspective of the whole hominoid evolutionary period. The past 5,000 years admittedly represent a period of extremely rapid change in man's ways of thinking and living and would, on artefact abundance alone, deserve recognition as an eminent archaeological phase, but the singularly human character trait, a deep fascination in our phylogenic roots, has always made the understanding of much earlier times a challenge to the academic community.

The technical innovations of metal working and the contrast with earlier agricultural and stone-tool oriented cultures have provided an extremely convenient nomenclature for phase description: Late Neolithic (LN), Early Bronze Age (EB) and so forth. Naturally, transition times, like LN to EB, occur at quite different times in various parts of the world but this rarely creates confusion once accompanied by a slight descriptive expansion (e.g. 'Iron Age Britain'). For earlier times there is the problem of a surfeit of conventions of time division, a situation largely created by historical circumstances rather than necessity. Once it had been recognized by eighteenth-century geologists that some division of the world's history was necessary, dissension sprang up as to what features of change, such as glaciation, flora or fauna, were truly generalized enough to be regarded as definitive.[33]

Perhaps the least controversial division is the broadest one dividing geological time into 'eras' (so that we live in the 'Cainozoic') and then splitting up the present era into 'periods', Tertiary and Quaternary, with the boundary between these matching the appearance and intercontinental spread of the mammals, *Bos*, *Elephas* and *Equus*.[34] In 1837, Schimper recognized that further division was feasible on the basis of glaciation effects, thus defining the 'epochs' of interest here as Miocene, Pliocene, Pleistocene and Holocene in a cold-warm-cold-warm sequence. Then the Tertiary/Quaternary boundary is also that of the Pliocene/Pleistocene (Fig. 1.3).

Of the epochs the Holocene is most difficult to define or even to justify as really existing separately from the Pleistocene. It is argued (and arguable) that the most recent worldwide warming which transformed northern Europe from a tundra belt into a deciduous forest region is a stable recovery from glacial conditions, even though temperatures typical of today are no higher than earlier interglacial times around 70,000 years ago (See Fig. A.2, Appendix A.) The Pleistocene/Holocene boundary has been defined on pollen distribution changes which, in antiquity, denote the swift upsurge of bush ground coverage,

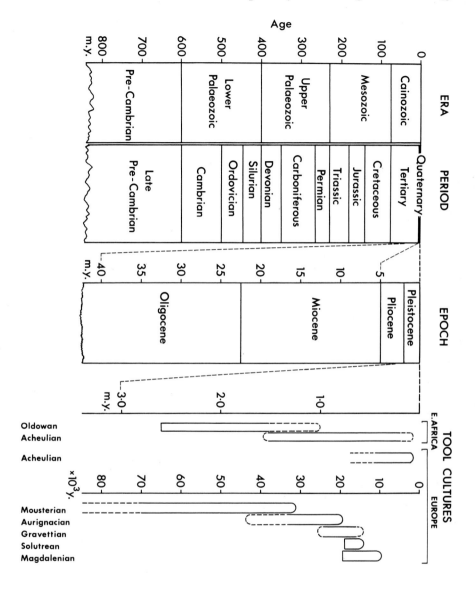

Fig. 1.3   Terminology of the geological and archaeological time scale, together
with that of the various tool cultures that developed in East Africa and
Europe during the past three million years. Time ranges when a
specific culture has been growing in importance or in decline are shown
in dashed extensions of the principal tool phase. The so-called 'Chellean'
culture in East Africa is now regarded as a developed form of the
Oldowan (c. 1·4–1·0 million years) and drawn here in the latter's range.

overcoming previous herbal control, particularly in the density of juniper shrub.[35] (We now believe that change occurred about 8300 BC.)

By far the most difficult convention to follow is that of the glacial/interglacial stratigraphy that has often been used to make further divisions in each epoch. The need for special nomenclature, like 'Weichselian', 'Hoxnian', etc., is understandable in that the reiterative nature of glacial advance and retreat allows ambiguity. However, the existence of three conventions for the Pleistocene, one each for Britain, Europe and North America (e.g. Ipswichian = Eemian = Sangamon), creates an undesirable complexity. Such terms are studiously avoided from this point onwards except in the climate discussion in Appendix A.

One interesting alternative means of Pleistocene subdivision lies in characterization of a site by its principal tool complexes, an aspect which appears to follow good sequentiality in time, albeit with regions of inevitable overlap. The Oldowan complex (which takes its name from the famous fossil locality of Olduvai Gorge where its earliest examples are known) is characterized by tools only crudely worked from pebbles gathered from local gravel. Each subsequent complex marks an advance in the ancient tool kit, starting with the evolution of the hand-axe and progressing to many types of implement for specialized purposes. The more common descriptive terms in European archaeology are given in Fig. 1.3 to key in the reader's sense of time when they occur in later sections and are more fully described as necessary. The lithic development in the American continent has also been studied in a similar manner.[36]

6 THE INVOLVEMENT OF SCIENTIFIC METHODS

Whatever scheme the archaeologist chooses, he must recognize that it offers only a relative chronology. The stage is then well set for the introduction of scientific dating methods which can unify the various classifications, whether climate- or artefact-related, into a scheme based solely on absolute age quotation.

To this end emphasis is laid on about a dozen concepts of material ageing, each with a portion of time scale over which it is most effective (Fig. 1.4). To avoid pre-empting the following scientific discussion the geological stratification derived in the last section has been matched to an age scale without lengthy comment here (Fig. 1.3). This matching latently underlines the remarkable rate of advance of science into archaeology. Very little of the scientific chronology is derived from research data more than two decades old, yet the case histories included in later discussion cover every continent (and even reach into ocean depths for some information) and span some thirty-five million years of the Earth's development, while extra inroads have been made in the realm of fine arts (see Chapter 10). It would be difficult to try and guess where this subject will be twenty years hence, but at least a mood of optimism is probably not misplaced.

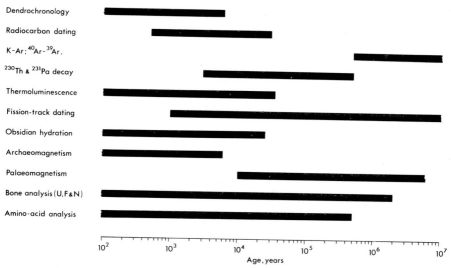

Fig. 1.4   Time range of application of the principal scientific dating techniques used in archaeological analysis.

The main techniques could well be supplemented in the future by other dating notions which, for reasons of brevity, can only be outlined and referenced here. For example, rock weathering is recognized as involving several time-dependent effects. The edge profile of a sandstone will be hyperbolic in outline with shape parameters that change with age.[37] Basalt will gain a weathering crust of distinctive colour with a thickness (d cm) that varies with time (t years) as:

$$d = a \, \mathrm{Log} \, (1 + bt)$$

Constants for Bohemian deposits have been reckoned as, $a = 0.46$ cm and $b = 10^{-5}$/year, offering a dating range of 500 to 10^7 years. Amongst young lavas features like change in acidity (measured as pH value) and elemental impurity composition seem to be time dependent.[38,39]

Ageing of parchment has been looked at in detail,[40] partly as a possible weapon against the document faker. Though the gross characteristics of the sheep (or goat) skin raw materials are very durable, their collagen fibres will degenerate slowly when exposed to water vapour, light and heat. An ancient document will have a low wet strength and be progressively more susceptible to shrinkage when exposed to heat the older the parchment is. This effect has been used to estimate the age of Dead Sea scroll fragments from Qumran to around the first century BC,[41] in the face of alternative claims that this material might even be of medieval origin.[42]

Finally, to wood, an appropriate material to discuss here as the following chapter is on dendrochronology. Recent advances in the

understanding of wood decay mechanisms have provided an explanation of a subtle cell-wall structure change with time.[43] The wall is
formed by deposition of water-soluble monomers which join together
to resist dissolution. Over centuries, however, some weaker bonds
break down and the so-called acetyl groups are leached out. At the
same time, acetyls provide some waterproofing to cell walls so that
their removal opens up the cross-linked lignin structure within. This
structure when treated in the laboratory with strong alkali solutions
yields up hemicellulose. By way of example, Florentine poplar
(*Populus nigra*) of fourteenth-century origin has been contrasted with
recent wood of the same species and gave a 45% lower yield of acetyl
content and a 30% higher yield of hemicellulose. Further, these changes
appear to have a linear time-dependence.

Whatever material an artefact is made of, one senses that one
structural feature will 'age' either through an intrinsic mechanism or
one environmentally controlled. The onus is on the scientist to identify
and evaluate that process and turn it to the advantage of present-day
man in understanding his past.

Chapter 2

Dendrochronology

1 BASIC DATING PRINCIPLES

1a INTRODUCTION

The science of dendrochronology was pioneered at the beginning of this century by A. E. Douglass, an astronomer by training, who set out to establish a correlation between the cyclic nature of sunspot activity and the magnitude of ring growth in trees.[1] Instead he recognized that these ring widths of timber in the semi-arid areas of Arizona and New Mexico were an accurate record of climatic variations of the past. As the pattern of width variations found in the pine construction-beams of the first site studied, Pueblo Bonito, was very distinctive and readily discernible at a host of other prehistoric sites in that region, many contemporary building phases could be cross-matched.[2]

This early work has been greatly extended with the establishment of the Laboratory of Tree-Ring Research at the University of Arizona. The catalogue of wood types now covered includes various pines (notably pondorosa, limber and bristlecone varieties), giant *sequoia*, fir, beech, juniper and sagebrush. The associated disciplines of dendroclimatology and dendroecology have already found several interesting applications such as the recognition of a twelve-year drought period, beginning in AD 1273, which may have contributed significantly to a fall in the prehistoric population in the Mesa Verde, Colorado, at that time.[3] (More recently, documentation of weather after the War of Independence has allowed many correlations between historical events and tree-ring behaviour.[4]) In wood behaviour itself interest in many of the species has been stimulated by their remarkable longevity. Ring sequences of the giant *sequoia* are recorded back to the third century BC [5] while one remnant of bristlecone pine has withstood the attack of the elements since the tree died some 9,000 years ago (Plate 2.1).

Marginal conditions of moisture precipitation like those of the arid zones of America are quite alien to the deciduous oaks of central and western Europe where temperature change and insect defoliation contribute more to the variability of the wood's annual growth pattern. Oak, because of its hardness, has been used in massive form since

2.1 Timber of the bristlecone pine (*Pinus aristata*) from the White Mountains of east-central California. (Photograph: J. A. Harsha. Courtesy of the Laboratory of Tree-Ring Research, University of Arizona, Tucson.)

Roman times—for example, to construct the catapult-firing platform excavated at the first-century fortress town of Vindolanda, in Northumberland. Even in regions of high conifer concentration this wood has been preferred for bell-supports in church belfries. Though there are no European trees more than 400 years old, a pattern of ring widths has been developed for the trees on the Hessian hills of southern Germany that stretches back, to AD 832, while a north German chronology has been built up around the Schleswig township (Plate 2.2), reaching the beginning of the fourteenth century. Other genera of trees, particularly silver fir, larch and beech, have played their part in extending our understanding of man's past.

1*b* ANNUAL TREE-RING GROWTH
At the beginning of the growing season the earlywood of large, thin-walled, xylem cells is generated through division of the cells of the

cambium that lies just within the bark. As the year passes the cells become smaller and their walls much thicker so that the boundary between the latewood and the following year's growth is usually clearly visible (Plates 2.3a, b and .4). The 'feeding' process of the timber is controlled by the production of carbohydrates and hormones in the foliage of the tree's crown (which also acts as the main transpiration area by which the tree 'breathes').[6] A sharp fall in the manufacturing

2.2   Schleswig Cathedral. (Photograph: courtesy of Landesamt für Denkmalpflege, Schleswig-Holstein.)

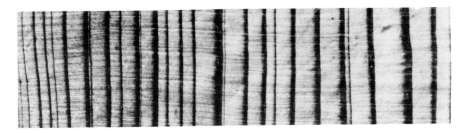

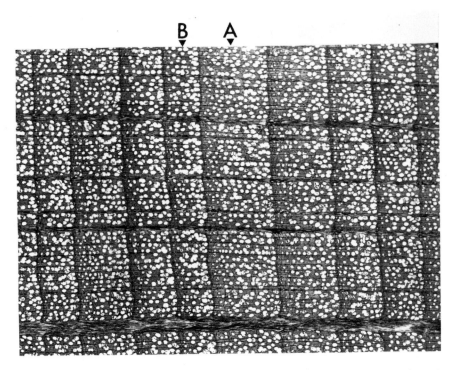

2.3   a. Sensitive ring-width structure of timber from the Betatakin ruins of
north-east Arizona. (Photograph: courtesy of the Laboratory of Tree-Ring
Research, University of Arizona, Tucson.)
b. Ring structure of 'diffuse-porous' beech. (Photograph: courtesy of
Professor W. Liese, Ordinariat für Holzbiologie, University of Hamburg.)

processes of the crown will be most strongly felt in the basal bark
regions of the stem in response to chemical depletion over the tree's
length. For very old trees the outer rings are usually much narrower
than those around the pith (see Plate 2.4) and they face greater competition for the food products of the crown because the bulk of the tree
has increased. Also, activation of cambial cell division occurs last in the
basal regions while annual growth may halt there first. Consequently
the outer rings of the lower parts of a tree will exhibit relatively higher

variability in width, sensitively following any change in the degree of food competition that might occur from year to year.

Wood from Arizona ruins records very violent fluctuations in ring width (often by an order of magnitude in successive years of growth— Plate 2.3a) and the quite sensitive pattern of beech illustrated in Plate 2.3b draws an example from European sources,[7] with ring A twice as wide as ring B. In contrast, in conditions of plentiful water supply (high rainfall or dense undergrowth cover that offers strong moisture retention) a 'complacent' ring series will result. The pine section of Plate 2.4 is typical of this complacency where ring-width variation in successive years rarely exceeds 20 per cent. It is clear from this example that comparison of widths must be made along a traverse moving radially out from the pith because ring-distortion is inevitable in localized stress regions such as a branch joint. Ancient man often introduced an unintentional pattern distortion when putting his cut beams under stress and causing the thin-walled early-wood cells to be crushed.

IC   DATING USING TREE RINGS

In living trees we have a precise date control with the bark ring corresponding to present day. Counting backwards from the bark towards the pith, ring by ring, measures the tree's age. But a section of ancient wood rarely contains a portion of bark, only a pattern of rings, each ring matching a definite, but unknown, calendar year in the past. So it is only the sensitivity of the ring-width structure that offers a means of cross-linking of the specimen wood to that of living tissue by a matching of their common periods of pattern variation. In Fig. 2.1 this matching procedure is illustrated for only three portions of timber but this 'bridging' process can be extended back to yield a complete absolute chronological record over many past centuries. There are some notable examples of violent fluctuations of ring width found so commonly amongst samples as to constitute a 'signature' for certain spans of years. The 'saw-tooth' sequence (AD 1529–41) in the south German hill oak ring sequence is such a signature (Fig. 2.2).[8] This type of behaviour speeds up the cross-linking procedure appreciably.

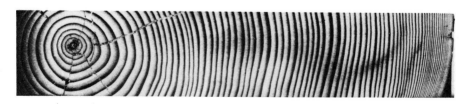

2.4   Full cross-section of a pine timber. Note the gradual decrease in ring thickness, moving from pith to bark. (Photograph: courtesy of the Laboratory of Tree-Ring Research, University of Arizona, Tucson.)

35

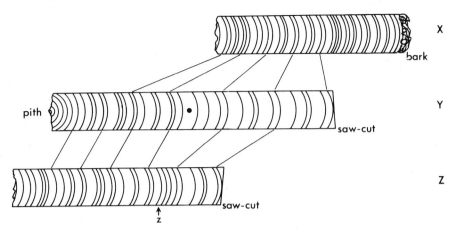

Fig. 2.1   Process of cross-matching ring sequences of three timber cross-sections. The section X is taken from a living tree so its bark date is known. The width variation, ring by ring, of an appreciable portion of the inner wood of X also occurs at the outer part of the older timber, section Y, cut in antiquity. (Note that it is the *relative* width of rings that defines the sensitivity of a sequence. As drawn here section Y timber had twice the growth rate of section X timber.) Another timber, section Z, matches section Y over portions of their lengths, but a region of hiatus following the narrow ring (z) is included. Variations like this are common, in practice, so synchronization procedures are employed, maximizing the frequency with which the ring-curves rise and fall together (reference 8).

Fig. 2.2   Portion of the ring-width pattern of the south German master chronology for oak. The inset covering the years AD 1528–42 illustrates the strong synchronization characteristics of the 'saw-tooth' signature: bold lines joining the datum points indicate a matching of direction of width change in any year for more than 75% of the timbers analysed (reference 14).

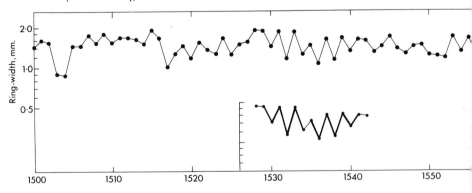

As no two trees grow in exactly the same micro-environment over the years a complete matching of ring patterns is highly unlikely. The sections X and Y in Fig. 2.1 are depicted as such an ideal situation but the section Z disagrees strongly in one ring (marked z) from the pattern of section Y. (No attempt is made to cross-link rings near the pith of the section (see Beam X of Fig. 2.1) since the growth rate of a tree during its early years tends to be highly variable.) Perhaps many of the upper branches had been removed by man for some domestic use, thereby cutting back the food production in the crown for particular years. A narrow ring (z) would result and, indeed, subsequent rings would reflect a gradual recovery to normality by a partial modulation of the ideal width sequence. On the other hand, nearby lumber collection could cause a growth spurt as the tree spreads its root system and seeks out fresh moisture supplies from the soil.

If, however, a reference ring sequence is sought, local factors of this nature must be largely eliminated so that observed variations in ring width can be safely attributed to broader regional climatic conditions. The Hessian oak reference curve illustrated in Fig. 2.2 for the span of years AD 1500–1620 uses the ring sequences of about ninety tree sections of that antiquity, simply averaging the width measured. An emphasis may then be laid upon certain portions of the curve using a 'synchronization' analysis that records the frequency with which the ring-curves rise and fall together. Such a procedure dramatizes the detail of the 'saw-signature' and draws attention to shorter-term, sharp, ring-width suppressions (note AD 1503–4 in Fig. 2.2).

The ring pattern of an undated oak section is then compared with that of the reference curve, and the synchronization analysis repeated, seeking the maximum level of agreement. How good that agreement will be depends upon the number of rings in the 'unknown' section. A pair of mismatched curves will agree to a 50% level (following a statistical randomness) with a standard deviation of $\pm\ 50/x\ \%$ (where x is the number of rings involved). To put these considerations into perspective most of the successful uses of oak dendrochronology discussed later

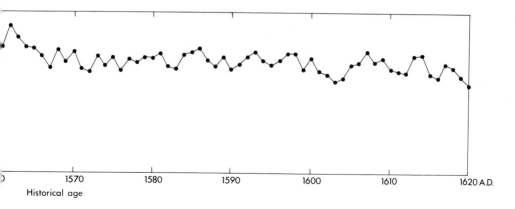

call upon a sequence of at least 100 rings and rely upon a synchronization of around 75% agreement or better.

For the Arizona woods which offer long ring-sequences and highly sensitive patterns in a single tree, some of the analytical effort is eased by 'skeleton' plots which record only those rings of appreciably different width from the norm and their relative position in the overall series.[9] This approach has been termed the Douglass System and has proved valuable not only in the semi-arid regions of Turkey and Egypt, as we might expect, but also in Alaska where temperature variation rather than limitation of moisture creates a high ring-width sensitivity.

On occasion the cross-linking may be possible only between portions of old wood and the ring-width data be unrelatable to a modern living tree sequence. Many 'floating' reference curves of this nature have been established which have appreciable archaeological impact, notably in the study of the Viking settlement, Haithabu. There the large number of features such as houses, water cisterns and defence palisades could be ordered, chronologically, relative to one another, despite much disturbance by later occupations of the area. Although such analysis is not absolute in the dating sense some pegging of the floating sequence's period is often obtained by a radiocarbon dating of a portion of the reference material.

1d   COMPLICATING FACTORS

Accuracy of this dating method strongly depends upon the reliability of equating a tree ring with the growth activities of a single year. However, some tree species have a tendency to form 'false' rings, usually as a fine structure of bands of developed latewood. An extreme case has been reported for a Texas yellow pine where early spring frosts created such havoc with the tree's growth that five rings were created in the seasons of 1936–7.[10] Microscopically the structure of a frost-damage ring is distinctive.[11] For the duration of the frost, peripheral contraction of external tissues (particularly in young trees) compresses the delicate cells in the cambial region and deforms them. The radial cell rows are laterally displaced and uneven in size. Subsequent recovery of the tree causes the damaged cambial derivatives to form a compact, dark band in the wood's cross-section.

Another mode of formation of false rings can result from insect defoliation which creates zonal aggregates of resinous cysts and cell trauma. However, this nutritional, rather than mechanical, disturbance produces no displacements in the radial cell pattern. For oak the observation of such anomalies is limited to a single instance, that illustrated in Plate 2.5, a microscopic section of a stake from the Neolithic settlement of Auvernier in Switzerland.

From the earlier discussion of tree feeding mechanisms it is understandable that some annual rings in a sensitive wood will be only partially formed or even absent altogether. Oak behaves benignly in this respect too, the rarity of missing rings being attributed to peculiarities in sap-flow processes of this ring-porous wood (differences in the pore-structure of hardwoods are discussed and illustrated in the HMSO publication *Forest Products Research, Bulletin 25*). In contrast, the diffuse-porous black alder, frequently found with oak at Celtic sites, is known to have 'lost' up to 45% of its rings across a sequence.[12] Oak typifies the 'ring-porous' structure, with large cells forming the pores in the earlywood and leading gradually to small compact cells in the latewood. (Plate 2.5). Diffuse-porous non-coniferous woods have large cells of a variety of sizes scattered through the year's growth, with the laying-down of a discernible latewood boundary occurring very late in the season (see Plate 2.3b for beech). Insect attack may be the cause of ring absence when of sufficient severity to bring the tree close to death.

An interesting use of frost-damage bands found in Canadian spruce has been to treat them as identifiers of the year matching the ring in which they occur.[13] These trees are also susceptible to the attentions of the spruce budworm (*Caeoecia fumiferana*) and the local absence of rings resulting from this insect's activities has been isolated by ring counting between two frost-marker points.

1e MEASUREMENT TECHNIQUES
Several forms of coring tools have been developed, notably the Swedish increment borer that has proved particularly valuable for sampling

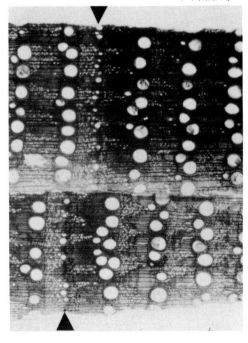

2.5 Ring structure of oak timber found at the Swiss Neolithic settlement of Auvernier, showing the only double-ring anomaly yet found in that wood-type. (Photograph: courtesy of Dr V. Giertz, Forstbotanisches Institut, Munich.)

living softwoods and yields a pencil-like, short cross-section.[14] Much longer sections are collected by using a power-driven extractor with a gimlet-type of detachable cutting head for softwoods and a chip-making corer for hardwoods that permits removal of short lengths as the cutting edge advances.[15] In cases where the wood (or charcoal) was water-logged in burial the material is usually impregnated with a water-miscible synthetic wax, polyethylene glycol, to preserve the material and prevent its deformation.[16] The softer materials can be razor cut and a sliding microtome will produce surfaces with good structure resolution on small sections. Precision sanding machines are required for preparation of longer sections like those of the prehistoric beams of ruins in Mexico. A dusting with chalk will bring up the cell detail in stronger contrast.

A small magnifying eyepiece with an incorporated measurement scale is then adequate for ring-width estimation. Where possible several traverses are run in differing radial directions in a search for missing rings created by the merger of latewood regions of rings exceptionally close together in some parts of the wood. An alternative approach has been employed for the study of oak beams removed from medieval and later buildings under restoration or demolition whereby the ring-pattern of a radially-cut sliver is picked out by using a photo-graph of the X-ray transmission of the wood.[17] The X-ray absorption in the sample relates to the density of the wood structure, with light photographic bands duly matching the compact cell growth of the latewood. Information about the widths of early and latewood is gathered separately, which allows some indirect detailing of a specific year's weather fluctuations.

Techniques of display of ring-width data have already been dis-cussed (i.e. synchronization and skeleton plots) and illustrated for oak in Fig. 2.2. For the longer-lived trees, like the giant *sequoia* and the upper timberline pine, varieties of limber and bristlecone (which have sequences extending over 3,000 years in many instances), pattern analysis is modified to account for the progressive ring-width decrease from pith to bark, a feature of the tree's ageing not connected with sequence sensitivity. Under these conditions an exponential curve is fitted to the simple width plot of the sample (Fig. 2.3 curve a).[18] A sequence of 'indices' is produced by dividing the measured ring width by this exponential's value at the same position (Fig. 2.3, curve b). As these indices do not vary as a function of the tree's age (or its speed of growth), the sensitivity of the sequence is expressed by the fluctua-tion about the base-line value of unity.

2   GENERAL APPLICATIONS TO DATING

2a   ENGLISH WEATHER PATTERNS OVER HISTORICAL TIMES

The widths and latewood densities may be compared with data on

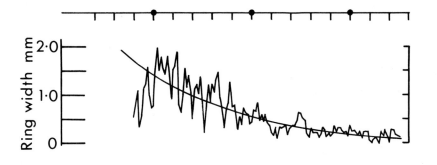

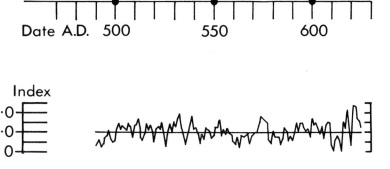

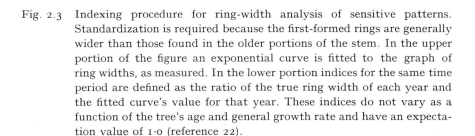

Fig. 2.3 Indexing procedure for ring-width analysis of sensitive patterns. Standardization is required because the first-formed rings are generally wider than those found in the older portions of the stem. In the upper portion of the figure an exponential curve is fitted to the graph of ring widths, as measured. In the lower portion indices for the same time period are defined as the ratio of the true ring width of each year and the fitted curve's value for that year. These indices do not vary as a function of the tree's age and general growth rate and have an expectation value of 1·0 (reference 22).

weather and crop productivity in historical documentation such as manorial accounts and diary recollections. Years of high density latewood seem to match records of high corn yield. In some rings the density decreases sharply late in the year, a feature that seems to be linked to extremely wet conditions in the late summer, a season of importance in medieval husbandry.

In more general terms we have already related a complacency in ring sequences to adequate moisture supply. Consequently times of excessively high rainfall have little impact upon the incremental growth of the tree once its appetite is satisfied. Thus droughts are the most significant weather feature, historically matching harvest difficulties and outbreak of fires.

During the Dark Ages Simeon of Durham noted many instances of fire devastation in the cities of York, Winchester and Southampton in AD 764 while the *Annals of Tighernac* report similar calamities in Ireland.[19] Bede marked out the year AD 737 for special attention with a comment on crop failure in the north.[20] In AD 783 the *Annals of Lorsch* (the Frankish chronicles of Emperor Charlemagne) comment that the continental summer was so hot that many men died of its effects. Remarkably all these events seem to be recorded in the construction oak of the dwellings in the Saxon village of Hamwih, near Southampton, through minima in the ring-width pattern. Also the later rings of the huts' beams suggest building began around AD 835 in good agreement with a coin find referring to Berhtwulf, king of Mercia during the following decade.

The thirteenth-century ring-width patterns show some of the greatest fluctuations amongst our English records.[21] We know that this period was exceptionally warm throughout the world, as glacial melting had advanced shorelines in land and left its mark amongst pollen records in regions never affected at any other time throughout the past two millennia. This warmth encouraged many years of high acorn yield, a fact noted by medieval farmers as this crop was a major source of feed for their pig-herds. Now in the rings widths we find these heavy fruiting years matched by a narrow ring as food supplies are deviated away from their vital function of vegetative growth.[22]

Even the best of weather that caused an abundance of fruit, wine and corn for the medieval farmers carried with it problems too, for warm winters encouraged breeding of the *Tortrix* caterpillar and shrub greenery was much destroyed by gourd worms. Of course, the effects of these creatures modify the tree-ring pattern, in turn, as discussed earlier.

2*b*   THE 'TIMBER-FRAME' TRADITION IN EUROPE
Many of the impressive churches, market halls and stately houses scattered over the length and breadth of north-west Europe date back as far as the twelfth century and stand as a fine testimony to the

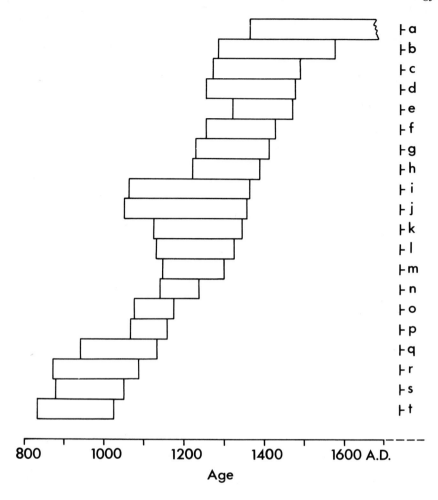

Fig. 2.4   The bridging process for development of the south German oak
master curve (reference 14). The sources of the reference material
(mostly from the Hessian region) are as follows:

a. Modern *Spessart* oak growing
   on the hills above the R. Main,
   a Rhine tributary.
b. Watterbacher, Haus
c. Büdingen, Schloss
d. Büdingen, Remigiuskirche
e. Büdingen, Stadtkirche
f. Aschaffenburg, Haus
g. Nieder-Weisel, Kapelle
h. Kassel, Brüderkirche
i. Gelnhausen, Brauhaus

j. Altenhausslau, Kirchturm
k. Gelnhausen, Haus Kuhgasse
l. Ebrach, Kloster
m. Büdingen, Remigiuskirche
n. Echzell, Kirche
o. Bösgesäss, Rost
p. Steinbach, Basilika
q. Ilbenstadt, Basilika
r. Büdingen, Schlosshof. Rost
s. Winkel, Graues Haus
t. Büdingen, Remigiuskirche

robustness of many of the local building timbers, particularly oak, beech and fir. Much of the wood is original and has supplied vital dendrochronological material which has solved a broad spectrum of historical, archaeological and architectural problems. At the forefront of this chronology building has been the study of the hill oaks (*Quercus petraea*) from the area bounded by the Danube and the Rhine, with concentration of sampling along the Rhine tributary, the Main. The bridging of ring sequences of living oak from Spessart and some twenty groups of construction oak, ending with that of the eleventh-century west wing of the Remigiuskirche at Büdingen, has now covered the span back to AD 832 (Fig. 2.4). The valley oak species, *Quercus robur* is almost entirely complacent. Its ring width would relate more strongly to felling than precipitation.

The scope of application of this south German master curve has proved surprisingly wide, reaching the region around the township of Trier in France.[23] and the medieval town of Zeigenhain to the north.[24] A large programme involving the French medieval market halls has been successful in clearing up many traditional architectural question-marks.[25] Three outstanding analyses have been carried out in British buildings; the Bailiff's House at Bewdley, the Priory House in Droit-wich (Plate 2.6) and the Vicarage at Berriew in north Wales. All three of these oak samples contained some timber where parts of the sap-wood still remained. (Sapwood is the term given to the young rings just inside the bark which, in the growing tree, contains living cells and reserve materials, like starch. Its texture is often spongy and its colour paler than the heartwood.) Normally the complete sapwood region of an oak occupies an inch of the tree's cross-section, so quite an accurate estimation of the thickness of the surface cutting made by the builder is possible. Thus the Droitwich Priory was dated to 1580, extrapolating from a ring sequence spanning 1384 to 1574 recorded in the timber.[26]

The Berriew Vicarage example raises an interesting point in that the house itself is precisely dated to 1616 by an inscription, while the ring-curve ends in a partially-formed sapwood ring matching May, 1615. Clearly little seasoning of the wood was contemplated, though verbal tradition has suggested a twenty-year storage period as common. There are many examples elsewhere that support a revison of the latter view. At the church of Filsch, near Trier, dated by inscriptions to 1780, the copper beech beams show rhombic distortion in their original rectangular cross-section. The measured 5% tangential movement matches well to the normal shrinkage that occurs during drying out of the wood. Thus the wood was worked in a fresh condition, a suggestion supported by the terminal ring dating to 1779. In Trier itself, in the south wing of the Cathedral, the ring pattern of the oak foundation beams of the choir stalls shows that the timber was felled *and* fashioned in the spring of 1311. A visually striking illustration of this point has

2.6 The Priory House, Droitwich. (Photograph: courtesy of the Planning Department, Worcester County Council.)

been observed in the flooring of a Romanesque house in Münstereifel where even axe cuts are readily recognizable and stored in the wood's 'memory' when worked in a sap-fresh condition immediately after felling. Also the dating of seventeenth-century Dutch paintings on oak panels (more fully discussed in section 3a) indicates that the period covering tree felling, board cutting and artist usage was often less than five years in all. Possibly it was desirable to allow some 'greenness' in the wood during cutting to combat wandering of the saw in production of these trim panels often only a quarter of an inch thick.

Attempts to link the ring patterns of north and south Germany have been unsuccessful, though it is notable that a Hanseatic trading ship, the *Bremer kogge*, has been dated to 1380 by its timbers, which were felled in the south at Weserbergland, and floated down to Bremen.[27] But a different master curve has been developed for the northern region centred about the township of Schleswig and covering many sites along the Elbe and the Weser.[28] Again the reference material was drawn from the oak-beamed churches and municipal houses of the area (plus a number of clock towers dating back to the sixteenth century). Attempts to extend this chronology to the Middle Ages have met serious difficulties, typified by many churches around Schleswig of Romanesque origin but kept in good repair by careful replacement of original beams at a later date. At the Cathedral (Plate 2.2) only Gothic timber had survived while adaptations of structure like that of the vaulted ceiling of the middle aisle are recorded now by roof trusses dating to the first quarter of the sixteenth century.[29]

The future may well see a change of emphasis away from the deciduous oak towards the softwood fir (*Abies alba*) for which a bridged chronology has already been built up by using living trees of the Bavarian alps and many older timber sources including beams from the tenth-century church of St Cyriak in Sulzberg that carried the ring pattern back to AD 820. The master curve includes timber from Switzerland and the Tyrol.[30] One startling feature to emerge has been the extremely tight correlation between the width variations of fir and oak over the latter half of the sixteenth century amongst the wider rings (Fig. 2.5).

2c A SURVEY OF OTHER ANALYSES, WORLDWIDE

It would be a formidable task to attempt a synopsis of the dating work already undertaken at the University of Arizona in Tucson, their experience covering more than 2,000 prehistoric sites from the American south-west and adjacent regions. *The Tree-Ring Bulletin* offers a comprehensive source of information about those analyses. However, one novel application reported in that journal caught the author's

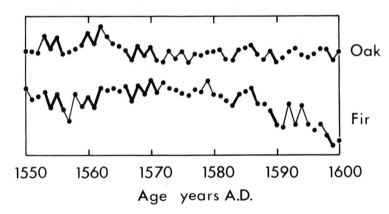

Fig. 2.5 Parts of the oak and fir master curves (AD 1550–1600). The vertical axis records the ring width in each type of timber. The data points are not linked if the ring width is less than 5 mm in either case, while only a fine link line is used if that level of variation is exceeded only in one tree type. Bold link lines indicate the ring width in both timbers is in excess of 5 mm. Clearly, with the finer rings excluded the two chronologies show excellent agreement (reference 30).

attention. In Arctic regions, along the open shores of the ocean and the Bering Sea, driftwood has been collected by the Eskimo communities for several centuries for building houses and making domestic utensils.[31] The tree rings of the construction planks mark the date of home building and hence the beginnings of occupation. Many of the wooden artefacts from within the house would carry the rings close to the outside of the log from which they fashioned, so that the latest period of occupation is recorded by the youngest item.

The Eskimos never seem to have found driftwood in such abundance that much of this material could be treated as expendable as fuel. (The survival of this driftwood is a testimony to the Eskimo's sense of economy in the past. In New Mexico, too, the store put by good timber preservation is illustrated by stockpiling habits of the pre-historic population of Chaco Canyon.[32]) Thus through the ideal preservation conditions of ground frost many early ruins of the past three centuries have been revealed intact during recent excavation.[33] Inland sites, too, have yielded some good cross-dating results with structures such as tepee-style graves almost always matching to patterns in live trees of the area. The relation of timber source regions to the beach finds is also expected to supply data on northern ocean currents, regarding speed and direction.[34]

Floating chronologies have been derived for a large number of archaeological sites including the Bronze Age fort of Buchau and the Neolithic settlement of Ehrenstein, both in Germany, and parallel developments at Züg-Sumph and Thayngen-Weier, in Switzerland.[35] Elsewhere ring sequences have been interpreted for the strengthening beams of the tomb of King Midas' father (in Turkey),[36] for a Japanese pagoda [37] and for the corduroy street levels of Novgorod in Russia.[38] The potential of specimens from Egypt has been noted since the climate there is conducive to good wood preservation.

SPECIALIZED DATING APPLICATIONS

3a EUROPEAN PAINTINGS ON OAK PANELS

Many of the leading artists of the seventeenth century worked in the Dutch lowlands and depicted peaceful village and riverside scenes on panels of oak. Notably prolific in this field was Philips Wouwerman (1619–68) and it was upon his paintings that workers at the Institute of Wood Biology of the University of Hamburg first concentrated their efforts.[39] Sequences of up to 250 rings are visible along the panel's edge, for this was normally manufactured by sawing radially across the heart of the wood core. To counter subsequent insect attack and warping of the board the sapwood was usually trimmed away, though six of Wouwerman's panels carried portions of it. The presence of sapwood rings allows the time of cutting of the timber to be estimated very accurately. This programme indicated that the artist normally used that wood within five years of the felling date. Eleven panels were linked together to form a floating chronology which allowed an ordering of Wouwerman's works in a relative time sequence (necessarily this chronology had to pre-date 1668, when the artist died). However, rather unexpectedly, synchronization was possible between the Wouwerman's sequence and the south German oak master curve (see section 2*b*). Besides producing an absolute dating scale for the paintings this matching suggested that the wood source for the panels was not a local one.

Two other works, *The Bleach* by Molenaer (1630–76) and *The Inn* by Dusart (1660–1704), fitted the same pattern but, in general, this situation seems peculiar to Wouwerman. Seven more of his panels suggested a different ring-curve that found cross-links in the works of more than twenty other Dutch artists of that period. This sequence is believed to be the reference curve for Holland covering the period of 1314 to 1666.

Dendrochronology has been able to contribute to academic problems

2.7   *Study of an Old Man*, attributed to Rembrandt (AD 1606–69). (Photograph: courtesy of Staatlische Kunstsammlungen, Kassel; catalogue number 233.)

of authenticity in works of Rembrandt (1606–69) and Rubens (1577–1640). For the former, the recent revision of the *Bredius Catalogue* by Professor H. Gerson suggests extensive misattribution. Thus the need for a Rembrandt master ring-curve was stimulated, leading to the analysis of some forty panels at Hamburg. *Study of an Old Man* (Plate 2.7), though signed and dated 1632, still faced expert criticism, but many doubts were dispelled by a tree-ring analysis that matched the Rembrandt master and suggested an oak felling date of close to 1610. Naturally any final authenticity pronouncement would have to be cautious as there are several examples of the re-use of old panels to produce imitations at a later date. Notable among these is the portrait in the Herzog Anton Ulrich-Museum (cat. no. 257) that is a copy of another painting on public display at the Den Haag Museum (cat. no. 556). The oak backings of both works fit the Rembrandt standard curve.[40]

But an imitator's use of 'out-of-context' wood is more readily discernible. One example where the evidence of dendrochronology and stylistic attribution may be at odds concerns the Rubens' work *Girl with a Mirror* thought to have been executed in 1620. However, the earliest felling date for the oak used in the panel mounting was 1635, not only incompatible with the stylistic attribution but scarcely early enough to have allowed Rubens to have used the wood before his death only five years later.

The reference curve built up from Rubens' panels probably represents the growth patterns of the woods around Antwerp where that artist spearheaded painting's contribution to the Flemish Baroque with a workshop output of prodigious extent. Flemish and German artists had received appreciable patronage from the English monarchy in the previous century when the post of Court Painter was held in high esteem. While in England their oak panelling seems to have been drawn from a limited stock of timber growing close to London. This is attested by the consistency of ring sequences found in portraits spanning 1530 to 1590, with that of *Archbishop Cranmer* by Gerloch Flicke, dating to 1546, visually matching Hans Eworth's *Viscount Montague* painted twenty-three years later.[41] Much of the weather pattern that influenced tree growth in north-west Europe appears to have been shared by south-east England, because the early rings of the Rubens-Antwerp reference curve cross-matched well to the Tudor period rings of these documented portraits. The English reference curve so built covers the period 1320 to 1547.

However, there are many Tudor portraits of unrecorded date, notably those of the monarchy itself. The Richard III exhibition mounted at the National Portrait Galley (London, 1973) had many such works, including seventeen representations of that king alone. The scientific study of four exhibits is of particular interest (Table 2.1).[42]

Table 2.1 : Dendrochronology of four Royal portraits of the Tudor period

Source reference†	Portrait	Period of reign	Panel date
P16	Margaret of York (Duchess of Burgundy)	—*	1520–1530
P40	Richard III (with The Broken Sword)	1483–1485	1572–1577
P42	Richard III	1483–1485	1512–1520
P45	Edward IV	1461–1483	1512–1520

†All four portraits are from the collection of the *Society of Antiquaries of London*. The P-references here are catalogue markings in *Richard III*, edited by Pamela Tudor-Craig.

*Sister of Edward IV and Richard III. Margaret held appreciable political power both during the lifetime of her brothers and subsequently, when her court was the centre of hostility to the Tudors.

(i) *P16; Margaret of York, Duchess of Burgundy*. The tree rings tend to match Netherlandish characteristics better than English, suggesting that the painting is a sixteenth-century import. But it is difficult to envisage the political context for this transaction so many years after the lady's death.

(ii) *P40; Richard III with The Broken Sword*. Some years ago X-ray studies of this picture revealed extensive alterations from an original format. The figure in the hidden painting has the humpback and withered left arm immortalized in Shakespeare's sixteenth-century tragedy. However, the tree-ring evidence adds nothing to the argument about Richard's true appearance since the panel dates well after the time when the description of those deformities was current.

(iii) *P42; Richard III*. This portrait is the only one extant that gives no hint of a physical deformity (usually suggested by an unevenness of shoulder heights). Though the panel does not date to the king's reign it carries so many detailed characteristics of that period that it is almost certainly a faithful copy of an original setting.

(iv) *P45; Edward IV*. The tree-ring pattern indicates that the panels for this work and P42 were *cut from the same tree*. Again the painting dates well after the portrayed king's reign.

No doubt the study now in progress of other panels from the Society of Antiquaries of London, including many 'arch-topped' portraits of the sixteenth century will throw fresh light on the history of painting during the Tudor era. But more gains may be expected much further back in English history, in Norman and Saxon times, for these panels supply another bridge to which earlier oak patterns may be linked. The movement in that direction has recently been illustrated by analysis of *The Life of Saint Etheldreda* (which originally formed part of the Shrine of Ely Cathedral during the latter part of the fifteenth century), the boards of which carry the ring pattern back to 1147.[43] Earlier material that should eventually be encompassed in this English analysis, includes important examples of waterlogged, preserved timbers. The clinker-built boat discovered during the widening of an old water-course near Graveney, in Kent, should supply reference material from the late ninth century,[44] while an oak-timbered well at North Elmham (a site believed to be tied to the bishopric for a Norfolk diocese during Middle Saxon times) should date to the early ninth century.[45] Even earlier, the remains of a Roman waterfront near the Tower of London, recently rescued from the river mud, should supplement tentative floating chronologies for that period that have already been established.

3*b* THE BRISTLECONE PINE AND THE RADIOCARBON METHOD

The longevity of the bristlecone pine (*Pinus aristata* Engelm) (Plate 2.1) was noted earlier. This comes about through the combination of several factors that can be summarized as follows.[46] The timber grows primarily at elevations of some 10,000 feet in the White Mountains of California. This region is protected by the Sierra Nevada against the rains of advancing Pacific storms. Though this creates quite an arid climate some advantage is gained in that low rainfall restricts growth wood bulk, straining the tree's reserves less in times of prolonged drought. In response to a low humidity the foliage remains compact, a feature that weighs against disease development. These mountain stretches lie well beyond the range of beetle attack and needle fungus (notably effective in wood destruction in the northern states) though the pine itself carries quite powerful fungus-resistant substances, like *pinosylvin*, to aid its survival. The tree is also thrifty with its feed supply by needle retention for about twenty years or more. The resulting stable photosynthetic capacity can alleviate stress on the wood's chemical stores for several years.

Ancient living trees, like a 4,900 year-old pine in the Snake Range of Nevada, provide a wide bridge between today and the distant past. But the bristlecone pine also resists rot, even in death, so that there are wood remains with ring sequences covering the last seven millennia.[47] The rings themselves are extremely sensitive in pattern, owing mainly to the marginal, semi-arid climatic conditions but also to a dolomitic soil with good drainage qualities.

Consideration of a precision of a single year in dating material of the fifth millennium BC is awesome, so it is understandable that, over the past decade, the scientific community have looked upon this wood as a vitally important reference material. The impact of this ring analysis has been particularly strong in a recent re-appraisal of the

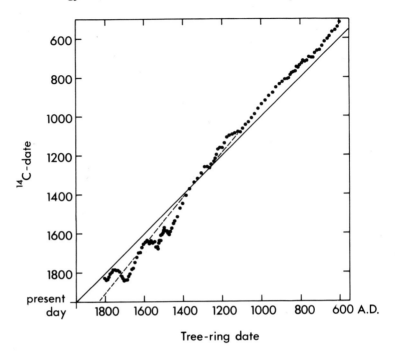

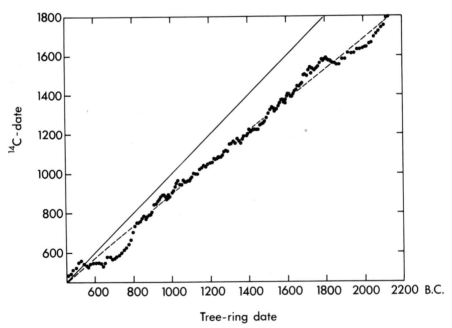

Fig. 2.6   Portions of the bristlecone pine calibration curve covering: a. present day to AD 600 and b. 500 BC to 2200 BC. The long-term trend of deviations is marked by a dashed line (^{14}C half-life of 5,730 years used in this case) (reference 51).

radiocarbon dating method (see Chapter 3).[48] Processing of wood samples taken at regular intervals along the various pine cores has indicated that a distinct discrepancy builds up between conventional radiocarbon (^{14}C) results and the tree-ring record as we move further back in time. This conclusion, first illustrated by H. E. Suess at La Jolla Radiocarbon Laboratory,[49] has been confirmed more recently by groups in Arizona and Philadelphia.[50,51] Extracts from the work of the latter are presented in Fig. 2.6a, b. Back to about AD 1300 the data is generally in line with the previous work by Hl. de Vries which suggested that late seventeenth-century wood samples carried a 2% radiocarbon excess.[52] The earlier period, back to around 600 BC, gave little cause for alarm with small deviation from conventional analysis. Then, earlier still, a steadily increasing discrepancy appears, reaching a level of more than 300 years at the end of the third millennium BC and around 700 years at the limit of availability of bristlecone reference material (see Fig. 3.5 also). Conventional ^{14}C-dates during this period appear to be consistently too young.

The introduction of a systematic correction in radiocarbon dates for early periods met a mixed reception in academic circles. Some pre-historians in Europe had already found even conventional ^{14}C-dates for the Neolithic era unaccepably old [53,54] so introduction of several hundred years more inevitably created further acrimony. In contrast, scholars of the detailed and abundant Mesopotamian cuneiform records had already noted apparent incompatibility between their estimates of the beginning of the First Dynasty of Babylon and ^{14}C-estimates for the time of the preceding Early Dynastic period, even though the latter grouped consistently around 2200 BC.[55] Also, in Egypt, records of astronomical events offered an independent chronology stretching back to 1872 BC (during the reign of Sesostris III of the XII Dynasty) with only minor uncertainties, usually amounting to less than twenty-five years.[56] Although the chronology building in the third millennium BC and before is a patchwork of evidence from many sources (notably the so-called *Turin Canon* and *Palermo Stone* king lists), the First Dynasty in Egypt was confidently placed at 3120 BC with no more than 100 years margin of error. It was amongst the tomb material related to this early period that radiocarbon re-calibration seemed most needed, with examples like the reed matting used in the brick course bonding in the superstructure of the Mer-Neit Tomb at Sakkara (Dynasty I, c. 3000 BC) dating conventionally to 2470 ± 60 BC.

It is noteworthy that a recent model put forward for the directions of cultural contacts through Europe during prehistoric times largely pivots on the acceptance of a long-term radiocarbon error term of the magnitude illustrated here.[57] Re-calibration of several dates for Iberian, Maltese and French megalithic tombs excludes the Near East as the source for their inspiration of design and decoration and the roles of the Aegean areas and western Europe as innovation regions are seen as reversed. On similar grounds, the origins of copper metallurgy are placed in the Balkans at close to 4000 BC, more than a millennium older than their supposed Aegean prototypes. Should either of these archaeological concepts be substantiated in the future the powerful role played by dendrochronology should be fully recognized.

The general long-term trend in the 'calibration' curves developed by the various laboratories are in reasonable agreement. (Reasons for the effect will be discussed in Chapter 3 from the radiochronologist's standpoint.) However, in the scientific community there is appreciable academic division about the short-term, sharp departures superimposed upon the general trend of increasing ^{14}C-error, both in terms of their interpretation and their very existence.[58] Regions of strong 'hiatus' suggested in the Philadelphia data are around 2200 BC, 700 BC, AD 350 and much of the period AD 1400 to the present day (Fig. 2.6a). The original La Jolla data also included these major excursions but suggested a great many more short-term fluctuations throughout the pre-Christian era.

These brief fluctuations create ambiguity in radiocarbon dates thus appreciably spreading the margin of error quoted on each age determination in some cases. For example, in the historical era studied by de Vries a conventional ^{14}C-age of AD 1850 matches tree-ring ages of AD 1790 and 1700. The Philadelphia reference curve has regions of such ambiguity over 15% of its length.

For the most part the radiocarbon dating technique is affected adversely by these short-term fluctuations but, in some special circumstances, the wandering nature of the calibration curve can be turned to advantage. This is illustrated in Fig. 2.7 for analyses of wood and charred grain samples collected from the Swiss Neolithic site of Gachnang-Niederwil.[59] In a region of rapid change of ^{14}C-activity grain harvests only a few years apart in true age will show a sharp difference in conventional radiocarbon results. The Niederwil grain yielded two clusters of ^{14}C-ages at about 3020 and 2820 BC in conventional analysis, even though the material was collected from between two successive floors of cleaved oak, each only used for a brief while before re-covering. During this time period the bristlecone pine calibration curve shows a sudden deviation which would match this sharp grain ^{14}C-change, over a tree-ring age range of 3640–3655 BC. Thus this period of site occupation is precisely and absolutely dated to this brief fifteen-year span during the fourth millennium BC.

Use of the sensitivity of the 'time-derivative' of the ^{14}C-content during sharp excursion periods has proved successful at two other Swiss Lake dwelling sites, Burgäschisee-Süd and Thayngen-Weier.[60] These two sites are regarded as contemporary with Niederwil (which was probably occupied for about seventy-five years) yet their oak timbers date about a century earlier than the charred grain samples discussed above (Fig. 2.7). It is possible that these oak analyses record

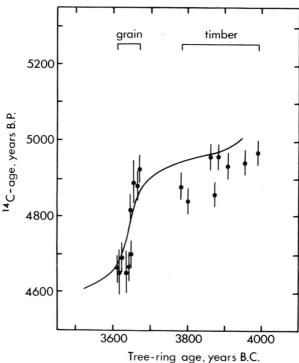

Fig. 2.7   Tree-ring and ¹⁴C-data for the Swiss Neolithic site of Gachnang-Niederwil (reference 59).

only an era of forest clearance activities near inhabited areas, the wood finding use in construction only a long while after. Settlement construction at the younger Swiss site of Auvernier (with a true age of c. 2700 BC) was dated in a similar manner utilizing a 'hiatus' zone around 3000 BC when the ¹⁴C-content changed by about 1 per cent in the space of only twenty years but then remained almost constant for the next century (see Fig. 3.5).[61]

Critics of this type of analysis mainly feel that direct archaeological application is rather premature, at present. There are question-marks not only about the mechanisms responsible for these radiocarbon deviations but, perhaps, about dendrochronological aspects also.

In this way the subject has moved full circle and focus has returned to the bristlecone pine itself.[62] (i) Does timber grown at such high altitudes present a true picture of the behaviour of other tree types at around sea level? (ii) Do the carbon-bearing fractions other than cellulose act as a reliable measure of atmospheric ¹⁴C-levels during timber growth? These questions remain unanswered as yet, although an independent calibration of the radiocarbon time scale is now in progress using fossil timber (both oak and pine) preserved in the peat deposits and lake sediments of Ireland.[63]

Chapter 3

Radiocarbon Dating

I BASIC DATING PRINCIPLES

I*a* RADIOCARBON PRODUCTION AND DISTRIBUTION

In the upper regions of the Earth's atmosphere there is a dynamic activity of nuclear processes as cosmic radiation first encounters the many types of atoms that make up our air. Some of the cosmic energy is converted into the production of neutrons which start off with high energies but gradually slow down after several atomic collisions. The slower, *thermal* neutrons as they are called, react efficiently with nitrogen through a chemical reaction,

$$^{14}N + n \quad \rightarrow \quad ^{14}C + H \quad\quad\quad (3.1)$$

No other neutron reaction in the atmosphere has a comparable likelihood of occurrence so that virtually every cosmic neutron eventually creates a ^{14}C-atom.[1] Initially the distribution of these atoms is non-uniform. The Earth's magnetic field deflects the electrially-charged cosmic rays so that the neutron flux in the stratosphere is much more intense near the poles than at the equator. However, at about 10 km above the Earth's surface, once the carbon has been converted to carbon dioxide, circulating air currents soon mix up the different parts of the atmosphere. In this way some 7·5 kg of ^{14}C is added to the world's carbon reservoir every year and distributed through it by a variety of mechanisms (Fig. 3.1).

The major intake of the atmosphere's carbon dioxide occurs at the ocean's surface by an exchange reaction, forming dissolved bicarbonates in the water. Gradually these bicarbonates find their way into the ocean depths with some of the carbon taking up a more substantial form as carbonate deposits or in marine shell structure. On land, plant life converts the carbon dioxide into foodstuffs through photosynthesis so that the carbon becomes organically bound in a living organism. In their turn, the plants are food for animals so that the ^{14}C moves onwards through various elements of the biosphere. Eventual death of vegetation or the animal life completes the cycle as the material decomposition releases CO_2 back into the atmosphere. The entire 'exchange reservoir' contains close to 4×10^{15} kg of carbon (93% of it

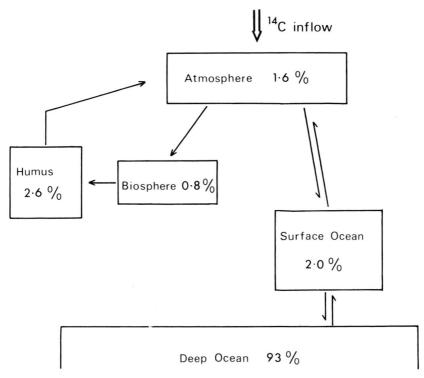

Fig. 3.1   Structure of the Earth's carbon reservoir.

in the deep ocean) of which the injected radioactive form ^{14}C contributes an average weight fraction of only $1 \cdot 5 \times 10^{-12}$. Most of the carbon is in the lighter isotopic forms of ^{13}C ($1 \cdot 1\%$) and ^{12}C ($98 \cdot 9\%$).

1b   RADIOACTIVITY OF NATURAL CARBON

Of the three isotopic forms of carbon only the much less abundant ^{14}C is radioactive. Its decay involves the emission of a low energy β-radiation through the reaction,

$$^{14}C \rightarrow {}^{14}\mathcal{N} + \beta^- \qquad (3.2)$$

Within a living organism the concentration of ^{14}C is steadily and continuously being replenished from new stocks in the atmosphere via the reservoir supply lines. However, at death the intake process ceases thereby setting a time zero ($t = 0$) when the radioactivity concentration is N_0. A quantity termed the *mean life-time* is symbolized by τ and conventionally quoted as 8,000 years for C^{14}. Then, decrease of concentration of the radioactive component follows the exponential law,

$$N = N_0 \exp(-t/\tau) \qquad (3.3)$$

(An alternative quantity more often quoted in this work is the radioactive *half-life*, $t_{\frac{1}{2}}$, equal to $0\cdot693\tau$. The ^{14}C half-life used conventionally is 5,568 years derived from the weighted average of three early determinations.[2])

The time zero for shell is marked by its period of crystallination out of the ocean's carbonates, i.e. a process of rapid growth. However, the annual rings of a tree each act as a briefly-lived unit so that a wood cross-section carries a complete sequence of radiocarbon contents from birth to death. Although movement of carbon between inner rings or their invasion by recent sap has been suggested, such a notion has been experimentally discounted,[3] at least for German oak, Douglas fir from Arizona and bristlecone pine from California. Though in the sapwood regions some transfer may occur the effective contamination is still limited as the main nutrient flow occurs in the most active outer portions of the trunk. Sharper time markers for the start of carbon's activity decrease are the one-year standing crops and fruits together with their man-made derivatives such as linen fabric and wines.

Within the framework of the natural, circulating reservoir shown in Fig. 3.1 we expect a recent form of any of these materials to emit radiation at a rate of close to 14.5 disintegrations per minute for a gram of natural carbon. Following the decay law of equation (3.3) preserved carbon-bearing remains 5,568 years old will contain only *half* their original ^{14}C-activity, provided the world's carbon reservoir was like that of today. Material twice as old (i.e. 11,136 years) will only be a *quarter* as active, and so on. This controlled loss of ^{14}C-activity with time is the basis of the radiocarbon dating method.

Historically, this elegantly simple dating principle resulted in its innovator, Professor Willard Libby, being awarded a Nobel Prize while early successes encouraged many institutions to add their weight to further radiocarbon research and application. The general applicability of the method over many millennia seemed well confirmed by age determinations like that of 3,620 years for deckboard from the funerary-ship of Sesostris III.[4] (His reign during the XII Dynasty in Egypt is marked by the earliest documentation of astronomical events, so that the burial is firmly set at 1831 BC.[5]) However, in recent years increased equipment sophistication has led to the raising of many detailed questions about the initial assumptions outlined here, *particularly the constancy of the exchange reservoir with time*. These questions dominate the discussion of this chapter and, in many cases, have determined the choice of examples presented.

1C THE 'FOSSIL FUEL' EFFECT

The activities of man himself have contributed much to the complications that beset the radiocarbon method at this time. In the latter part of the nineteenth century the Industrial Revolution set in motion an injection process which has stocked the atmosphere with steadily

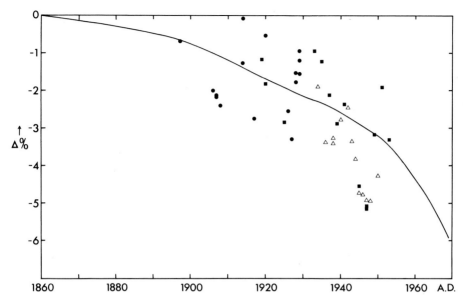

Fig. 3.2   Variation of atmospheric ¹⁴C-concentration arising from the fossil-fuel
effect. The theoretical curve is compared with data points gathered
from ¹⁴C-analysis of pre-1950 wines (solid circles), malt whiskies
(solid squares) and flax seeds (open triangles) (reference 9).

increasing amounts of *in*active ¹²C. Oil and coal combustion has
re-introduced carbon that had settled out of the reservoir circulation
many millions of years ago. The 'fossil fuel' effect has caused a dilution
of natural ¹⁴C-concentrations which has accelerated appreciably in the
past two decades (Fig. 3.2).

The influence of this effect upon dating has been aggravated by
inertia in the mixing phase of the exchange processes between the
atmosphere and the oceans, with time lags of transfer averaging around
twenty years.[6] Although fuel burning has added only about 0·3%,
by weight, more carbon to the reservoir, up till now, wood growing in
the mid-1950s was already recording a ¹⁴C-concentration 2% below the
expected uncontaminated level.[7] The fossil fuel effect gives recent
material a false antiquity of up to about 160 years.

The ¹⁴C-changes over the past century have been considered theoreti-
cally with due note being taken of the differing rates of exchange
between the various parts of the reservoir and the input rate of artificial
carbon dioxide estimated from documentary sources of power con-
sumption worldwide.[8] These theoretical predictions are summed up
in Fig. 3.2 and compared with kindred ¹⁴C-variations in sensitive
media like flax seeds, vintage wines and malt whiskies from Scotland.[9]
(In the latter group quality control of the manufacturers ensures that
the source of barley used is established firmly and excludes mixture of
grains from various regions.) The overall picture of fossil fuel take up

in the biosphere seems to be well understood. As by far the main industrial impact post-dates 1890 it has been possible to take account of it in the development of radiocarbon standards (see section 3.1.*f*).

1*d* WEAPON-TESTING EFFECTS

The onset of the thermonuclear era in 1952 caused a high-altitude neutron injection into the northern stratosphere which created a new source of ^{14}C-production with which to contend in dating research. By 1963 the air of the troposphere was recording a ^{14}C-concentration twice as high as the cosmic-induced level as the radiocarbon input rate outstripped the ability of the exchange processes at the ocean surface to spread the fresh material through the reservoir. The introduction of an international moratorium at that time, restricting bomb testing in the atmosphere and oceans, has allowed the circulatory pattern to begin to re-establish its equilibrium. Once completely absorbed weapon-testing ^{14}C will have artificially increased the radioactive fraction of the world's carbon inventory by close to 3%.[10]

This extra ^{14}C, particularly that produced in high latitudes where the majority of the natural radioactivity originates, has been extensively used as a 'tracer' to define the paths and speeds of carbon transfer through the many sections of the reservoir. The carbon dioxide mixing between the stratosphere and troposphere takes up to four years, somewhat more slowly than fallout material like strontium (stratosphere residence time 1·5 years [11]), but the latter may attach itself more readily to settling particles. Interhemisphere mixing in the troposphere takes only about one year. The 'hold up' at the ocean's surface matches that of the fossil fuel absorption, i.e. ten to thirty years, but mixing is rapid and thorough in the shallow waters through wind action and convection currents. Transfer mechanisms are far slower in the ocean deep as its colder waters have to move all the way to the polar regions before re-surfacing and reacting once more with the atmosphere. Long residence times for inorganic carbon in this condition creates an apparent age for it of more than 1,200 years in some regions.[12]

In contrast the plants of the biosphere immediately utilize any troposphere enrichment and many organisms clearly reflect the bomb-carbon build up. Malt whiskies of Scotland, derived from a barley crop, record the annual synthesis (Fig. 3.3) as do post-1953 vintage wines[13] and grasslands from all latitudes.[14] The plant life is also sensitive in the growing season to the so-called spring leakage in the stratosphere when air currents facilitate stratosphere-troposphere movements of ^{14}C. Related annual oscillations in the ^{14}C-content of the atmosphere are particularly clear in the post-1963 period.

The human link in the biosphere 'compartment' of the carbon reservoir exhibits some interesting features with soft tissue and bone marrow following the bomb-carbon trends of Fig. 3.3 while bone collagen and mineral lag behind by some ten years or more in their

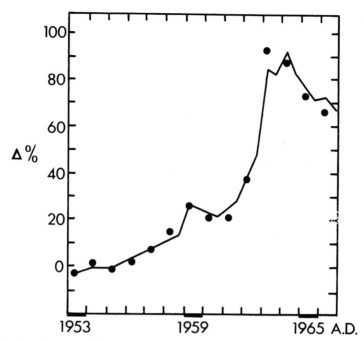

Fig. 3.3   Correlation between ^{14}C-concentrations in atmospheric carbon dioxide and in vintage whiskies (data marked in solid circles) (reference 9).

artificial ^{14}C-assimilation.[15] In the marine food chain there is a great variability in the measured ^{14}C-uptakes of several creatures over this high injection era. The algae (*phytoplankton*) at the ocean surface readily absorb the activities of the water's carbonate and bicarbonate and the minute organisms that feed on them (*zooplankton*) follow suit.[16] Fish, like cod and whiting feed on these organisms but other species, like skate, seem to be bottom feeders and thus carry a normal, low ^{14}C-content. All these life forms play a significant role in the reservoir composition as they eventually become the deep-sea marine sediments and petroleum beds that make up the bulk of the carbon inventory.

This varigated series of carbon-rich, organic and inorganic materials represent the detailed components of the exchange reservoir. They indicate the need for clear definition of what was used in analysis when a radiocarbon date is reported.

1*e*   ISOTOPIC FRACTIONATION

The movement of radiocarbon illustrated by this weapon-testing data highlights the complexity of the finer structure of the exchange reservoir. Additionally, at each transfer stage, account must be taken of slightly differing efficiencies of movement of the heavier, active ^{14}C-atoms and of both the lighter, stable forms, ^{13}C and ^{12}C. This 'isotopic fractionation' leads to relative 'ageing' effects of different components in the reservoir, with some enrichment of radioactivity of ocean carbonates compared with the atmosphere above and some depletion in the land plants and their by-products.[17] It is usual to keep track of this effect using the much more abundant ^{13}C isotope though its enrichment due to fractionation is only half that of ^{14}C. To obtain the magnitude of deviation from the normal natural level a quantity, Δ, is defined as,

$$\Delta\%_{00} = \delta^{14}C - (2\delta^{13}C + 50) \cdot \left\{ 1 + \frac{\delta^{14}C}{1000} \right\} \%_{00} \qquad (3.4)$$

where $\delta^{13}C$ and $\delta^{14}C$ are the observed deviation (expressed in parts per thousand) from the ^{13}C and ^{14}C laboratory standards (see section 1f). Examples of the effect that may be drawn from the 'fossil fuel' research data in the literature (Fig. 3.2 and Table 3.1) while typical levels of $\delta^{13}C$ for the various sections of the carbon reservoir are indicated in Fig. 3.4.

Table 3.1

Sample*	$\delta^{14}C\%_{00}$	$\delta^{13}C\%_{00}$	$\Delta\%_{00}$
Malt whiskey, 1937	-11.4	-19.9	-21.4
Malt whiskey, 1939	-34.9	-28.1	-29.0
Vintage wine, 1907	-47.3	-38.3	-21.9
Vintage wine, 1907	-27.0	-27.8	-21.5
Flax seed (Belfast), 1934	-34.9	-33.2	-19.1
Wool (Yorkshire), 1851	-30.4	-31.8	-17.2
Wool (Yorkshire), 1851	-23.1	-27.5	-18.3

*Extracted from fuller data given in reference 9. $\delta^{14}C$ and $\delta^{13}C$ carry measurement errors of about $5\%_{00}$ and $0.5\%_{00}$ respectively, in each case.

Although the figures listed here are somewhat selective some illustrate well the need for proper allowance for fractionation. Note particularly the tightening in the match of Δ-values for the two annual pairs (the 1851 wool and the 1907 wine). It must be remembered that changes of $10\%_{00}$ represent an age error of some eighty years. The whiskies of 1937 and 1939 would seem to differ in an age around 190 years without correction, but the 1937 level of $\delta^{13}C$ of $19.9\%_{00}$ is anomalously low. The example of flax has been included as its man-made derivative, linen, is occasionally found in archaeological contexts. The level of $\delta^{13}C$ quoted for the 1934 seed is only about 7% higher than the average for the subsequent fourteen years. (The contribution to seed growth of inactive or non-contemporaneous carbon in the soil seems to be negligible.) Using the average of $\delta^{13}C = 31 \cdot 0\%$ instead of the value directly related to the material would still introduce age errors of around thirty-five years. These examples stress the importance of this refinement in laboratory procedure particularly when handling material from recent times (see also section 3.1.*h*).

The reasons for carbon isotope fractionation are multifold [18,19,20] over and above the macroscopic reservoir features of Fig. 3.4. Some of the many observations in this subject are listed here for reference purposes:

(i) An intrinsic difference in synthesis has been recognized between various tree species: European larch has a CO_2 fractionation factor $1 \cdot 1\%$ more than oak in a similar climate.[21]

(ii) In a worldwide sense fractionation in marine plankton varies in the $\delta^{13}C$-term by as much as $0 \cdot 23\%$ per °C. (reference 22).

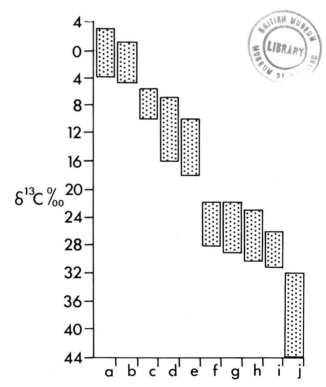

Fig. 3.4 Carbon isotope ratios of various carboniferous materials: a. carbonates; b. volcanic carbon dioxide; c. atmospheric carbon dioxide; d. marine plants; e. marine organisms; f. coal; g. land plants; h. liquid hydrocarbons; i. organic sediments; j. natural gas (reference 18).

(iii) Even the small 0·1–0·2°C drop in mean global temperature since 1940 has been related to a δ^{13}C-increase of about 2‰ over the past decade.

(iv) On land, grasses in low latitudes across the world grow in extreme micro-climatic conditions directly above the soil in warm, dry areas. Their δ^{13}C-values averaged close to 13.8‰ during the weapon-testing era. However, several feet above ground level the fractionation reflects only general climatic conditions (δ^{13}C −24·6‰ for banana leaves in the Canary Islands) and is in far less contrast with temperate counterparts (−27·6‰ on average).

We must anticipate similar levels of variability in isotopic composition of archaeological organic remains and take account of it in final assessment of the radiocarbon dating accuracy.

A similar remark is appropriate for inorganic remains. A recent study of skeletal remains at Mostin, northern California, considered the influence on bone composition of a dominance of freshwater fish in local diet.[23]

One general conclusion worth stressing is that isotopic fractionation *increases* with *lowering* of temperature. The use of the dating method covers at least one important glacial period, some 20,000 years ago, and an era of warm oscillations (the Alleröd period) around 11,000 years ago.

1*f* STANDARD MATERIALS FOR RADIOCARBON DATING

The three effects discussed above, fossil fuel production, weapon testing and isotope fractionation, combine together to set stringent controls upon the standard materials used in this work. Also, with the proliferation of the laboratories now undertaking dating, such standards are essential to allow correlation of results from different sources. There are no lack of basic carbon standards of detailed chemical purity, but two find most use in radiocarbon analysis.

(i) *As a* ^{13}*C-standard* a calcium carbonate from the Cretaceous Peedee formation of South Carolina is used and labelled *PDB belemnite*. Carbon dioxide generated by solution of this material at 25·2°C in 100% H_3PO_4 acid is analysed in a mass spectrometer and the isotopes of this gas determines the zero on scale of fractionation of Fig. 3.4. The abundance of the natural rock supply gives this belemnite its strongest appeal though the NBS Graphite standard *21* has also been considered (δ^{13}C of −27·8‰ on the PDB fractionation scale). Equation (2.4) in the last section indicates how this standard is employed after definition of the unknown sample's δ^{13}C value through,

$$\delta_s{}^{13}C‰ = \left\{ \frac{(^{13}C/^{12}C)_s}{(^{13}C/^{12}C)_{PDB}} - 1 \right\} \times 10^3 \qquad (3.5)$$

As a geological mineral the source of this standard is free of either of the man-made carbon contaminations.

(ii) *For a* [14]*C-standard* the National Bureau of Standards (Washington, D.C.) holds a stock of oxalic acid (COOHCOOH.2H₂O) as a universal reference. This acid is a recent preparation so that it contains some excess activity from the weapon-testing effect. However, wood of AD 1890 (when the Industrial Revolution was scarcely under way) has a measured activity close to 95% that of the modern acid preparation. The accepted ^{14}C-activity standard [24] is taken as 0·95 A_{ox} and the measured deviation of the unknown sample from the standard is given by

$$\delta^{14}C = \left\{\frac{A_s}{0\cdot95\ A_{ox}} - 1\right\} \times 1000 \qquad (3.6a)$$

The oxalic acid itself is somewhat susceptible to isotopic fractionation during laboratory conversion to carbon dioxide. Measurements on twenty different preparations from the acid show a $-19\cdot0\%_0$ $\delta^{13}C$ deviation from the belemnite standard. The correct oxalic activity is derived from the measured level A_{ox}^m, by the relationship,

$$A_{ox} = A_{ox}^m \left\{1 - \frac{2\ (19\cdot0 + \delta^{13}C_{ox})}{1000}\right\} \qquad (3.6b)$$

Artificially-produced *sucrose* is being considered as an alternative, as its fractionation during the oxidation of sample preparation seems very reproducible.

Once the sample's isotopic fractionation has been allowed for, equation (3.4) gives a value of Δ for the true radiocarbon content difference from the present-day natural level. An age is then calculated from,

$$t = \tau\ Log_e \left\{\frac{1000}{1000 + \Delta}\right\} \qquad (3.7)$$

As a simple example to illustrate use of these equations, if A_s is half the oxalic acid standard's activity, in the absence of any isotopic fractionation, $\delta^{14}C = \Delta = -500\%_0$. The naperian logarithm of 2 is 0·693 so that $t = 0\cdot693\tau$. Thus the age equals the half-life of radiocarbon, as it should.

1g   MEASUREMENT TECHNIQUES AND SAMPLE PREPARATION

The means by which the radiocarbon activity of an archaeological sample is determined is complicated by two inherent properties of [14]C:

(i) The beta radiation emitted during the radioactive decay, indicated in equation (3.2), is as a spectrum of energies, the maximum of which is only 160 keV. Such low energy radiation is only very short ranged: for example, the maximum penetration into aluminium would be around 130 microns. By incorporating the carbon into the structure of the counting device itself the recording of the presence of ^{14}C has been kept at quite an efficient level. A Geiger detector requires a filling gas for operation so that deliberate use of the sample converted to that condition is now common.

Carbon dioxide (CO_2) has the great advantage of simple production procedure but there is a tendency for some electronegative impurities, like chlorine, to follow a similar chemical path so that they also occur in the filling gas. Their presence is detrimental to the counting characteristics.[25] Methane (CH_4) is more complex to produce but the presence of impurities is less important. It can also be used at much higher pressures in the counting system increasing the radioactivity concentration in the detection volume. Acetylene (C_2H_2) has also gained some popularity as it is diatomic in carbon so that the counting gas is that much stronger in the radioactive element.[26] Its preparation chemistry is daunting compared with carbon dioxide but, like methane, it is quite tolerant to impurities.

There is the alternative approach available whereby the sample is prepared as a solvent, like benzene. Such liquids scintillate when the energy of radioactive decay is released in its volume and electronically there is no problem in detection of these light pulses. A small sample of original carbon compound gives a compact liquid sample in which the radioactivity is intensely concentrated. The highest yields of benzene (98% or more) have been achieved in the reaction procedure:[27]

$$\text{Sample} \xrightarrow{O_2} CO_2 \xrightarrow{Li} Li_2 C_2 \xrightarrow{H_2O} C_2 H_2 \xrightarrow{\text{catalyst}} C_6 H_6$$

using a vanadium-activated silica-alumina catalyst for the acetylene-benzene conversion stage.[28] Five grammes of carbon in the sample yield a litre of acetylene.

An important advantage of this liquid sample technique has been the removal of low temperature equipment necessary for vacuum line operation in gaseous preparations. Also the isotopic composition of the final benzene product is very close to that of the raw material at the beginning of the chain as the carbon yield is so close to 100%. In contrast we have already noted a weakness in this respect in the conversion of the oxalic acid standard to carbon dioxide gas (see section 1*f*).

(ii) Whatever mode of counting is employed the equipment is just as sensitive to a background of extra pulses particularly those induced by incident cosmic rays. A simple Geiger counter detection system would measure around 800 counts per minute unrelated to ^{14}C-activity in its filling gas. Although some of these counts, perhaps ten to twenty, can be attributed to trace levels of other radioactive impurities in the construction materials of the Geiger tube itself, by far the major problem arises from the ionization of the chamber gas by cosmic-ray muons.[29] Consequently the counter tube is surrounded by a bundle of shield counters which react to the outside radiation and switch off the central detector for the brief duration of the background interference. Use of this anti-coincidence electronics inside radioactivity-free lead or iron shielding (to cut off more general radiation backgrounds) can keep extraneous rates of uncertain origin down to around one count per minute.

Notably this low background is still of a similar magnitude to that of a gramme of archaeological carbon. Also the cosmic-radiation intensity tends to fluctuate throughout the counting period which may be two days or more for older material. When the latter effect is a practical limitation the liquid scintillation approach is strongly favoured as automatic sample changing devices can switch in a 'blank' non-radioactive batch for a brief spell of counting to follow short-term disturbances.

The considerations of low ^{14}C-activity and the continuous presence of a significant and somewhat variable background indicate the problem of applying the radiocarbon dating method to material more than about 30,000 years old (equivalent to about five half-lives of ^{14}C). This time limit has been doubled using the chemistry expedient of *isotopic enrichment* (by deliberate fractionation) though the amounts of raw sample required is far greater.[30] Such an approach is quite rare, as yet, as the prevention of contamination in very low-activity work is problematical. However, there are no doubt several archaeologial problems that could justify such specialized effort as alternative scientific dating methods at that period of the past are scarce.

Contamination, in general, creates some specific problems in radio-carbon dating samples, particularly in bone. Almost all impurities found in wood, charcoal or fabric remains are swiftly cleansed of any 'old' calcium carbonate (deposited out of ground water percolating through the burial medium) using a weak solution of hydrochloric acid (HCl). Also any modern carbon excess derived from absorbed humic acids in the soil can be removed using sodium hydroxide (1N NaOH solution).[31] But with unburnt bone, where porous structure tends to encourage uptake of pollutants, the original *collagen* component is somewhat difficult to recover independently. A preferred procedure is to initially remove the mineral substances and some of the organic extras from crushed bone using an 8% HCl solution, a treatment which also breaks some of the hydrogen bonds of collagen, rendering the latter soluble in a subsequent wash of hot water.[32] Other organic pollutants, like the humic acids and root remains, remain in a residue. The same treatment has been suggested to extract the similar portion of shell's structure, concioline. The pure gelatine produced in each case can be dissolved and used directly as a liquid scintillator.

1h QUOTATION OF RADIOCARBON DATES

The bulk of the published results for radiocarbon dating and research is to be found in *Radiocarbon* (originally a supplement of the *American Journal of Science*). As the most widely recognized and most fully-used scientific dating technique in archaeology it has been the first method to mature to conventional ways of data presentation. In particular the Cambridge Radiocarbon Conference in 1962 agreed that: (i) all dates should be calculated using the *Libby half-life* of 5,568 years (see section 1b) even though recent determinations that average about 5,730 years are generally accepted as correct.[33] (Retrospectively this 3% short fall of the original half-life value was in evidence in Libby's original fit of an exponential decay curve to data for known age samples.[34]) (ii) Ages are then quoted as 'years BP' (Before Present), with a modern zero point of AD 1950. When a date is quoted in terms of AD or BC such notation often implies that the more recent half-life value may have been used and the accompanying text should record the correction made. A typical format for a published radiocarbon date would be as follows:

LAB-NO	GENERAL MATERIAL DESCRIPTION	RADIOCARBON AGE ($\pm$ 1δ) $\delta^{13}C = 0\%_0$

Fuller sample description (both as to its material nature and archaeological context). Details of collection are sometimes added. *Comment* (usually by site excavator): cross-references to other similar sites and alternative dating information. Any likelihood of carbon contamination is also noted.

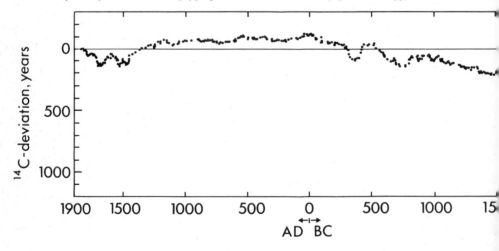

Fig. 3.5 Complete bristlecone pine calibration curve covering the past 7,400 years (^{14}C half-life of 5,730 years used in this case) (reference 35).

Each laboratory has a short identifying letter sequence (e.g. UB for Queen's University, Belfast) and it is generally agreed that quotation of a radiocarbon date in other publications without a numbered identifier is of little value. Some further comments on dating accuracy will be made below (section 1*i*) but purely in terms of convention the standard deviation ($\pm$ 1δ) reflects only the statistics of the counting procedure. For sample and background count rates of S and B, respectively, over a counting period of t, the net count due to ^{14}C is given by $\{(S - B)t\}$. A standard deviation on this count is given by $\{(S + B)t\}^{\frac{1}{2}}$.

1*i* LONG- AND SHORT-TERM FLUCTUATIONS IN THE RADIOCARBON INVENTORY

The inadequacy of an error level quoted only in terms of counting statistics has recently been emphasized by long- and short-term deviations of the ^{14}C-dates from direct correspondence to 'calendar' years. These deviations, evidenced by tree-ring study of the bristlecone pine, are illustrated in Fig. 3.5, for the 7,400 year span for which this timber is available.[35] (The derivation of the so-called 'calibration' curve was discussed in the last chapter as an application of dendrochronology.[36]) Certainly introduction of corrections to conventional radiocarbon dates for long-term deviations (seemingly of as much as $+700$ years at the beginning of the fourth millennium BC) has an appreciable effect upon archaeological interpretation. Re-orientation of cultural and technological links in European prehistory example this.[37] But from the radiochronologist's standpoint the long periods of man's evolution which this dating method covers and that pre-date the tree-ring data are also very important. Thus a major part of recent research in this topic has sought physical mechanisms that could be

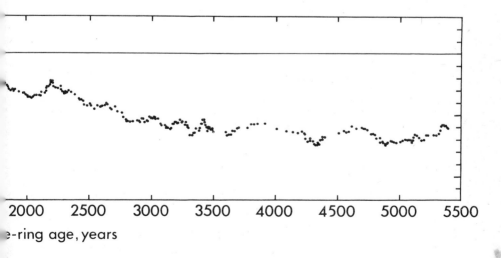

2000   2500   3000   3500   4000   4500   5000   5500

e-ring age, years

responsible for these deviations, to enable some prediction of radio-carbon behaviour in those earlier times.

Whatever hypothetical mechanisms are suggested they must be seen to work in the 'test-zone' covered by the bristlecone pine chronology. Three factors have been considered in detail:

(i) change of ^{14}C-production rate in the stratosphere caused by changes in geomagnetic field intensity,

(ii) change in the ^{14}C-production rate via modulation of the cosmic-ray flux by solar activity, and

(iii) changes in the distribution of the radiocarbon throughout the various components of the exchange reservoir.

In the movement of carbon down through the various atmospheric levels and into the biosphere (which contains the bristlecone pine timber) the inpact of any fresh input is heavily attenuated.

In mixing with the bulk of the worldwide carbon inventory the integrated effect of any brief additional ^{14}C-influx will create only a minor perturbation in the biosphere. A more gradual variation will appear as a modulation on the radiocarbon change with time.[38] Such a long-term modulation would result, for example, from the sinusoidal variation of the Earth's geomagnetic moment (M) over the past millennia (Fig. 3.6a).[39] The deviation, Δ^{14}C%, of measured radiocarbon content from that of recent wood (in practice, it is a pre-industrial era fir from Oregon that sets the zero deviation) shows a similar sinusoidal change with time (Fig. 3.6b).[40] Its period is about 10,350 years which compares reasonably well with the value of this parameter for the M-variation, 8,900 years. Also, in keeping with the reaction characteristics of the exchange reservoir, there is a slight lag in phase of a few hundred years between the ^{14}C-response and the M-variation.

On the basis of this visually strong correlation (Fig. 3.6) it is accepted that the change of the Earth's field intensity is a primary contributor to ^{14}C-variability with time. After this the changes in global climate superimpose another long-term variation. Appreciable quantities of 'old' carbon are locked up in ice which plays no part in the circulatory processes of the reservoir. The gradual increase in temperature since the last Ice Age will have resulted in a steady decrease in ^{14}C-concentration as melting ice swelled the bulk of the oceans. It has been estimated that a practical rate of injection of this fossil carbon of about 0·8% per millennium would join with the geomagnetic data to give excellent agreement about periodicity of the ^{14}C-changes.[41]

Other parameters effected by temperature such as ^{14}C-transfer rate into the oceans and quantity of planktonic life at sea are considered to cause only minor disturbances to the ^{14}C-distribution about the world.[42] The same can be said of the atmosphere's carbon enhancement caused by man's forest clearances in prehistoric times. The mean age

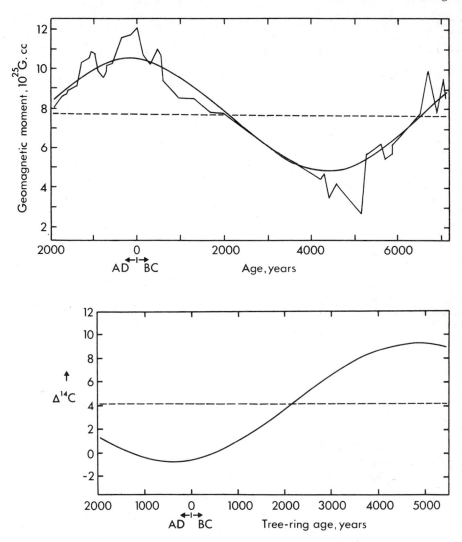

Fig. 3.6   a. Variation of the Earth's magnetic field intensity during archaeological times in Europe. (Data gathered from sites in Czechoslovakia,
Hungary, Poland and Turkey.) A smoothed sinusoidal curve is fitted,
with an equation:

$$M(t) = \left\{ 2 \cdot 8 \sin \frac{2}{8900} (t + 405) + 7 \cdot 7 \right\} \times 10^{25} \text{ Gauss. cc.}$$

This function's period is approximately 8,900 years, its maximum
value is at AD 130 and its minimum value is at 4320 BC (^{14}C half-life
is 5,730 years in this calculation) (reference 39). b. Deviation of the
[14]C-content of wood dated by dendrochronology from that of a recent
wood (specifically Oregon fir pre-dating the industrial revolution)
over the past seven millennia (reference 40).

of the timber and the associated humus would be only about 300 years, thus creating only a small fossil fuel effect as far as radiocarbon dating is concerned.

Once the general trend of geomagnetically-induced ^{14}C-variations are stripped away from the tree-ring calibration curve (Fig. 3.5) we are still left with many short-term fluctuations unexplained. So far these have been most closely tied to cyclic behaviour of solar activity as a periodicity of about 400 years in the ^{14}C-data is in agreement with aurora observations.[43] A high sunspot activity influences matters in two ways:

(i) intensification of the weak interplanatory magnetic field so that the cosmic-ray flux is subdued close to the Earth and

(ii) modification of the cosmic-ray energy spectrum creating a bias away from the slower particles that are responsible for ^{14}C-production.[44]

However, sharper activity changes probably do not explain the much shorter ^{14}C-fluctuations that may occur within a decade or so: the carbon reservoir's attenuation mechanism sees to that. These rapid changes might be explicable in terms of violent ^{14}C-enhancement created by solar flares, or, more probably, by short-term climatic variations.

To appreciate the role of climate in this part of the discussion it should be recalled that the deep ocean has an apparent age of about 1,200 years or so (section 1*d*). Purely in terms of relative bulk of carbon content the whole amount in the atmosphere must be trans-ferred to the ocean sixty times over, i.e. complete atmosphere-to-sea transfer over some twenty years. Short-term temperature variations on this time scale will influence the ^{14}C/^{12}C ratio in the atmosphere as fractionation is modified in the sea-surface exchange process. One example of strong climate/^{14}C-fluctuation correlation of this nature is thought to be the sharp excursion during the eighth century BC which matches significant climatic change in northern America and central Europe during the so-called Grenz-Horizont period.

Thus to attain the objective of understanding the likely effectiveness of the radiocarbon dating method back in time between 10–40,000 years ago the behaviour of the Earth's magnetic field and climate must be predictable. For the former of these we run into new problems over and above simple north-south dipole intensity changes of the type described earlier. There is also abundant evidence of geomagnetic excursions that completely reversed the field's direction or almost did so at various times throughout the world.[45] One clearly recorded in aboriginal fire-places at Lake Mungo in Australia carried with it an appreciably higher field strength (by about 50%), a feature bound to create a large ^{14}C-hiatus during and after the excursion interval of roughly 3,000 years.[46] (The timing of this excursion is around 30,000 BC by radiocarbon dates for the area, but the accuracy of this analysis is probably plus or minus a couple of millennia in the light of the foregoing discussion.) Equally troublesome is the indication of a long period of low field intensity after that time during which the atmospheric ^{14}C-concentration probably rose by more than 33%. Dating for the last glacial period and its termination (around 20,000 years ago) could be underestimated by more than 2,000 years.

It is a pity that climate plays a secondary role in long-term ^{14}C-deviations as our knowledge of temperature variations in the past is comparatively good. Ice cores from Greenland[47] carry a reliable climate indicator for the past 85,000 years in their oxygen isotope ratios ($^{18}O/^{16}O$), with fractionation responding at about 0·7‰ per °C.[48] The general picture of timing and extent of glacier advance can probably be estimated quite accurately (see Fig. A.2, Appendix A).

At one time it seemed that better chances of interpretation of early radiocarbon dates lay with two of the older archaeological sciences, varve chronology and sedimentation rate determination. For the former, counting of the clay layering of Swedish varves and of the algae-microfragment sediments of lake varves in Minnesota both confirm the ^{14}C-deviations over the past seven millennia. However, before that time the Swedish material suggests a reversion as earliest varve counts (c. 10500 BC) match their conventional radiocarbon ages once more.[49] This is seen to fall in line with geomagnetic predictions of sinusoidal variation of ^{14}C-excess (Fig. 3.6). In contrast the Minnesota material indicates a ^{14}C-excess of about 4 to 9% over that same period.[50] Meanwhile the interpretation of lake sedimentation *rates* in many parts of the world suggests even higher divergence of ^{14}C-dates with a continuation of the rising trend of ^{14}C-concentration back to about 12000 BC, at least. Thus it now seems that reconciliation must be achieved between these various data sources before any independent attack on the problems of radiocarbon dating can be contemplated.

So many of the finer details of the radiocarbon variations remain unresolved that no strong attempt has yet been made to routinely correct older conventional dates, least of all those prior to the bristlecone pine era. All results in the following sections are quoted strictly within the conventional framework though in many cases the reader may be tempted to adopt at least one form of correction factor to produce more absolute ages and possibly a more realistic error than the one quoted.

2 GENERAL DATING APPLICATIONS

The impact of the radiocarbon dating technique is best illustrated by the fact that almost all the other scientific approaches to archaeology discussed in this book evidence their reliability by comparison with its time scale. In particular, ^{14}C-dates are now turning pollen zonation into an ancillary source of chronology and consequently placing time markers on many of the important periods of climatic change that influenced man's recent evolution and choice of habitat (Fig. A.1, Appendix A). Perhaps the most general feeling that is derived in reviewing some twenty years of routine application of this method is that classical techniques in archaeology previously kept chronology short, tightly weaving cultural links (and the succession of technological advances) into quite narrow time periods.

These points can be illustrated by examples in British archaeology.[51] The beginnings of the Neolithic period are synchronized with the '*Ulmus* decline' that occurred throughout north-western Europe. The sudden fall of elm pollen concentration is offset by the appearance of agricultural weeds that indicate forest stripping and animal husbandry. (Young elm shoots provide excellent fodder for cattle.) The consistent dating of this horizon throughout the land to 3000 BC, or a few centuries earlier, lies more than a millennium beyond previous classical estimates.[52] Also the extent of the Neolithic period is estimated at about 1,200 years, many centuries more than expected. More recently, near the end of the Bronze Age, the signs of worsening climate around the eleventh to eighth century BC (as noted in the previous section) are clearly to be seen in the arrival of much new insect fauna, notably the beetle, *Prostomis mandibularis* (F), which lives in wood that is in an advanced state of decay.[53] Rotting timber and sodden forest humus gave way to marshland and peat bogs over which man built sturdy trackways of oak. These, in turn, yielded fresh surfaces for active growth of *Sphagnum* moss which, in death, accumulates as peat growth to form blanket bogs. This anaerobic peat overlay forms an excellent preservation medium for the trackway beams and several have been excavated in fine condition. These beams and their enveloping peat all offer excellent material for radiocarbon analysis in areas like Thorne Moor and Shapwick Heath.

Like the trackways that stand in buried isolation there are many wooden artefacts of uncertain typology which are now placed in a preliminary age sequence. Into such a category fall the many prehistoric boats of widely differing design, like the elaborate construction of those found at North Ferriby (Plate 3.1) where the heavy oak planks are stitched by slender lengths of yew. The Neolithic peat deposits also preserved some rare specimens of yew long-bows, including one fashioned from flat wooden staves bound with leather (Q-646; 4650 ± 120 BP). Here again, with no stylistic guidelines, ^{14}C-dating was necessary to place these weapons apart from their younger counterparts of the Early Bronze Age also shaped from yew branches (Plate 3.2: Q-684; 3680 ± 120 years BP).

Frequently, individual burials pose a similar problem of context loneliness not just in Britain but throughout the world. Though the radiocarbon dating range is extremely short compared with the whole

3.1 Prehistoric sewn boat excavated at North Ferriby, Yorkshire. Radiocarbon age, 2700 ± 150 years BP (BM-58). (Photograph: courtesy of the National Maritime Museum, London.)

3.2 Early Bronze Age yew bow found deep in the peat near Cambridge in 1885. Radiocarbon age, 3680 ± 120 years BP (Q-684). (Photograph: courtesy of the Pitt Rivers Museum, Oxford.)

five million-year time span of hominid development reviewed in various parts of this book the method's contribution has been appreciable, if only because it covers the transitional period of Neanderthal man to Modern man and the spurt of human versatility that went with it. We now know that this transition occurred about 40,000 years ago in Europe and at least five millennia earlier in Africa.[54] In the latter case much of what is known of that early period has been pieced together at the site of Border Cave, northern Natal, South Africa, where fine preservation conditions protected fragile evidence of man's occupation some 50,000 years ago, like bedding twigs and leaves, feathers and even insect wings.[55] Ground haematite pigment from these levels and in all deposits down to bed rock indicate mining activities (probably at the local Ngwenya source of Lion Cavern) while 35,000 year-old notched bones reveal an example of simple counting.

Though of quite different antiquity burials in the Border Cave area show one distinctive feature in common with younger, dated skeletal finds elsewhere, the liberal use of red pigments (where necessarily cinnabar served as a substitute for ochres) for ceremonial purposes. Examples include the Neanderthal site at La Chapelles-aux-Saints, France,[56] the *Paviland Man* from Wales (18460 ± 340 years BP: BM-374),[57] the permafrost-sealed graves of Sungir in northern Russia, the 8,000 year-old platform shrines of Catal Huyuk and the elaborate Shang Dynasty tombs in China of the second millennium BC. Age determination of these sites and of many other important burials, like that of the rare *Nevada Indian mummy* from the New World (Plate 3.3) (c. 500 BC),[58] stand amongst the ^{14}C-dating methods major contributions.

In recent archaeological periods the development of man can be charted out in a series of transition zones such as those associated with metallurgical innovation or with the development of farming or with introduction of ceramics and variations of their styles. In these aspects nowhere has the impact of ^{14}C-dating been greater than in northern and western Africa. Analysis covers the period of replacement of a quartz microlithic tradition with a stone axe + pottery culture in Nigeria (c. 3600 BC) recorded at the rock shelter of Iwo Eleru (Plate 3.4) and the cattle husbandry recorded in cave paintings at Tassili n'Ajjer in the Sudan (c. 3000 BC).[59] Later, in contrast to the order of events in Europe, it seems that the beginnings of Iron and Copper ages in West Africa were almost contemporary and date close to the fifth century BC, while a bronze-casting era was comparatively delayed to the end at

3.3 Indian mummy from Chimney Cave, Lake Winnemucca, Nevada. Radiocarbon age for bone collagen, 2500 ± 80 years BP (UCLA-689) and for skin
tissue, 2510 ± 80 years BP (UCLA-690). The surrounding vegetal clothing
yielded 2590 ± 80 years BP (UCLA-692). (Photograph: courtesy of Dr P. C.
Orr, Western Speleological Institute, Santa Barbara, California.)

77

3.4   Rock shelter at Iwo Eleru, Nigeria, where a stone-axe and pottery culture replaced a quartz microlithic tradition, c. 3600 BC. (Photograph: courtesy of Professor T. Shaw, University of Ibadan, Nigeria.)

the first millennium AD.[60] Also many of the highspots of Nigerian verbal legend have been pinpointed, with the dating of several royal graves of Ife, like that of the twelfth century ruler, Lafogido. (The ancestral hero, Oronmiyon, is reputed to have set out from there to found the Edo dynasty in Benin and, out of respect for him, each king's head was sent back for burial.)

[14]C-dating has begun to lay a sound foundation for our under-standing of farming structure in Neolithic times and its development from supplementation of a diet based on hunting to a primary role in settlement life.[61] The earliest site of Zawi Chemi Shanidar, northern Iraq c. 9000 BC, traces out, in its successive cave deposits and make-shift huts, a transfer in interest from wild goats to domesticated sheep many of which were killed young to provide food and skins.[62] There are several sites of this nature in France and one excavated at La Adam Cave on the Black Sea coast but they lack any absolute chronology so

it is impossible to judge if their development was truly contemporary with the Iraqi site. Cereal cropping was also well under way by the eighth millennium BC in the Near East and it seems likely that Europe entered a similar phase quite shortly afterwards. The fixed chronological point of 6220 BC for such farming at Nea Nikomedeia, Macedonia, certainly post-dates extensive wheat, barley and flax growth at Argissa, Thessaly, a 'tell' settlement of unknown antiquity.

Some of the potential of radiocarbon analysis in a study of much more recent material, of the medieval period and later, has been realized despite the sharpness of ^{14}C-fluctuations over the past few centuries (Fig. 3.5). In conjunction with judgments of experts of medieval architectural history many anomalies in construction of the great barns and market halls of France and England have been clarified.[63] On a much smaller scale several parchment manuscripts and charters of the Renaissance period have been successfully studied[64] and the dating method's application to authenticity problems amongst such documents given consideration. Forgery detection of paintings (using the medium, linseed oil) has been suggested searching for the much higher activities of ^{14}C associated with post-1952 weapon testing.[65]

3 SPECIALIZED DATING APPLICATIONS

3a THE ROOTS OF IRON AGE INDUSTRY

The displacement of bronze by iron for weapon manufacture carried with it many changes in the international power scene throughout the first millennium BC. In China the advent of the long iron sword added to the invention of the crossbow to transform military strategy during the restless era of Chinese history known as the 'Warring States' period (475–221 BC). In the West, almost a millennium earlier, the Egyptian army of Rameses had been ruthlessly crushed by the Hittite troops of Muwatallis, with his iron-sworded regiments and squadrons of iron-tyred chariots. Some centuries later the fate of control of the fertile Nile region of Egypt had largely hinged upon the superior armoury that iron offered when a fully-equipped Assyrian army routed the incumbent Nubian forces in 666 BC. Iron also brought with it some improvement in the lot of peasant farmers as well, offering sturdy shares for the ox-pulled plough, plus hoes and woodworking adzes.

From a chronological standpoint it is fortunate that charcoal played an important role in early iron manufacture. The metal would be too soft to work conveniently but for the carbon impurity it gathers from the smelting fuel during ore reduction.[66] Consequently furnace remains, forge hearths and slag debris (Plate 3.5) supply ample material for radiocarbon analysis. A combination of ancient documentation, this scientific data and some folklore has made possible the tracing of iron development across the African continent, over the past three millennia.

3.5   Iron slag rich in carbon nodules, associated with the ancient iron-smelting furnaces of the site Kgopolwe 4 at Palabora. Radiocarbon age, 280 ± 60 years BP (Y-1658). (Photograph: courtesy of Professor N. J. van der Merwe, State University of New York, Binghampton.)

This information is summarized here in conjunction with the map of Fig. 3.7.

Wrought iron and steel production using a bloom furnace (operating at about 1150°C) was developed by the Hittites as early as 1800 BC and in usage there and in the Babylonian Empire during Hammurabi's reign (c. 1750 BC). Despite bitter experience in war, the Egyptians had only absorbed iron into their technology to a limited degree by the twelfth century BC, yet far less sophisticated nomadic groups of Phrygians had swarmed through the Hittite capital of Hattusas only a few years earlier and promptly embargoed iron export, clearly appreciating the metal's value. Two centuries later the upheavals of the northern lands had subsided and a Phoenician civilization had crystallized, controlling the major ports of Ugarit, Byblos, Sidon and Tyre. Their maritime dominion spread to the north-west coast of Africa (leading ultimately to colonization at Carthage) and iron technology went with the trade.

At this stage there is no dating evidence to suggest that the spread of iron working into West Africa came from anywhere other than Phoenician settlements via caravan trade routes. The Nile regions

continued to accept this metallurgical transition only cautiously and the major industry that emerged there in the Nubian region of Meröe only flourished after 400 BC. The southward movement is recorded in its passage through Nigeria by the closely-dated furnace site of Taruga (fourth to fifth century BC) of the Nok culture.[67]

Fig. 3.7 The chronological development of Iron Age industry in Africa as indicated by radiocarbon analysis. Related sites are as follows: B = Babylon; Ht = Hattusas; By = Byblos; S = Sidon; T = Tyre; C = Carthage; Mp = Memphis; Th = Thebes; M = Meröe; Ak = Aksum; Nt = Ntereso; Ta = Taruga; Sa = Sanga; F = Furi i mine; Ma = Machili; Ka = Kapula; Pa = Palabora; Tk = Talaky (references 66, 68).

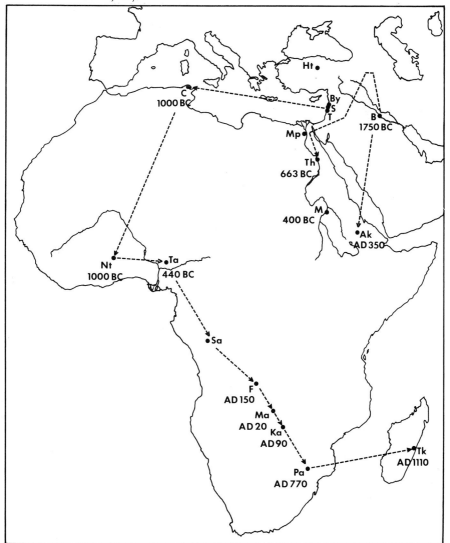

Tenuous radiocarbon links through Angola and the Congo carry the iron chain to the Transvaal at sites like Palabora which was fully operative by the ninth century AD.[68] There these restless tribes chose to settle and develop a metal industry that continued until the beginning of this century.[69] The present-day archaeological site consists of grass-covered mounds of slag and furnace debris scattered over the plain that lies beneath the Lolwe hills. From excavations here we can begin to appreciate the high value put on early metal work with an exchange rate of around six iron hoes to a head of cattle and use of the same implements as bridal price payment.

The African routes of Iron Age development are primarily built on charcoal remains found in association with the metal artefacts. However, recent assay of the iron itself had indicated that its own content of carbon is sufficient to allow direct dating. The wrought iron of the Hittites would carry only about 0·06% carbon at most: an upgrading to steel requires the incorporation of more carbon (0·1–2·0%) by a long high temperature heating. These levels would typify the carbon contents in iron of the West from its origins through to the late fourteenth century AD.[70] In contrast the ancient iron from China was produced by blast furnace treatment of the ore (at about 1400°C). The 'cast' iron that results from this method of manufacture contains much more carbon (1·5–5·0%) than western material. Steel, which appears in that area in the third century BC, was produced by oxidation of some of this high carbon content.

For the past 500 years blast furnace preparation has dominated the iron industry but important changes have occurred in the source of fuels. Up until the beginning of the eighteenth century coal, in its raw form, had been avoided as it produced inferior iron alloys with a high sulphur content. However, attitudes changed swiftly after the introduction of 'coke' furnaces at Coalbrookdale, England, in 1709, so that, by the middle of the nineteenth century, charcoal had been almost completely displaced as a fuel throughout Europe. (The Swedish iron industry was exceptional in delaying its switch from charcoal to coke until well into the twentieth century.) Coke was first used in the United States, in Pennsylvania, shortly after 1830. This technological change is evidenced in the ^{14}C-content of the iron's carbon as the fossil fuel inclusions will show no radioactivity. Some illustrative material is presented in Table 3.2.

It is worth recording here the potential of this work in authentication of cast-iron sculptures of the Ming Dynasty (c. fifteenth to sixteenth century AD) depicting Buddhist deities. These are usually of sufficient bulk to permit adequate metal sample (some 50 g) to give a good carbon yield. Radiocarbon dating of wooden sculptures is open to question on the grounds of availability of old timber but the charcoal used in cast-iron making will be derived from freshly-cut wood still 'green' with sap and thus contemporary with the sculpture. In addi-

Table 3.2: ^{14}*C-dating of iron artefacts*

Source (archaeological date)	Artefact	% carbon	^{14}C-date (years)
Sian, China (Han Dynasty, 221 BC–220 AD)	Stove grating	3·2	2060 ± 80 BP (Y–1511)
Loyang, China (Warring States, 480–221 BC)	Pole supports	3·1	2380 ± 80 BP (Y–1513)
Roman Fort at Inchtuthil, Scotland (AD 85)	Nails	0·22	1850 ± 80 BP (Y–1510)
Hopewell Furnace, Pennsylvania (AD 1771–1845)	Furnace debris	2·0	200 ± 60 BP (Y–1506)
Trading Post, South Dakota (AD 1870–1900)	Stove part	3·0	c. 25,000 BP (Y–1505)

tion, the mistaken use of modern coke in a forgery's production would make authenticity judgment even more clearcut.

3*b*   THE RANCHO LA BREA TAR-PITS OF CALIFORNIA
Contamination of sample is a problem in radiocarbon dating that has received much attention as it is a more limiting factor on the range of the method deep into the past than the ^{14}C-half-life. For example even

3.6   The tar-pits at Old Hancock Ranch house, Rancho La Brea, California. (Photograph: courtesy of Dr R. L. Reynolds, Natural History Museum, Los Angeles County, California.)

a 1% addition of modern material to organic remains that are truly 60,000 years old will yield a laboratory age of only 34,000 years.[71] Several cleansing laboratory procedures are now standard (section 1g) to cope with normal levels of carbonates and humic acid in burial media. In rare cases this treatment is inadequate and specialized extraction methods are called for. For organic remains, like peat, that are likely to be in prolonged contact with ground water the limitation of dating to a pure component of cellulose is advocated.[72] However, perhaps the most remarkable radiocarbon dating achieved in the face of adversity relates to the petroleum-impregnated bones from the Tar-pits of Rancho La Brea. in California.[73]

Tar seepage from underlying oil-bearing strata creates an unusual form of stratigraphy with only a few stable regions of oxidized asphaltum and compacted clay.[74] These reflect a period of quiescence in an otherwise dynamic activity of oil and gas in mixing entombed remains (Plate 3.6). The Rancho La Brea area is a site of active oil seepage that may have looked like water pools to the local animals which, on approach, became trapped in the surrounding tar. Carnivores sought to feed on these victims and so, in turn, were ensnared as well.[75] Consequently the tar, which acts as a fine preservative, now contains a very comprehensive representation of the fauna of the Los Angeles Basin area during the Pleistocene era. Many of the animals are now extinct, like the almost legendary sabre-tooth tiger (*Smilodon cali-*

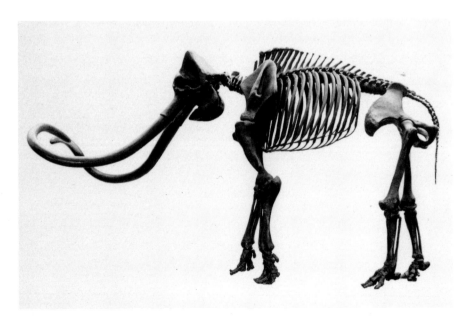

3.7 Mounted skeleton, *Mammuthus imperator*, reconstructed from bones found at the Rancho La Brea tar-pits. (Photograph: courtesy of Dr R. L. Reynolds, Natural History Museum, Los Angeles County, California.)

fornicus) and the Imperial mammoth, yet their intact skeletal remains have allowed their complete reconstruction (Plate 3.7). To the list of the ill-fated ancient local inhabitants we should add *Homo sapiens*, together with a multitude of bird and insect species and remnants of coniferous trees.

The tar-soaked wood offered suitable radiocarbon material as the contaminant could be treated well with xylol washing. But there remained a question-mark whether such analysis would be directly linked to nearby bone remains in the face of possible context turbulence. The petroleum was more insidiously incorporated in the La Brea fossil bones themselves so a method of microanalysis of collagen amino acids was adopted.[76] Such amino acids would not be present in the tar-pit matrix materials so they can present no spoiling problems.

After routine cleaning of the bone, including decalcification, the collagen-petroleum residue was hydrolyzed in $6N$ HCl. The resulting hydrolyzate was then divided in a chromatograph-column of Dowex 50-WX8 resin charged with $4N$ HCl. Elution with $5N$ NH_4OH freed the sorbed amino acids which could then be converted to highly purified CO_2 suitable for a proportional counter. Separate gas chromatography of a portion of the purified acids, seeking a hexane extract, checked for any residual petroleum contamination.

Several dense mid-shaft femoral bone sections from the sabre-tooth tiger yielded dates ranging between 10700 and 29700 years BC, comparing well with associated wood analysis and showing, surprisingly, good increase of ^{14}C-ages with greater depth.[77] Conservative estimates of 40,000 years have been suggested for the range of antiquity of fossil assemblages in even deeper parts of these tar deposits.

Such amino-acid analysis has a potential for dating other seep sites rich in faunal remains, for example at McKittrick and Carpinteria (also in California) and at Talara, in Peru.[78] Some improvements of technique are also envisaged if other sources of contamination, like impregnated preservatives, are feared. A major constituent of bone collagen, hydroxyproline, is rarely present in other proteins and this could also be obtained in pure form using similar chromatographic methods.

Chapter 4

Radioactive Decay Techniques, including the Potassium-Argon and Uranium Series Methods

1   INTRODUCTION

The time range of applicability of the radiocarbon dating method is limited by the half-life of the *parent* isotope in the decay process (^{14}C), 5,730 years. A sample more than 50,000 years old will contain less than 0·2% of its original ^{14}C-activity, a level which would be submerged in background signal in laboratory analysis. But there are many other natural isotopes in archaeological and geological materials with quite different decay half-lives which are potentially usable for dating purposes in a similar manner. For example, silicon-32 (^{32}Si), which is created by interaction of cosmic-ray particles with argon nuclei in the atmosphere, has been considered recently for the dating of the biogenic content of lake sediments [1] as that isotope has a half-life of about 650 years and a readily-measurable beta-radiation emission with a maximum energy of 0·21 MeV.

However, few of the decay schemes discussed here behave quite so simply. One group of important isotopes, all components of the decay series of uranium or thorium, acts as *pseudo-parent*, becoming the head of radioactive chains in some artificial way (Table 4.1). In the case of lead extraction from galena ore, ^{210}Pb is carried through with the metal while radium separates out and is then removed in the resulting waste.[2] Then this lead isotope is 'unsupported' by its long-lived precursor, radium-226, so that subsequent decay follows with the short half-life of twenty-two years. Similarly ionium (^{230}Th), when it is precipitated in ocean sediments, loses the support of its parent uranium which remains in solution in the sea water.[3] Both ^{210}Pb and ^{230}Th have been successfully applied to dating problems (section 4.2).

Otherwise the emphasis is laid on the *daughter* product growth with the parent assumed to have remained almost unchanged since the onset of the decay period. Amongst the most important of these in geological work is the rubidium-strontium decay (^{87}Rb–^{87}Sr) with a half-life of 5·0 × 10^{10} yr, which has been used to date the earliest granites of

Table 4.1: Radioactive decay characteristics for uranium and thorium

Uranium-238 decay series		Uranium-235 decay series		Thorium -232 decay series	
Isotope and emitted radiation	Half-life	Isotope and emitted radiation	Half-life	Isotope and radiation emitted	Half-life
^{238}U	4.5×10^9 years	^{235}U	7.1×10^8 years	^{232}Th	1.4×10^{10} years
↓ ^{234}Th	24.1 days	↓ ^{231}Th	25 hours	↓ ^{228}Ra	5.7 years
↓ ^{234}Pa	1.2 minutes	↓ ^{231}Pa	3.4×10^4 years	↓ ^{228}Ac	6.1 years
↓ ^{234}U	2.5×10^5 years	↓ ^{227}Ac	22 years	↓ ^{228}Th	1.9 years
↓ ^{230}Th	8.0×10^4 years	↓ ^{227}Th	18.6 days	↓ ^{224}Ra	3.6 days
↓ ^{226}Ra	1620 years	↓ ^{223}Ra	11.2 days	↓ ^{220}Rn	54 seconds
↓ ^{222}Rn	3.83 days	↓ ^{219}Rn	3.9 seconds	↓ ^{216}Po	0.16 seconds
↓ ^{218}Po	3 minutes	↓ ^{215}Po	1.8×10^{-3} seconds	↓ ^{212}Pb	10.6 hours
↓ ^{214}Pb	27 minutes	↓ ^{211}Pb	36 minutes	↓ ^{212}Bi	
↓ ^{214}Bi	20 minutes	↓ ^{211}Bi	2.2 minutes	64% ↗	1.0 hours
↓ ^{214}Po	1.64×10^{-4} seconds	↓ ^{207}Tl	4.8 minutes	^{212}Po	
↓ ^{210}Pb	22 years	↓ ^{207}Pb		↓ 36%	3×10^{-7} seconds
↓ ^{210}Bi	5 days			^{208}Pb	
↓ ^{210}Po	138 days			↓ ^{208}Tl	1.0 hours
↓ ^{206}Pb				↓ ^{208}Pb	3.1 minutes

Earth's history (to about 4.0×10^9 yr).[4] However, in archaeological terms this decay is too slow to be of any value: even for a quite high rubidium content of 100 ppm in a sample, after a million years the ^{87}Sr content will be less than 4×10^{-10}. Instead attention is focused on the argon-40 build up from the radioactive component of potassium, ^{40}K, which follows a half-life of 1.30×10^9 yr. It is this *K-Ar dating method* [5] that forms the theme of the first section of this chapter.

I POTASSIUM-ARGON DATING

Ia THE DECAY OF POTASSIUM-40

Of the total potassium content of a mineral only 0·0118% is in the form of the radioisotope, ^{40}K. This isotope decays in a rather unusual manner with two possibilities of daughter products, calcium-40 and argon-40. As illustrated in Fig. 4.1, 89% of the potassium disintegrations lead to ^{40}Ca through a beta-radiation emission (maximum energy, 1·33 MeV) while the remaining 11% convert to ^{40}Ar, with gamma-ray emission (energy of 1·46 MeV), by a nuclear rearrangement process known as K-electron capture. A high temperature heating of the mineral in antiquity will drive out all the argon accrued over earlier geological history, as this element is gaseous. Once the mineral has cooled its constituent potassium will begin to replenish the argon stock from its newly-set zero concentration. The ^{40}Ar in the sample (age of t years) measured in present day is given by

$$^{40}\text{Ar} = (0\cdot11) \,.\, ^{40}\text{K} \,.\, (\exp \lambda t - 1) \tag{4.1a}$$

where λ is the decay constant for the complete ^{40}K-decay, equal to $5\cdot30 \times 10^{-10}$ yr^{-1}. (The decay constant is defined by $\lambda \,.\, t_{\frac{1}{2}} = 0\cdot693$. For the ^{40}K decay, each branch carries its own λ-value of $0\cdot58 \times 10^{-10}$ yr^{-1} and $4\cdot72 \times 10^{-10}$ yr^{-1} for K-capture and β-emission respectively.) Even for the huge time span of twenty million years covering hominoid development discussed below, this age equation can be justifiably simplified to a linear relation:

$$^{40}\text{Ar} = (5\cdot82 \times 10^{-11}) \,.\, ^{40}\text{K} \,.\, t \tag{4.1b}$$

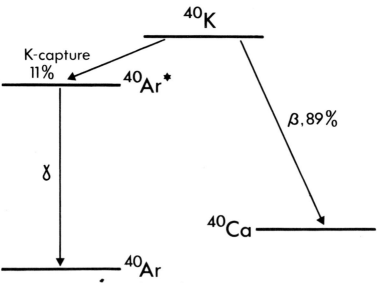

Fig. 4.1 Decay scheme of potassium-40.

Features that give this method its strength in archaeological analysis are:

(i) Potassium is a common elemental constituent in many of the Earth's minerals. Indeed in some minerals like micas and alkali feldspars it is a major component of the crystal structure and present at 3–10% concentration.[6] Volcanic pumice and obsidian carry about a 3% potassium content.

(ii) Argon is an element detected with particularly high sensitivity in a mass spectrometer. Detection limitations are set mainly by the argon background level in the instrument and the handling capacity of its argon gas extraction system.[7] A practical lower limit of age determination of about 10^4 yr is usually considered reasonable on these grounds.

1b DATING COMPLICATIONS AND REMEDIES

The breakdown of the basic assumptions of K-Ar dating quickly narrows down the choice of minerals that can be successfully analysed. The sources of these difficulties may be summarized as follows:

(i) *Argon excess* at the 'time zero' point is typified by the gas retention of deep-sea basalts. When the magma erupts into the ocean environment previously-formed Ar is held by high hydrostatic pressures while the rock is chilled into rapid consolidation.[8] The mineral, hornblende, has been shown to suffer from this problem,[9] sometimes exhibiting a starting 'antiquity' of as much as fifty million years. Pyroxene also is often unreliable as even trace levels of argon excess can heavily overshadow the decay effects of its inherently low potassium content (rarely greater than 0.2%). This 'swamping' of the historically-accrued ^{40}Ar by an inherent component has also posed severe problems in the dating of recent lava flows even if the potassium content is high and even though such materials de-gas in the volcanic process quite well.[10]

(ii) *Atmospheric argon contamination* in present day was recognized in the early stages of this subject. Many minerals adsorb argon not only on the outer surface but on crystal cleavages, at intergranular boundaries and at lattice imperfections like gas 'bubble'-cavities.[11] Extra argon may be supplied by the melting equipment used by gathering the gas stored in the sample.[12]

A simple solution to this second factor would seem to lie with the isotopic breakdown of argon in the air, as $^{40}Ar:^{38}Ar:^{36}Ar = 296:0.19:1$. The presence of ^{36}Ar in a sample acts as a tracer of the atmospheric contamination. This works well if the initial argon excess discussed above is of minor importance or its isotopic composition is the same as that of the air. Unfortunately many authors have noted that the latter notion is frequently erroneous.[13] Though sophisticated graphical techniques of handling batches of data, termed 'isochron' plots and 'initial argon' diagrams, have met with some success, conventional K-Ar dating is treated as suspect when applied to single samples. Only recently, with the development of the refinement of 'age-spectrum' analysis (discussed in section 4.1c), have these problems been overcome.

Both factors (i) and (ii) lead to overestimation of age, if ignored. Other factors cause underestimation:

(iii) *Argon loss by diffusion* is a common phenomenon in the potassium-rich feldspars, orthoclase and microcline, so these minerals are rarely studied by the conventional technique. Though the gas mobility is largely controlled by temperature other parameters play a part, particularly in glassy structures. Electron microprobe studies of basalts have illustrated that if the post-volcanic cooling was slow enough K-bearing crystalline inclusions of well-defined lattice structure retain argon well while a more rapidly chilled glass matrix will not. Also, in *obsidian*, weathering hydration causes an acceleration of argon release.[14] In several forms of rock other alteration mechanisms such as a re-crystallization of a potassium salt or breakdown of feldspars to form kaolinite also upset the K/Ar ratio.

Even minerals that are normally regarded as reliable for dating purposes (like biotite and sanidine) can suffer diffusion losses if they occur in grain sizes of dimensions comparable with the argon diffusion length of the argon gas in that mineral. Regions of crystal damage or alteration to fine-grained by-products all supply gas outlet paths. Understandably one of the initial studies of a material submitted for K-Ar dating is a detailed petrographic analysis seeking these forms of sample disorder and the presence of sound minerals.

(iv) *External contamination* sources can carry the age estimation into error in either direction. On the one hand fresh materials may be deposited in pores (notably calcite or chlorite) or the present-day measure of the K-content upset directly by chemical attack that results in some ion substitution and leaching. On the other hand even minute additions of non-contemporaneous, older materials can be quite disastrous. This problem is particularly important in deposits of volcanic glass falls (tuffs) which could gather some wall rock from the lava vent or subsequently collect extraneous material carried by ground water percolation. Consequently 'whole-rock' K-Ar analysis by conventional means is rarely treated as reliable and most attention now focuses on specific mineral extracts. It is these considerations that substantially dictate the sample size eventually processed and thereby set a practical lower limit of around a million years or so in age determination.

1c EXPERIMENTAL PROCEDURE

The standard technique of flame photometry is used for total K-content determination, with the ^{40}K-concentration subsequently estimated on the basis of its known abundance.[15] (Accuracy of around $\pm 1\%$ is regarded as quite practical for K-contents of more than 1%.) Argon analysis follows a more complex course beginning with a surface etching in warm hydrofluoric acid. Apart from the convenient removal of adhering matrix material from a specific mineral extract this acid treatment will achieve a significant reduction of the atmospheric argon component that lies mainly in the outer layers of the crystals.

Furnace heating up to about 1800°C (to completely melt the sample), under vacuum, leads to extraction of all the argon gas together with other inert noble gases (like helium and radon) and several other impurities. Some purification is possible in the furnace itself, using 'getter.'-materials (such as zirconium and titanium sponge) which preferentially absorb various gases. However, the cleansing stage is usually extended by feeding the gas mixture first through a 500°C furnace containing copper chips and copper oxide powder (thus trapping hydrogen and oxygen extras), then into an 850°C furnace containing titanium granules (taking out carbon monoxide and dioxide and any nitrogen).[16] All the noble gases will move freely through these systems and they are collected only when absorbed onto cooled charcoal.

The slight differences in atomic mass, M, of each isotope of the argon is detected by a mass spectrometer. Ions produced by exposure to low energy electrons (emitted from a hot tungsten filament) are beamed through a magnetic field that diverts their path through a circular path. The radius of that path is proportional to $\sqrt{M}$ so that the various isotopes arrive at a detector along different, spaced paths. At each detection position the incident number of ions is a measure of the original concentration of the gas at the spectrometer's input. The sensitivity of the equipment is evaluated by addition of an ^{38}Ar 'spike' of known concentration to the sample gas at the ionization stage.[17] Recent improvements in this form of spectroscopy, using a cyclotron resonance principle, have appreciably heightened its sensitivity and reproducibility.[18]

1d THE AGE-SPECTRUM APPROACH

In the earlier discussion errors and limits of the order of a million years or more were quoted. Clearly these uncertainties could only be tolerated in geological dating analyses and put a large question-mark about the applicability of K-Ar dating in the archaeological era. Indeed only when suites of minerals extracted from 'young' materials are internally consistent in their ages or when detailed site stratigraphy is satisfied do workers in this field breathe easily over conventional results.

However, two new developments have altered the pattern of development of this technique quite dramatically. First, in response to the additional interference in the conventional approach, that of sample inhomogeneity (which introduces errors when K- and Ar-contents are assessed on different portions), the '^{40}Ar-^{39}Ar method' was developed in 1966, whereby mass spectroscopy is used exclusively.[19] The isotope, ^{39}Ar, can be produced by fast neutron irradiation in a nuclear reactor:

$$^{39}K + n \rightarrow {}^{39}Ar + p \qquad (4.2)$$

The total amount of ^{39}Ar produced in this way will depend upon a combination of factors in the neutron treatment, such as n-flux intensity and its energy spectrum, nuclear cross-section for the reaction as well as total potassium content of the sample (of which ^{39}K is the most abundant isotope). If the irradiation is expressed as a composite factor, G, we may write isotope concentrations as

$$^{39}Ar = {}^{39}K \cdot G \qquad (4.3)$$

Combined with the conventional dating equation (4.1b), we have the age, t years, as

$$t = (1 \cdot 72 \times 10^{11}) \cdot G \cdot \frac{^{40}Ar}{^{39}Ar} \cdot \frac{^{39}K}{^{40}K} \qquad (4.4)$$

where the ratio of potassium-isotope contents is fixed and equal to $7 \cdot 9 \times 10^3$ (see section 4.1a). The value of G can be measured directly by arranging a standard of known age alongside, so that the only argon-isotope ratio stands as unknown.

The complicating factors surrounding this approach largely focus on the need to create sufficient ^{39}Ar for accurate evaluation while keeping down the interference effect of the reactions,

$$^{40}K + n \rightarrow {}^{40}Ar + p \qquad (4.5a)$$

$$\text{and } {}^{40}Ca + n \rightarrow {}^{36}Ar + n + \alpha \qquad (4.5b)$$

The first of these reactions arises in part from the inevitable slight 'contamination' of the neutron beam with a lower energy component. A flux of 10^{14} neutrons per cm^2 is typically satisfactory for material around 10^5 years old and the artificial ^{40}Ar production would only become significant for a flux two orders of magnitude greater.[7] The interference at ^{39}Ar caused by the calcium reaction only exceeds 1% when the ratio K/Ca $\leqslant$ 0·03. This constraint is easily satisfied by the archaeological materials commonly analysed, usually by many orders of magnitude, and only amongst the Ca-rich plagioclase feldspars is the limiting condition even approached. The important geological minerals have to be treated much more cautiously.[20]

Nothing in this argon-isotope technique copes with the other conventional difficulties of gas retention and/or diffusion loss. For this a sample de-gassing technique has been formulated where a series of ages are evaluated after successive heating steps leading up to complete

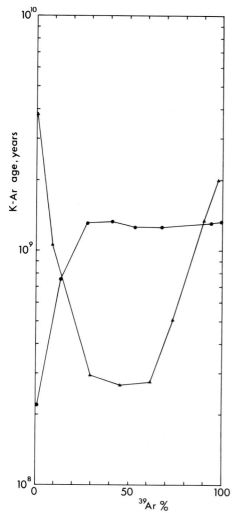

fusion.[21] This is illustrated for two minerals of great antiquity, a biotite from Marble Mountains in California and a whole rock sample from an intrusive diabase dike in Liberia (Fig. 4.2). Each portion of each mineral when heated after neutron irradiation shows an ^{39}Ar loss as the gas is forced to diffuse out. The ^{39}Ar released at each step measures the integrated effect of each heating cycle.

For the biotite the lower temperature ages are low but eventually a plateau develops in this 'age spectrum' at around 1,300 million years. There is evidence here of some ^{40}Ar loss by diffusion. Parent potassium in regions of the crystal that allowed such loss in the past will also give up its artificially-induced ^{39}Ar when heated. The fraction of potassium in diffusion-resistant regions gives rise only to stable ^{39}Ar that remains until complete fusion while its concentration can be calculated from equation (4.3). That same potassium fraction gave us the measured

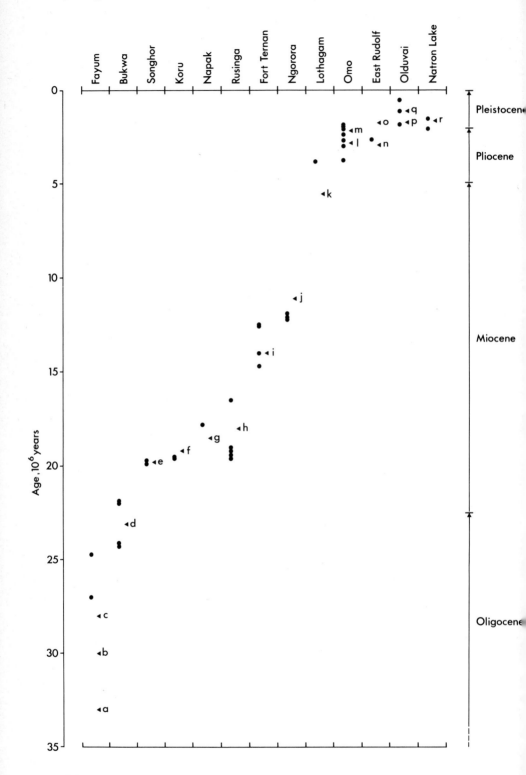

Fig. 4.3   Hominoid chronology derived from the K-Ar dating method.
Data charted here for thirteen sites are presented in column form with
data points to the left recording K-Ar age determinations while
lettered markers to the right suggest the hominoid's likely age inferred
from site stratigraphy relative to the dated regions. Hominoid species
are listed here together with source of K-Ar analysis, plus related
references (in parentheses).

Fayum (Egypt): a. *Oligopithecus savagei*, b. *Propliopithecus haeckeli*,
   c. *Aegyptopithecus zeuxis* (Plate 4.1). Basalt capping the youngest
   Oligocene deposits (23).

Bukwa: d. *Limnopithecus legetet*. Lavas above and below the fossiliferous
   sediments (26).

Songhor: e. *Limnopithecus* species (*legetet* and *macinnesi*), *Dryopithecus*
   (*Proconsul*) specia (*africanus*, *nyanzae* and *major*), *Dryopithecus*
   species (*gordoni* and *vancouveringi*). Mica from near the base of tuffs
   that yield the bulk of the mammalian fauna (25, 26).

Koru: f. similar to Songhor material. Biotite related tuff (25, 26).

Napak: g. *Limnopithecus* species (*legetet* and *macinnesi*), *Dryopithecus*
   (*Proconsul*) major. Mica from tuff (level I) (26).

Rusinga Island: h. *Limnopithecus* species (*legeget* and *macinnesi*),
   Dryopithecus (*Proconsul*) species (*africanus*, *nyanzae* and *major*).
   Lava rich in melanepheline, overlying fossil horizon, Nepheline
   separate underlying fossil horizon (27).

Fort Ternan: i. *Ramapithecus wickeri*, *Limnopithecus* species, *Dryopi-*
   thecus species. Biotite from tuff horizon immediately underlying the
   fossiliferous strata and an overlying phonolite lava (26). The
   $^{40}Ar/^{39}Ar$ 'age spectrum' technique was used for the phonolite
   study.

Ngorora: j. *Hominoid*, the find represented only by the crown of a single
   molar. Underlying lavas and 'derived' feldspars in the sediments
   (28).

Lothagam: k. *Australopithecus africanus* (hominid mandibular fragment). A basalt sill intrusive into the middle faunal level, Lothagam
   2, which lies well above the hominid fossil level (29, 30).

Omo (Usno Formation): l. *Australopithecus* species of two lineages:
   (i) a robust series, similar to the Olduvai genus, *boisei* and (ii) a
   gracile series comparable with the genus, *africanus*.
   Glass from an underlying tuff (29, 31).

Omo (Shungura Formation): m. similar to Usno Formation material.
   Feldspar from a series of tuffs two of which bracket the fossiliferous
   zone (31).

East Rudolf: n. *Homo* (species indeterminate) (cranium 1470); o.
   Australopithecus boisei (see Plate 4.2). Sanidine feldspar phenocrysts
   extracted from a sediment termed the KBS Tuff of the Koobi
   Fora formation. Hominid n was found in the Karari Escarpment
   area while hominid o originates from the lower tuff of the Ileret
   area. The $^{40}Ar/^{39}Ar$ 'age spectrum' technique was used for the KBS
   tuff material (32–34). Stratigraphical relationships and fauna of these
   deposits are discussed in references 35–38 while the most recent
   hominid finds and their genus attributions are discussed in references
   39 and 40.

    Olduvai Gorge: p. *Homo habilis* (type cranium *H.7.*) *Australopithecus boisei*. Several anorthoclase extracts from different strata of a volcanic tuff, Bed I (16, 41–43). q. *Homo erectus* (cranium, *H.9*, on Bed II). Continued representation of this Homo species is found throughout the Middle Pleistocene, in Beds III and IV. Post cranial remains of Hominid, *H.28*, from the latter is illustrated in Plate 4.3. Biotite from Middle or Lower Bed II (16, 44–46). A more recent anorthoclase K-Ar marker date is recorded, related to the tool industry transition of a developed Oldowan form to early Acheulian.

    Natron Basin (Humbu Formation): r. *Australopithecus* species in the robust group (the *Peninj* mandible), though there are strong *Homo* affinities when compared with the cranium, (*H.9.*) from Olduvai (labelled q above). Olivine basalt overlying the fossil stratum (47). Basalt flow underlying the fossil stratum, in the upper part of the Sambu lavas (48).

[40]Ar stored so that these two elemental concentrations satisfy the stability requirements basic to K-Ar dating.

The diabase example shows quite different characteristics. The initial rapid ˙fall in the spectrum indicates the release of weakly-bound excess argon of atmospheric origin. After a brief levelling the apparent K-Ar age rises steadily up to the fusion point. This rise is attributed to release of much more tightly-bound excess argon (probably trapped during rock formation). The appreciable magnitude of both interfering excesses is noteworthy. Clearly, inclusion of these components in argon assessment after complete fusion in the conventional manner would be disastrous. (In fact a plagioclase extract etched with hydrofluoric acid dated to 570 millions years.)

While this stepwise heating goes a long way to improving age determination of younger materials by minimizing the sources of confusion, the diabase example indicates that caution is still necessary. The plateau region in Fig. 4.2 at around 270 million years is still believed to be about 40% too high. If this is due to some potassium leaching in the distant past, it remains undetected by any feature of this sophisticated analysis.

1e K-Ar DATING OF HOMINOID DEVELOPMENT

In the light of the recent technical advances just described it is the coming decade, perhaps, that will supply a much more comprehensive application of K-Ar dating. Amongst the earlier acceptable studies the comprehensive assessment of chronology amongst North American fossil mammals is particularly important.[22] Dating covered the whole of the present Cenozoic geological phase (some seventy million years of faunal evolution) and identified the initial eight to ten million year phase as one of rapid evolution, filling the ecological niche created by dinosaur extinction.

K-Ar results have vitally influenced the build up of a framework for cross-linking in time of Man's ancestors throughout the world. The fossil finds of Egypt and East Africa, with their thirty-five million year development span, lie at the heart of this study, as shown in Fig. 4.3 (together with the source of the K-Ar data and find sites in East Africa recorded in Fig. 4.4). The nature of the fossil sampling amongst these sites is highly variable with Bukwa represented by only three teeth and Ngorora yielding up only a crown of a molar while Rusinga supplied an abundance of finds.

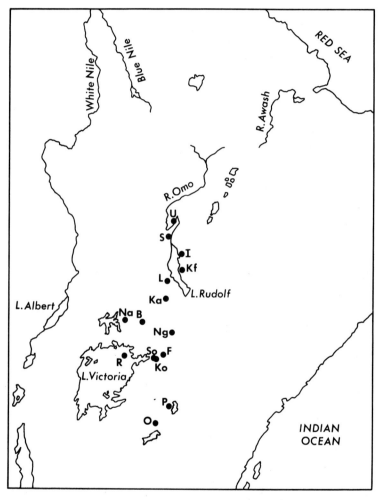

Fig. 4.4   Principal fossil-find sites in East Africa: U = Usno Formation (Omo Basin); S = Shungura Formation (Omo Basin); I = Ileret (East Rudolf); Kf = Koobi Fora (East Rudolf); L = Lothagam; Ka = Kanapoi; Na = Napak; B = Bukwa; Ng = Ngorora (Baringo Basin); R = Rusinga Island; So = Songhor; F = Fort Ternan; Ko = Koru; P = Peninj (Natron Basin); O = Olduvai Gorge.

No attempt is made here to sharply define, with confidence, the stages at which the various branches of the hominoid family tree became separated into the three sub-groups—extinct genera are quoted in parenthesis—: Hominidae (*Australopithecus, Ramapithecus*), Pongidae (*Dryopithecus, Aegyptopithecus*), Hylobatidae (*Pliopithecus, Limnopithecus*), leading ultimately to modern man, the great apes and the gibbons, respectively. This separation is made largely on dental evidence for the very early material, rather of necessity as jaw fragments constitute the bulk of our finds.[23] In simple modern-day terms an ape's jaw has four incisors at the front which are separated from the other teeth to provide space for large interlocking canines, plus groups of molars that run in parallel rows into the skull. A human jaw carries small canines and all the teeth touch while the molars complete a curve that is widest at the rear of the mouth. Subdivision of hominid types amongst the younger finds is tenuously related to morphological characters of the braincase and face as well.[24]

The sequence begins with a date of twenty-seven million years for a basalt lava in the Jebel et Qatrani Formation of the Fayum in Egypt which lies well above the fossiliferous horizons. The earliest hominoid, *Oligopithecus savagei*, could well be the ancestor of the very ancient pongids, *Propliopithecus haeckeli* and *Aegyptopithecus zeuxis* (Plate 4.1). An eroded specimen, *Aeolopithecus chirobates*, not charted here, could be the hylobatid forerunner of the *Limnopithecus* species that form a

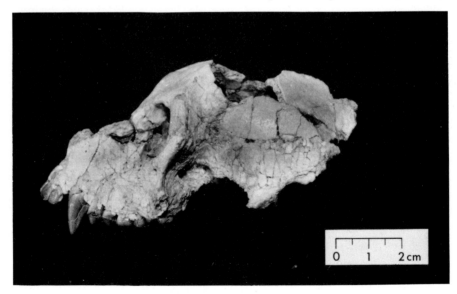

4.1   Fossil remains of *Aegyptopithecus zeuxis*, found in the Fayum, Egypt. This specimen, regarded as of the pongid group in dental characteristics, is believed to be about twenty-eight million years old. (Photograph: A. H. Coleman. Courtesy of Professor E. L. Simons, Yale Peabody Museum, Yale University, New Haven, Connecticut.)

large part of our hominoid evidence throughout the following fifteen million years. The rest of the finds during that period are all designated as pongid of the *Dryopithecus* species. It is indicative of the fineness of division between pongid and hylobatid form at that time that one of the latter, *L. legetet,* has recently been re-assigned by one expert, to join five *Dryopithecus* forms.[25] (The subgenus, *Proconsul,* has been recognized for some time in three forms, *africanus, major* and *nyanzae,* the first two of which may be ancestral to the present-day chimpanzee and gorilla, respectively.) [26,27]

The hominid/pongid division seems to occur shortly before fourteen million years ago at which time *Ramapithecus wickeri* emerges at Fort Ternan, probably forging a link between earlier pongids and the pseudo-human australopithecines. Unfortunately, at this vital point in hominid evolution a blank period of almost nine million years begins when only the Ngorora tooth provides a fossil record.[28] Quite suddenly we are able to attribute the lower jaw found at Lothagam, Kenya, with confidence to the hominid group, *Australopithecus africanus,*[29] even though it is appreciably sturdier than the modern-day structure. Geographically the fossil hunt is now focused on the eroded, barren regions that surround the present extent of Lake Rudolf which lies on the Kenya/Ethiopia border. The lake has been able to avoid drying up during the past millennia of arid climate in the region because the Omo river to the north is well-stocked by rainfall in the high mountain ranges of Ethiopia (Fig. 4.4). Today the dense forests crowd in about the narrow meander of the river but at the time when the early hominids were herding their animals at the lakeside the whole surrounding plain was submerged. The Usno and Shungura formations of the Omo Basin have yielded up a plentiful supply of remains of two australopithecine species, one, a robust form similar to that labelled *boisei* when first found at Olduvai and the other, a gracile form comparable with the *africanus* group.[30,31]

Our record of occupation sites amongst hominid groups begins around 2·6 million years ago with the excavation of stone artefacts and broken-up bone heaps in the Koobi Fora area, east of Lake Rudolf.[32-35] The organization of movement for hunting and scavenging by a group which shares food and a community spirit, albeit quite tenuous, is now in evidence. The Omo finds had alerted the scientific community to the potential of this region and of the Ileret region further north, so that various disciplines have been able to gather together to evaluate not only the hominid fossils but also the vertebrate fauna chronology, geological and palaeomagnetic stratigraphy and the environment of sediment deposition as indicated by algae content.[36-39] A picture emerges of at least three hominid lineages including both forms of australopithecines found at Omo (like the cranium KNM-ER-732 shown in Plate 4.2) and a genus, *Homo,* of highly speculative attribution. (The last of these include the cranium *1470,* which may

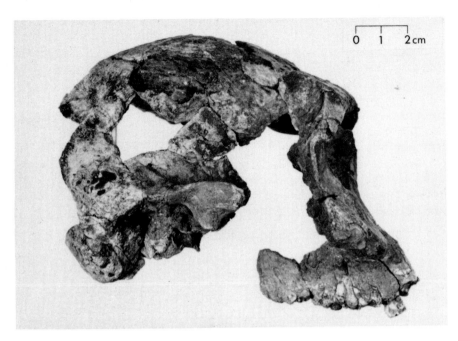

4.2 *Cranium 732*: an important australopithecine specimen found at Ileret, East Rudolf, in the lower tuff. Its age is, at present, estimated at 1·6–1·8 million years. (Photograph: courtesy of the Kenya National Museum, Nairobi.)

date to around 2·9 million years ago.) Amongst the twenty new hominid specimens recovered in 1973 alone, one exceptional mandible (*1482*) has been linked to a singular Omo find referred to as *Paraustralopithecus* that may be a remnant of an earlier population on the verge of extinction.[40]

Whereas East Rudolf may stand as the watershed of pseudo-human pongids and genuine proto-hominine stock the younger specimens of Olduvai Gorge to the south, in Tanzania, indicate that the *Australopithecus/Homo* dichotomy has been resolved. The *boisei* species of the former and the *habilis* species of the latter occur in the same stratigraphy (termed *Bed I*).[41,42] Now that the fossils are much more complete than the Miocene material discussed earlier, intercomparison of cranial and dental structure and post-cranial components becomes more detailed. For example, the type cranium (hominid, *H.7*) of *Homo habilis* is seen to share morphological similarity to the species, *Homo erectus* (H.9), that emerged about 0·5 million years later but contrast with a cranium (H.24) in the same stratum (designated *Bed I*). It has been suggested that these differences may represent nothing more than sexual dimorphism in the *habilis* grouping.[43]

The hominid chronology is now far less dependent upon K-Ar dates. Rather the stone implement industry that gradually expands both in size and diversity of form throughout the period of *habilis/erectus* transition allows archaeological cross-linking of a more classical nature. At Olduvai the tool assemblages, termed *Oldowan* and *Acheulian*, mark the transition in stratigraphy from Beds I to IV respectively.[44] (In part, this change is defined by the emergence of the hand-axe and the cleaver.) The latter industry dates to about 0·5 million years by which time hominid bone structure had developed to accommodate habitual upright biped motion (Plate 4.3).[45,46] The transition between these two industries is dated to around 1·3 million

4.3 Post-cranial remains of Hominid *H.28* (*Homo erectus*) from Bed IV, Olduvai Gorge. (Photograph: courtesy of Professor M. H. Day, St Thomas's Hospital, London.)

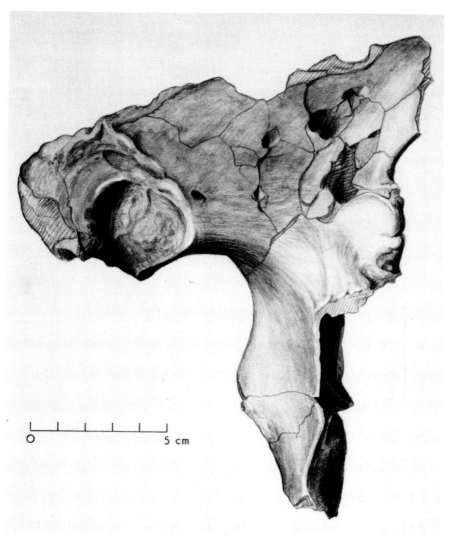

0   5 cm

years both at Olduvai and at Lake Natron, further to the north-east.[47-51] A mandible of robust structure found at the latter site and stratigraphically below the early Acheulian assemblages may mark the final record of australopithecine activity before extinction.

This section has concentrated upon the evidence of evolutionary characteristics of hominoids. It is worth stressing that K-Ar dating supplies a chronological framework for the much broader links between sites supplied by other faunal remains, particularly fossil *Suidae* and *Proboscidia*.[52] (There are three living species of suid in Africa, the warthog—*Phacochoerus africanus*—, the bushpig—*Potamochoerus porcus* —and the giant forest hog—*Hylochoerus meinertzhageni*. The dominant species amongst the Proboscidea, the elephant, exhibits three main generic lineages represented in the late Pleistocene by the groups *Mammothus*, *Elephas* and *Loxodonta*. The last of these leads to the living african elephant, *L. africana*.) Indeed such faunal correlations drew attention to the inadequacy of several early K-Ar ages for the hominid-bearing site of Kanapoi which has recently been assigned to the period between Lothagam and Omo, Shungura Formation, at around four million years ago. Also the availability of twelve different fossiliferous units in the Baringo area provides the stratigraphic evidence for the fourteen to five million-year range which, it will be recalled, is served only by a single tooth from Ngorora.[53]

1f LINKS TO OTHER HOMINOIDEA, WORLDWIDE

Hominid development seems to have been confined to Africa until the mid-Miocene, about 13 million years ago. However, forerunners of the other living hominoids, the orang-utan, gibbons and siamangs, were widely distributed over the whole of South-East Asia well before that time. The movement of hominoids out of Africa into Eurasian regions probably began some seventeen million years ago. Hylobatids of the genus *Pliopithecus* appear at around that time in Europe and became extinct around eight million years ago. The extant European form is probably derived from Asian stock the earliest record of which has recently been found at Haritalyangar in India, in deposits that are about eleven million years old.

Pongids of the genus *Dryopithecus* are generously represented in fossil finds from many sites. Unfortunately none of these sites carry direct radiometric ages, though related sediments have been analysed. Two species, *D. fontani* and *D. laietanus*, are represented in Europe, both more advanced than African species and probably dating to around thirteen million years ago.[54] Neither species seem to have a lineage to any living pongid. Many dryopithecine examples recovered from the Siwalik Hills in India and the Salt Range in Pakistan probably date to between sixteen and ten million years. One species, *D. indicus*, may be ancestral to the extinct hominoid lineage, *Gigantopithecus*, which was first discovered in Pleistocene deposits in China some thirty years ago.[55]

The pongid/hominid link species, *Ramapithecus*, is to be found in the Siwalik region also (genus *punjabicus*).[56] As in Africa the Late Miocene Asian deposits provide no hominoid fossils in their faunal remains upon which to forge evolutionary links, so we can only hypo-thesize that this species is the Miocene forerunner of hominidae in Asia.

Up to 1970 the seriation of South African early hominid sites was based on relative faunal ages only, even though much of the basic descriptive terminology of the subject stems from the first fossil finds unearthed in that area. For example, Professor Dart's discovery of the face and braincast of a small child at Taung, in 1924, together with the recovery of adult specimens from quarries at Sterkfontein and Makapansgat a few years later, defined the genus, *Australopithecus africanus*. The gracile skull from Sterkfontein contrasted with a much larger variety found at Kromdraai in 1938. The latter, together with material from Swartkrans, provided a separate genus, *Australopithecus robustus*.

The fossil record of *Elephas recki* at Makapansgat links closely to the well-dated counterparts of East Rudolf and Omo (Shungura Formation). On the evidence of fossil suids, Sterkfontein and Makapansgat hominid finds are of similar antiquity, i.e. about 2·5 million years old.[57] Similarly faunal comparisons between Swartkrans and Olduvai (Bed I) suggest an age for the South African site of 1·8 million years, perhaps a little more.[58] Kromdraai is probably slightly younger.

The Taung skull is now the subject of detailed reappraisal.[59] This has been activated by a new series of dates estimated for the first opening of these cave sites by the effects of erosion and valley widening along the river gorges of the Highveld.[60] The Taung cave only became available as a catchment area around 0·87 million years ago, while the hominid-bearing strata lie somewhat above bed rock. This data rejects the previous thinking that the Taung juvenile is the holotype of *A. africanus*. Instead this skull would seem to be a late survivor of *A. robustus*, contemporary with proto-human stock, *Homo erectus*.

Finally, any discussion of the chronology of the worldwide network of hominoid finds must include a reference to early man in Java, the dating of which has support from K-Ar determinations, albeit in a rather controversial manner. The mandibular fragment of a species, termed *Meganthropus palaeojavanicus* and found in the Djetis beds of Sangiran, was underlain by a pumic tuff recently dated to 1·9 million years.[61] The australopithecine character of this find is not surprising. However, the matching strata at the site of Modjokerto further to the east of the Island has provided an infant skull with strong *Homo erectus* affinities. This fossil alone, if its early age stands up to future scrutiny, would be sufficient to require radical revision in our present human palaeontological interpretations.

2 URANIUM-SERIES DATING

2a THE THORIUM-EXCESS METHOD

Development of dating methods based upon the decay of the uranium radioactivity sequences (^{238}U+, ^{235}U+) stem from the early research of Joly who illustrated that the radium contents in deep-sea sediments far exceeded that of terrestrial materials.[62] This has been attributed to the almost complete absence of all the uranium daughter products from natural waters caused by the very low solubility of the two radioisotopes early in the two decay chains, ionium (^{230}Th) and protactinium (^{231}Pa), respectively.[63] (See Table 4.1). Instead the precipitation of these isotopes leads to their concentrations in recently deposited sediments being in excess of that compatible with radioactive equilibrium.

A sediment's ionium, when no longer 'supported' in the radioactive sense, will decay in concentration with a half-life of close to 75,200 years.

The profile of ionium concentration with depth would be exponentially decreasing from the upper surface of the deposits if three assumptions are satisfied:

(i) that there is no migration of thorium after deposition,

(ii) that the concentration of the ionium has been constant in the surrounding water during the period to be dated,

(iii) that the sedimentation occurred at a constant rate.

Evidence that chemical exchange is restricted to the early stages of the sedimentation cycle suggests factor (i) creates no dating problems.[64] Tests of the validity of the other two factors has often been based upon separate analysis of the much longer-lived thorium isotope, ^{232}Th ($t_{\frac{1}{2}} = 1\cdot4 \times 10^{10}$ years) which is treated as following the same chemical paths as ionium, being of the same elemental family. In a steady situation the ^{232}Th would be at a constant level throughout the depth profile while, in the face of any perturbations, the isotope's concentration could be used to normalize data from successive strata.[65] However, several criticisms have been expressed both on evidence of lack of reliability of some dating results[66] and on evidence that the two thorium isotopes often have different physical origins within the same sediment.

A more reliable approach has been recommended whereby a similar depth profile is obtained for protactinium (^{231}Pa) with age determination now related to this isotope's half-life of only 32,500 years. The ionium/protactinium concentration ratio is a measure of age in terms of their half-life difference of 42,700 years. The greater effectiveness of this method stems from the similarity in which both these isotopes arrive in the sediment.

The 'thorium-excess' technique has so far proven of little importance archaeologically in a direct manner but has supplied the recent time markers for magnetic intensity and climatic variations of the past 1·2 million years [67] and for associated faunal analyses of the past 2 million years.[68] Illustration of this work is given in the Appendix A.

2b   THE THORIUM-DEFICIENCY METHOD

Materials formed in the oceans, like corals and molluscan shells, will be deficient in ionium and protactinium. Thus any calcereous fossil contains uranium but very low concentrations of its daughters. If the fossil remains as a 'closed system' over the archaeological period then the extent to which ^{230}Th and ^{231}Pa have grown in again acts as an age indicator (Fig. 4.5).[69] For example, a 75,000 year-old sample should have radioactivity contents expressed by the ratios,

$$\frac{^{230}\text{Th}}{^{234}\text{U}} = 0.50 \text{ and } \frac{^{231}\text{Pa}}{^{235}\text{U}} = 0.80$$

An 'open system' can be defined as one in which such a pair of analyses are not concordant.

Corals seem to be the only material which at present can be treated as regularly reliable and give accurate results because their uranium uptake is quite high (about 3 ppm). Dating of reefs in Barbados has supplied valuable information about marine strandlines that indicate the sea level at times in the past and thus act as a measure of glaciation on a worldwide scale.[70] Also an isolated age has been determined for an Acheulian biface tool found encrusted in marine molluscs in exposed scarps at Dallol, Afar in Ethiopia.

In contrast, molluscs seem to be of little value for dating as the major portion of their uranium is secondary uptake located on grain boundaries and thus susceptible to migration. Instead a complex, dynamic

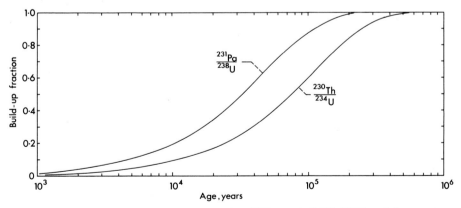

Fig. 4.5   Temporal changes in the ^{231}Pa/^{238}U and ^{230}Th/^{234}U-activity ratios (reference 69).

'open system' model has been advocated in which a mobile uranium component moves through the shell and leaves it while associated decay products are retained.[71] Evidence of the mobile component's passage is given by the occurrence of protactinium in excess of that appropriate to equilibrium with the retained uranium. This approach has met with some severe criticism and scepticism.[72] Technical factors that relate to the mechanisms of shell formation and subsequent protection after the death of the carrier organism have been studied and possible conditions for 'closed' dating of some molluscan species given consideration.[73]

Uranium uptake by bone is the basis of a chemical means of distinguishing old bones from new (see Chapter 9). Thus we would expect that a present-day uranium content is only the end point of a continuous growth over the entire burial period. As this mechanism would induce an 'inertia' in the build up of ionium and protactinium, radiometric ages should tend to be too low. This has proven to be true in practice except in a few instances where good age determination is thought to be indebted to the presence of ground water forming a closed system rapidly after bone placement. Examples include vertebrate fossils from Sacramento, California,[74] and faunal remains related to Acheulian artefacts in the Isimala Beds of Tanzania.[75] However, a date of 130,000 years for the earliest example of *Homo sapiens* found in the Kibish Formation of Ethiopia [76] is now in question and its correlation to skull specimens of 'Rhodesian Man', found at Broken Hills and Saldanha,[77] is now possibly invalid.

2c DATING OF LEAD WHITE PIGMENT USING LEAD-210 DISEQUILIBRIUM

The manufacture of lead white pigment involves the extraction of the elemental metal from the sulphide ore, galena. Within the ore there are trace levels of uranium and its decay descendants all in radioactive equilibrium. However, this equilibrium is severely upset by the high temperature of smelting, as the waste slag products carry away with them a major portion of the radium (^{226}Ra) present: only ^{210}Pb survives this treatment to be carried through with the metal itself into the pigment's constitution.

Left unsupported by its radium ancestor ($t_{\frac{1}{2}} = 1620$ years) the ^{210}Pb-concentration decays away, following its half-life of only twenty-two years. Equilibrium is established once more after about 200 years or so, when a decay balance is struck with the traces of ^{226}Ra that were retained (Fig. 4.6).[78] The concentration of ^{226}Ra can be measured by picking out its α-radiation of decay (4·78 MeV) in an alpha spectrometer. The ^{210}Pb-concentration is measured less directly by similar study of its α-emitting decay product, ^{210}Po. (Its own β-activity, though also countable, would have to contend with much higher levels of

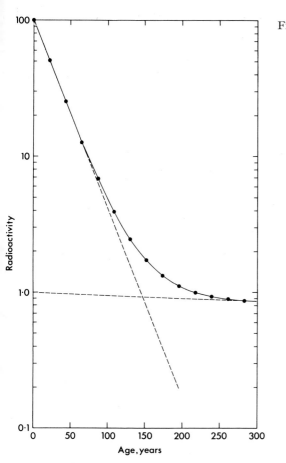

Fig. 4.6 Recovery of radioactive equilibrium of
the ²¹⁰Pb-content of
a lead white pigment.
The initial activities of
²¹⁰Pb and ²²⁶Ra im-
mediately after pig-
ment manufacture are
shown here with a
starting ratio of 100:1
(reference 79).

background activity caused by cosmic rays and impurities in the detection equipment.)

The drastic reduction of radium content caused by ore refinement can bring its radioactive concentration down to as low as 0·1 dpm/g. (dpm/g = disintegrations per minute per gram of lead.) This activity in a sample of pigment that can be taken from a painting without undue damage (perhaps 10 mg) will begin to approach the background counting of around 10^{-3} dpm of the spectrometer itself. The ²¹⁰Po-activity of a recent pigment may range between 1 and 150 dpm/g dependent upon the source of the original ore. Thus dating is only practical back to the late eighteenth century at best and sometimes no further than the middle of the last century, dependent upon the initial ²¹⁰Pb-content of the pigment.

The present-day ²¹⁰Pb and ²²⁶Ra-concentrations (Pb_t and Ra, respectively) can be related to the pigment's original lead isotope content at the time of manufacture, Pb_0, by an age equation,

$$Pb_t - Ra = (Pb_0 - Ra) \exp(-\lambda t) \qquad (4.5)$$

where $\lambda = 0.031$ year^{-1} and t is the time since the ore separation was carried out.

Unfortunately, without knowing what ore source was used no Pb_0-level can be predicted, even roughly, so absolute age determination is ruled out. However, it is quite practical to assess the authenticity of some paintings as the works of Han van Meegeren, the acknowledged imitator of Vermeer's work, illustrates (Table 4.2).[79]

Table 4.2: Radium/lead analysis of paintings in the Vermeer style attributed to Han van Meegeren (1889–1947)

Painting Description	^{210}Po-content (dpm/g)	^{226}Ra-content (dpm/g)
Supper at Emmaus	8·5	0·8
Mary Magdalen washing Christ's Feet	12·6	0·26
Woman reading music	10·6	0·3
Woman playing a mandolin	8·2	0·17

In 1937, the renowned scholar, Abraham Bredius, sent a shiver of excitement around the art world with his discovery of *Supper at Emmaus*, an early Vermeer. His attribution was swiftly supported by many other Dutch experts, such as the Schneiders of the Mauritshuis at The Hague, and duly the painting took an honoured place on the walls of Rotterdam's Museum Boymans. But, in reality, this work was a forgery. This only became known when the Dutch police, in 1945, took a wealthy expatriate, Han van Meegeren, into custody on suspicion of collaboration with the Nazi regime.[80] This accusation was based on van Meegeren's involvement in the sale of another 'Vermeer' (entitled *Woman taken in Adultery*), to the Reichsmarschall, Hermann Goering. The penalty for such a crime could be death and van Meegeren had no stomach for even the thought of such a fate. He confessed, not to a war crime, but to art fraud on a grand scale, encompassing the acclaimed Boymans 'masterpiece', a recent Rijksmuseum acquisition, *The Washing of the Feet of Christ*, *The Mandolin Player* (Plate 4.4) and works in the style of Frans Hals, Pieter de Hoogh and Ter Borch. To prove his claim van Meegeren was obliged to add *Jesus in the Temple* to his Vermeer oeuvre, under police supervision.

In the case of the *Woman playing a mandolin* we can consider the present-day ^{210}Po-content of 8·2 dpm/g and ask what level that would have been in about 1660 when Vermeer produced works of this luminous and serene type. As the van Meegeren/Vermeer time span is equivalent to about thirteen half-lives of ^{210}Pb we can estimate a minimum seventeenth-century post-smelting value of the related ^{210}Po at the unrealistic level of 10^5 dpm/g. A similar argument applied to the other paintings listed in Table 4.2, indicates their fraudulent nature, too.

4.4 *The Mandolin Player*, a Han van Meegeren imitation in the style of Vermeer. (Photograph: courtesy of the Rijksmuseum, Amsterdam.)

Pigments with very similar ^{210}Pb and ^{226}Ra-concentrations cannot immediately be pronounced as ancient. It could be argued that smelting might only create a small separation in some instances. However, all reported analyses offer no examples amongst works confidently attributed to the nineteenth and twentieth centuries where disequilibrium is still not clearly discernible. In contrast all works of the Vermeer period so far analysed exhibit radioactive steadiness.

Chapter 5

Thermoluminescence Dating

1 BASIC PRINCIPLES

1a INTRODUCTION

Time and again recent excavations have been stimulated by chance discovery, during ploughing or trenching, of concentrations of pottery fragments. Pottery is certainly the most common artefact of the past ten millennia and its change in shape, decoration and technique of manufacture provides a sensitive chronological system in its own right, in many parts of the world. This system is strictly relative although there are several time markers, supplied by historical records and science, that may allow a certain pottery style to be a definitive dating tool for certain periods. For example, we have seen that several Minoan wares are dated by their presence in well-documented Egyptian tombs while some characteristic Romano-British wares are fixed to within a decade by associated coin finds.

There are some obvious limitations to the cross-linking methods of this nature, in pre-record, pre-metal eras and in regions, like West Africa, where pottery technique and style seem to have remained static over many centuries. Certainly the radiocarbon dating of associated organic remains has radically improved our knowledge of the earlier ceramic times, but in the past decade the emergence of the *thermoluminescence* method offers an equally potent technique, as it is directly applicable to the ceramic fabric.

1b THE TL AGE EQUATION

Thermoluminescence (TL) is the light emitted when a crystalline material is heated to around 500°C, appearing in addition to normal incandescence generated at that high a temperature. The light represents a release of energy stored in the crystal lattice (as electrons trapped at regions of imperfection) following long-term exposure of the mineral to nuclear radiation. Consequently geological minerals, like quartz, calcite and the various feldspars, emit vast levels of TL when heated in direct reflection of their long period of dosage.

These same minerals were frequently added to a potter's raw clay stock to give his fashioned ceramic a 'breathing' capacity and strength

110

to face the rigours of kiln-firing. This firing, usually to temperatures between 700°C and 1100°C, would drive off any geological TL in the mixture. Thus when the finished pottery began its life, perhaps as a cooking vessel or storage unit, it contained no stored TL energy whatsoever. Such wares would probably survive only a decade, at most, before damage and disposal. The major part of its archaeological life-time will have been spent in a condition of disuse in a burial context of soil.

The natural radioactivity (as uranium, thorium and potassium-40) in the pottery fragments (termed 'sherds') and in the burial medium supply a fresh and steady source of radiation dose year after year until present day. Gradually the TL energy builds up: the natural TL measured in the laboratory now is directly related to the total radiation the ceramic has experienced since a 'time zero' was set by the original firing (Fig. 5.1).

The mixture of minerals occurring in pottery fabric all have their own sensitivity to radiation. In general, feldspars tend to respond much more strongly than any quartz present, though the latter mineral shows a high degree of sensitivity variation, a factor that is controlled in part by firing and cooling conditions. Thus each pottery fabric has to be calibrated for its TL response, so that a quantity termed *equivalent dose*, Q, can be defined through,

$$Q = \frac{\text{Natural TL}}{\text{Sensitivity (TL per rad)}} \qquad (5.1)$$

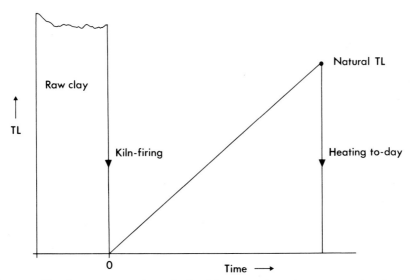

Fig. 5.1   Simple representation of the 'time zero' setting process in thermo-luminescence dating of pottery.

The radiation unit introduced here, the *rad* is equivalent to 100 ergs of energy absorbed by 1g. of material. Natural radioactivity supplies around 0·2 to 1·0 rad per year to pottery.

Standard techniques of radioactivity assessment ('alpha counting' for uranium and thorium content [1] and 'flame photometry' for potassium content [2]) allow an estimate of the annual dose-rate to be obtained. Assuming the archaeological TL grew linearly with time (a notion that is questioned in section 1*i*), as shown in Fig. 5.1, an age equation follows:

$$\text{Age, (years)} = \frac{Q \text{ (rads)}}{\text{Dose-rate (rad per year)}} \qquad (5.2)$$

Notably the half-lives of decay of the three natural radioisotopes are all well in excess of 10^8 years so that they do supply a constant

Fig. 5.2   Plot of the α-radiation dose contained within the volume of a quartz grain (radius a = 45 microns) beyond a depth of penetration, x. Differences in range of travel for the various energies of alpha radiation result in dose arising from the ^{238}U decay chain being more severely attenuated than that of the ^{232}Th decay chain (reference 11).

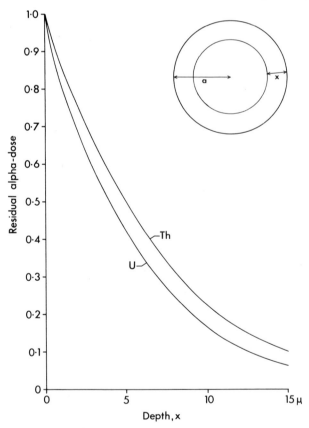

dose-rate over the comparatively short archaeological period. This dose-rate portion of the age equation is susceptible to change, however, not through any radioactive decay effects, but under the influence of environmental factors (section 1*h*).

1C RADIATION DOSIMETRY IN POTTERY

The nuclear energy released in the pottery fabric and in the surrounding burial media takes three forms: α-, β-, and γ-radiation, each of which has quite distinctive properties. (^{40}K emits only β- and γ-radiation. Its decay scheme was given in Fig. 4.1.)

(i) *α-radiation* has a very short range in clay fabric. Even the most energetic emission of ^{212}Po in the thorium decay series (8·8 MeV) will travel only about 45 microns. (See Table 4.1 for details of energy distribution in natural radioactivity and interpretation in terms of α-ranges in Table 5.1 here.[3]) Thus it is a source of radiation truly internal to the ceramic itself. But within that fabric there is an important inhomogeneity related to the uranium and thorium distribution. Most of the crystalline inclusions (particularly quartz) which are the source of the TL signal are virtually radioactivity free.[4] Those which are greater than 90 microns in diameter contain an inner volume that experiences no alpha dose at all.[5]

The gradient of the α-dose distribution across the body of such large crystals is quite steep (Fig. 5.2). More than 50% of the whole dose

Table 5.1: Energy distribution of natural alpha radiation and associated ranges in a clay matrix

	Uranium-238 decay chain			Thorium-232 decay chain	
Isotope	*Energy (MeV)*	*Range (microns)**	*Isotope*	*Energy (MeV)*	*Range (microns)**
^{238}U	4·20	14·6	^{232}Th	4·00	13·6
^{234}U	4·77 (72%) 4·72 (28%)	17·2	^{228}Th	5·42 (71%) 5·34 (29%)	20·8
^{230}Th	4·68 (76%) 4·62 (24%)	16·9	^{224}Ra	5·68 (95%) 5·44 (5%)	22·4
^{226}Ra	4·78	17·5	^{220}Rn	6·28	26·6
^{222}Rn	5·49	21·2	^{216}Po	6·77	30·0
^{218}Po	6·00	24·6	^{212}Bi (36%)	6·09 (30%) 6·05 (70%)	25·1
^{214}Po	7·68	36·7			
^{210}Po	5·30	20·2	^{212}Po (64%)	8·78	45·3

*Where an isotope emits more than one alpha a weighted mean of the range for each energy is taken.

absorbed is taken up in an outer shell of 10 microns thickness in a 90 micron grain. Once the effects of this gradient are averaged over the crystal volume we find that the dose is attenuated to a level of only 24% of that in the surrounding clay matrix. For much larger crystals, of dimensions close to 1 mm, α-dosage is of negligible importance.

Dating analysis must also take into account a second factor that reduces the α-dose but has nothing to do with grain size attenuation. Within the vicinity of its short path α-radiation will create a core containing a high density of excited electrons. Trapping of electrons at imperfections near this core will then be a highly competitive process. In the wake of the α-radiation's passage many electrons will simply return to their original crystal site. Consequently much of the α-radiation energy is wasted in non-trapping processes.[6]

In contrast, longer-ranged β- and γ-radiations create much lower electron densities in their path and so, in terms of activation of TL energy storage, they are much more efficient than α-radiation. This relative efficiency is expressed by a factor, termed a '*k*-value' which is measured by the ratio:[7]

$$k = \frac{(\text{TL/rad})_\alpha}{(\text{TL/rad})_\beta} \tag{5.3}$$

This quantity has to be determined for each pottery fabric, using a laboratory α-radition source of known strength. *k*-values ranging between 0·08 and 0·25 are common, though that of quartz is sometimes much lower, at around 0·02. (This latter point has important consequences in the theory of the quartz-inclusion technique discussed in section 1*e*).

(ii) *β-radiation* is emitted as a complex energy spectrum for each nuclear disintegration (Table 4.1).[8,9] ^{40}K-decay involves only one such spectrum with energies ranging from 0 to 1·33 MeV (Fig. 4.1) and an average energy of 0·58 MeV. The uranium (^{238}U and ^{235}U) and thorium decay chains give multiple spectra with ^{214}Bi providing the highest β-energy (1·78 MeV) in the uranium series and ^{212}Bi providing the highest β-energy (2·09 MeV) in the thorium series. The average energy carried by each entire decay chain is 2·25 MeV and 1·40 MeV respectively.

β-radiation has a range of travel which, of course, depends upon the initial energy, but, in general terms, is far more penetrative than α-radiation. For example, 1 MeV β-radiation has a range of 1·6 mm in quartz. It may still be treated as an internal radiation source for the sherd's dosimetry, though, as a precautionary measure, the 1 mm 'transitional' zone near the surface which is effected by soil β-dose, is usually stripped away before sample preparation. Now, while there is some grain size attenuation of β-dose it is an order of magnitude less severe than that appropriate to α-dose.[10]

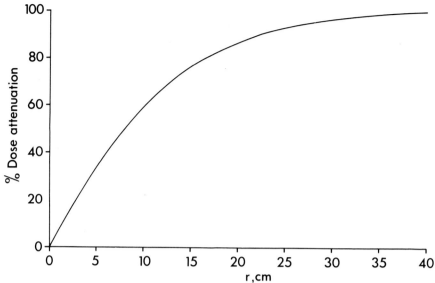

Fig. 5.3 ^{40}K γ-radiation dose at the centre of a spherical mass of compact radioactive soil medium (density assumed to be 2·7 g/cc.) as a function of sphere radius. r. The effective attenuation is expressed as a percentage of the dose provided by a sphere of infinite radius. The γ-radiation attenuation characteristics of ^{238}U and ^{232}Th decay chains are similar to the ^{40}K example here, if rather more severe: at $r = 10$ cms, the dose fractions are 59% (^{40}K), 63% (^{232}Th), 65% (^{238}U) (reference 11).

(iii) *γ-radiation* supplies the major *external* contribution of radiation dose, together with a small cosmic-ray component (about 0·02 rad.yr^{-1}). Radioactivity in burial soil even 20 cm or more away from the sherd's location supplies a significant amount of γ-dose (Fig. 5.3).[11] The γ-radiation from ^{40}K has only one energy, 1·46 MeV, but that of uranium and thorium has many components. The total γ-energy associated with each of the latter decay series is 1·91 MeV and 2·43 MeV, respectively.

From this discussion it is apparent that there are only two ranges of grain size for which the dosimetry is likely to be straightforward: {a} fine-grains of around 4 microns that experience almost all the dose components in the pottery fabric (smaller grains, particularly sub-micron ones, are difficult to handle from a practical standpoint); {b} grains of such large dimensions that α-dosage is unimportant, but not so large that β-attenuation effects are at all critical. The choice of 90 micron diameter quartz crystals for such analysis is explained in section 1e.

1d THE FINE-GRAIN TECHNIQUE: SAMPLE PREPARATION
Carefully controlled crushing of the sherd allows the recovery of the crystalline inclusions in the same size range as they were when embedding in the clay matrix.[12] A procedure commonly employed is to squeeze

several fragments from the inner parts of the sherd between the faces of a V-shaped trough supported in vice jaws. The brittle fired clay readily separates from inclusion surfaces and then, as a powder, acts as a buffer against damage of the harder quartz and feldspar grains. The whole powder sample is divided up in grain size during settling from an acetone suspension. Only material less than 8 microns in diameter remains in liquid decanted after two minutes. After a further twenty minutes many of these finer grains will have settled. Only sub-micron grains remain suspended so these can be conveniently poured away.

The 1–8 micron material, when reshaken in acetone, can be conveniently pipetted in equal portions into flat-bottomed glass tubes, each carrying a thin aluminium disc at the bottom. A 50°C evaporation removes the surplus acetone to leave a series of individual disc samples each carrying about 1 mg of evenly-spread pottery. Reproducibility of deposition between discs is around ± 3%.

Still concentrating on dosimetry aspects, at this stage, it is valuable to take some typical levels of pottery and soil radioactivity contents and turn the energies of α-, β- and γ-radiation discussed above into annual dose-rates, here quoted in rads per year.

	α	β	γ
^{238}U (3 ppm)	0·86	0·039	0·036
^{232}Th (12 ppm)	0·85	0·026	0·063
K (2%)	0	0·172	0·052
Total dose input (rad yr^{-1}):	1·71	0·237	0·151

For a k-value of 0·14, the 'effective' α-dose becomes 0·24 rad yr^{-1}. But for this allowance for such inefficiency it is clear that the α-dose contribution would swamp all other components. As it is, each radiation form is of equal importance in dose-rate evaluation.

1*e* THE INCLUSION TECHNIQUE: SAMPLE PREPARATION

The initial acetone washing of a vice-crushed sample during the preparation stage of the fine-grain technique leaves grains and fragments larger than 8 micron in size as a residue. Now this coarser material is gently mortar-crushed and passed through a magnetic separator which sorts the required crystalline minerals out of the clay ground mass that contains small levels of responsive iron impurity.

Some discolouration of the crystalline extract is usually apparent. This is caused by diffusion of some of the elemental constituents of the host clay matrix (like iron, aluminium and sodium) into the outer regions of the crystals, a process activated by the high temperatures of kiln-firing.[13] Impurities of this type can serve as TL centres in their own right, but they have the undesirable feature of being in the part of the inclusion which suffers the major α-dosage (see Fig. 5.2). Under these conditions any simple principle of minimization of that dose component is immediately violated. But treatment of the extract with 1N solution of hydrofluoric acid overcomes this problem very effectively. For a 100 minute etching time many minerals, like feldspars, are dissolved away. Quartz, while resisting acid attack, still loses a shell about 12 microns thick, and, with it, about 85% of the α-dose contribution (Fig. 5.2). Quartz grains that survive this treatment carry a residual α-dose of 6%, or less, of the total annual level.

Quartz grains of a diameter, circa 90 microns are most suitable for routine analyses as they usually provide a significant proportion of the total inclusion content. For this grain size a β-dose attenuation factor of ×0·94 is appropriate. The HF etching treatment suggested above takes away those regions of the quartz that stop the very low energy component in the β-radiation spectrum, thereby requiring a further ×0·94 factor to be included in the analysis.

1*f* THE TL DETECTION SYSTEM

Either in fine-grain or quartz-inclusion form, archaeological samples give a very weak TL intensity (typically, about 10^5 photons per second).[14] The design of apparatus developed to optimize detection of such low light levels is schematically presented in Fig. 5.4. The optical system is biassed towards the blue end of the electromagnetic spectrum (c. 3800–4500 Å) using filters like the Corning (5·58) or (7·59) in front of a photomultiplier tube with a 'bialkali' ($K_2Cs\,Sb$) cathode which has a

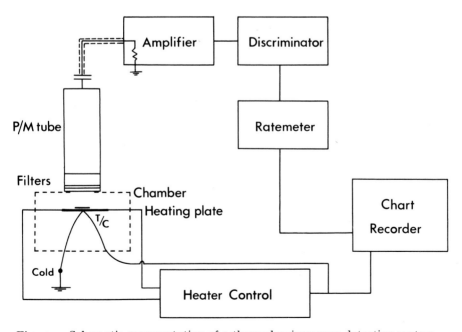

Fig. 5.4   Schematic representation of a thermoluminescence detection system.

peak response in the same region. This arrangement also rejects the large majority of the incandescent glow which is dominantly red in colour. A heat-reflecting filter (Chance-Pilkington HA3) is sometimes included to enhance this rejection.

The pulse output of the photomultiplier's anode is electronically amplified to give a spectrum of pulse heights ranging from 0 to 15 volts. A 1 volt threshold set in the discriminator unit takes out the smaller pulses which arise not only from the true TL signal but also from the background of electronic noise. Many of the pulses larger than 5 volts are caused by extraneous scintillations due to radioactivity in the photomultiplier glass structure and cosmic-ray excitation. As these events are quite rare the pulse-rate counting approach illustated here minimizes their significance. The refined signal from the ratemeter feeds the vertical axis of the chart recorder.

A thermocouple welded beneath the nichrome heating strip converts the temperature during the heating cycle into an electrical current that drives the horizontal axis of the chart recorder. The essential requirement of the heater control is reproducibility. For convenience a linear heating rate is usually imposed, using servo-control, operating at around 20°C per second.

Within the heating chamber itself the sample is kept under an atmosphere of an inert gas (either nitrogen or argon) containing minimal levels of oxygen and water vapour impurity (usually less than 2 ppm of either). In this way non-radiation-induced ('spurious') TL is adequately quenched.[15] The origins of this form of TL are ill-understood. The only obvious features are that it is associated with surface charge on the pottery grain's surface (often enhanced by grinding procedures) and most responsive to chemically reactive gases like oxygen. As spurious TL is mainly yellow to red in colour of emission (around 5500 Å) the optical system outlined above also has an advantage of rejecting much of this unwanted light signal.[16] The literature also contains several recipes for sample pre-treatment to minimize this problem.[17,18]

1g GLOW-CURVE ANALYSIS AND TL STABILITY

The plot of TL intensity *versus* temperature is termed a 'glow-curve'. Typical forms of this curve for fine-grain and quartz inclusions from pottery are shown in Fig. 5.5 i, ii and 5.6 respectively. To understand the structure of glow-curves it is necessary to look at the nature of the TL energy storage process in somewhat greater detail.

The thermal stability of electron trapping depends upon the tightness of binding between the electron and the particular defect involved. The higher the temperature at which a peak occurs in the TL glow-curve, the stronger is the binding effect.

For many of the lower temperature peaks even ambient ground temperatures are sufficient to disrupt the electron-defect link. For

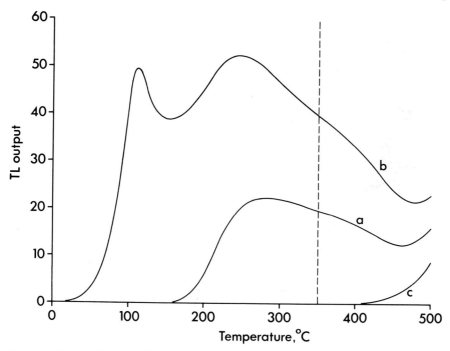

Fig. 5.5 (i)   a. Natural TL glow-curve from a fine-grain pottery sample.
               b. Glow-curve from Natural TL + TL induced by laboratory irradiation.
               c. Background incandescence.

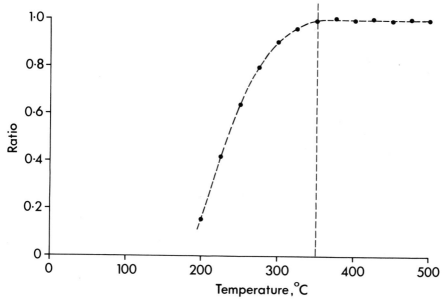

Fig. 5.5 (ii)   The 'plateau' test, checking the stability of TL storage over archaeological times.

example the 110° peak that is frequently observed in pottery analysis and attributed to quartz in the fabric has a half-life of only 145 minutes at 20°C. It is scarcely detectable in a radiated sample left for a day before glow-curve measurement. The resistance to electron 'leakage' rises at a very rapid rate (roughly by an order of magnitude for every 35°C, according to normal TL kinetic concepts) so that we are thinking in terms of decay half-lives of about 10^4 years around 300°C, 10^7 years at 400°C and so on. Considerations of this nature explain the absence of low temperature peaks in the natural TL curve as it reflects the influence of sample storage over the archaeological period. Stability can be studied for each sherd by seeking a 'plateau' in the ratio of the natural TL ordinate to the laboratory-induced TL ordinate at the same temperature (Fig. 5.5, lower portion).

As shown in Fig. 5.5 the TL curves for fine-grain samples tend to be 'smeared out' and built up with appreciable overlap of many glow-peaks derived from a broad suite of minerals. Also their curve shapes are extremely varied as the mineral mixture may take many forms. In contrast, once etched free of extra TL centres near the surface, the quartz glow-curves for pottery assume an almost universal form, independent of where in the world the material originates (Fig. 5.6).[19] The more intense 110°C peak is used in TL dating in a manner quite different from that described here (see the 'pre-dose' technique in Appendix B) and often accompanied by the 'shoulder' peaks at around 160°C and 225°C. For routine dating analysis attention is focused upon the two overlapping peaks at 325°C and 375°C. Though the 325°C peak dominates the high temperature region in the illustration it is equally as common to find the 375°C peak is the stronger of the two.

'Plateau' testing in inclusion analysis is complicated by the rapid fall away of the glow-curve either side of such well-defined peaks. Fortunately detailed kinetic studies indicate decay half-lives for storage at around 20°C of more than 10^7 years for both these peaks, so stability analysis is obviated.

The evaluation of the quantity, equivalent dose (Q), defined in section 1b, is approached in the same way in both the fine-grain and quartz-inclusion technique, as it is just the amount of additional laboratory dose required to increase the high temperature TL level to twice that of the natural glow-curve (Fig. 5.5, upper portion) (see also Fig. 5.7, more fully discussed in section 1i).

Beyond this point the discussion of TL dating will concentrate on a variety of correction factors, under the headings of 'environmental effects', 'supralinearity' and 'anomalous fading', each of which have a different level of significance in each of the two techniques of grain size selection that is employed.

1*h* ENVIRONMENTAL EFFECTS

(i) *Water uptake*. Archaeological contexts even within a metre or so

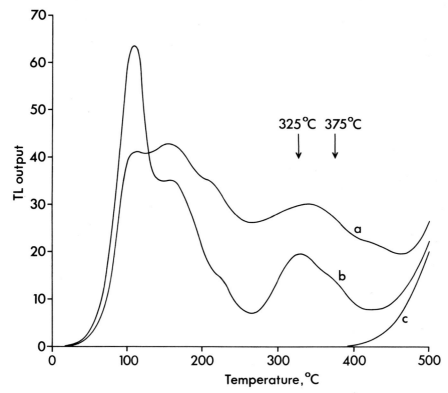

325°C 375°C

Fig. 5.6   a. Typical glow-curve obtained from an irradiated portion of coarse-grained crystalline minerals extracted from pottery.

b. Glow-curve of the same crystalline extract which has been reduced to quartz only, by hydrofluoric acid etching. Apart from complete solution of several less resistant minerals, such as feldspars and calcite, the acid also takes away surface regions of the quartz grains, removing impurities introduced by high temperature diffusion during kiln-firing (reference 19).

of the ground surface are almost invariably soaking wet. The water uptake of the buried pottery and its surroundings has a direct impact on the dose-rate experienced, by acting as a radiation absorber in its own right. The internal α- and β-radiation crosses a succession of thin clay walls and fine pores (varying in diameter from 0·1 to 10 microns in typical fabric) while giving up its energy to the various TL minerals embedded in the structure. Air in the pores will scarcely slow the radiation at all, but a water filling will appreciably shorten each path length. In fact, water absorbs α-radiation almost 50% more effectively than clay [20] so the associated dose-rate reduction is expressed by the equation:

$$\alpha_{\text{wet}} = \frac{\alpha_{\text{dry}}}{1 + (1 \cdot 50) \, (fw)} \tag{5.4}$$

where w is the saturation water uptake (as a fraction of the sherd's dry weight) and f is the fraction of that water retained in the burial circumstances.

Water absorbs β-radiation about 25% more effectively than clay so a further equation results:

$$\beta_{wet} = \frac{\beta_{dry}}{1 + (1 \cdot 25)\,(fw)} \qquad (5.5)$$

The value of w varies from about 0·05 to 0·30 in pottery. The much less-tightly packed burial soil may hold as much as 40% water, by weight, so that γ-dose reduction factors are often very severe. However, now the water is only 14% more effective as an absorber than the soil. The suite of equations for this effect is completed with

$$\gamma_{wet} = \frac{\gamma_{dry}}{1 + (1 \cdot 14)\,(f_1 w_1)} \qquad (5.6)$$

The subscript, 1, is used to distinguish f and w values of the soil from those of the sherd itself.

As moisture retention is effected through capillary action at pore walls the moisture content of soil is much more susceptible to seasonal fluctuations than that of the sherd. Unfortunately little research data is available to put a figure to such fluctuations. In Britain, $f = 0\cdot95$, with an uncertainty of only 0·05, would seem reasonable but Mediterranean and Near Eastern sites require more thought. At many sites the true condition is probably controlled as much by the region's water table as rainfall variations through the year. A broader range of $f = 0\cdot6$ to 1·0 is often used, with reservation.

(ii) *Radon emanation.* In both the uranium and thorium decay series there is one radioactive product (radon-222 and thoron-220, respectively) that are inert gases. They are both highly mobile until radioactive decay, as their daughter products are chemically reactive. As thoron has a half-life of only 54 seconds few of its atoms progress beyond the pottery pores. In contrast the radon half-life of about 3·8 days enables that gas to move into the burial medium and, in part, find freedom in the atmosphere. Such movement carries with it a partial loss of internal dose to the extent that 60% of the α- and β-contributions would be lost in a condition of 100% radon emanation. Fortunately, measured loss levels rarely exceed 20%, but this still produces errors in internal dosimetry of about 5%. Emanation effects in soil are likely to be far more significant as close to 96% of the uranium chain's γ-radiation energy is post-radon.

The presence of water, in the sherd and the soil, acts as an inhibitor to radon movement but only in so far as the diffusion distance is reduced from several metres to a couple of centimetres.[21] That distance is still comparable with or rather greater than the thickness of most sherds.

Thus, even in wet conditions, internal dosimetry can be upset by emanation effects. It might seem that external dosimetry would be somewhat steadier while water restricts radon movement, as the range of γ-radiation is so much greater than possible diffusion displacements. In fact in the soil we must contend with a quite different mechanism, that of direct transportation by ground water flow, which is capable of carrying this radioactivity several metres from its source.

In general it is felt that water uptake and radon emanation effects are far less predictable in evaluation of the external dose-rate. Additionally it is that dose-rate which suffers at the hands of any non-uniformities of radioactivity in the burial medium. Scattered pebbles or rock fragments of broken walls and ramparts can act as radioactivity hot spots (or the very opposite) while closely adjacent strata of different constituency may provide a partial dose-rate somewhat different from that expected from the sherd-bearing soil.

At the site itself it is sometimes possible to bury a small capsule containing a radiation-sensitive phosphor in the relevant trench section for a year, so that it records directly the environmental dose-rate that the pottery experienced in the past. In this way seasonal fluctuations in dose-rate are integrated as they were in antiquity, though it is acknowledged that year-by-year variations are not taken into account by this approach. These problems have been studied in detail in the process of dating Bronze Age ceramics from Denmark.[22]

1*i*   CORRECTION FOR SUPRALINEARITY IN RADIATION-RESPONSE

In the age equation (5.2) it was assumed that TL grows uniformly with radiation dose. In reality, some non-linearity is common, with a distinctive form: (i) at smaller doses the sensitivity (TL per rad) is low but gradually increasing; (ii) at higher doses (typically around 300 rads) the growth curve becomes linear (Fig. 5.7, curve a). Extrapolation of this linear portion backwards gives a positive intercept, I_0, on the dose axis. In TL dating this effect poses problems because the information about original low dose curvature and, hence, the magnitude of I_0, is lost once the archaeological dose has carried the TL response into the linear region. The means of investigation of this so-called 'supralinearity' involves regeneration of a 'second-glow' TL response curve after draining of the natural TL (Fig. 5.8, curve b). Then the query posed is whether or not the supralinearity intercept defined by this fresh growth curve, I_N, is a reliable laboratory equivalent of I_0.

(i) *Quartz supralinearity*. If, during drainage of the natural TL, no change occurs in the way in which the TL trap associated with the glow-curve peak captures electrons, then we expect the second-glow response curve will repeat the TL growth form as it was in antiquity (and partially recorded in the first-glow response, in application of

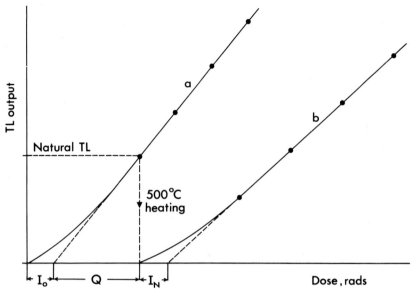

Fig. 5.7   Supralinearity in the radiation response of pottery minerals (references 19, 23 and 24).

additional laboratory radiation). Then the slopes of these two response curves would be parallel over the linear portion. On the contrary, if the TL trapping mechanism is modified by the heating process in some way, a 'parallel-slopes' criterion of this nature will not be satisfied. Then, extending this argument, I_N is only expected to equal I_0 if that criterion is upheld.

In principle this kind of logic could be applied to the TL response of any mineral. In practice the quartz peak at 375°C has proven to be regularly 'benign' while that at 325°C, in a 'malign' manner, often changes its slope and intercept. In a test programme on quartz extracts from Romano-British wares from seven archaeological sites (Plate 5.1) TL ages were within 5·4% of their known ages, on average, when a benign supralinearity correction was included. Analysis of some sherds at the 325°C peak in a malign condition yielded TL ages sometimes in error by as much as 41%. Values of I_N ranging from 0 to 260 rads were recorded with supralinearity contributing as much as 55% of the total archaeological dose, in one instance.

(ii) *Fine-grain supralinearity.* It is unusual to find first- and second-glow responses with parallel slopes for fine-grain disc samples, mainly because heat-induced colour changes that occur during measurement of the natural TL modify the clay's optical transparency. The empirical use of I_N amongst a large group of known age sherds (mostly Romano-British) indicated the value of some supralinearity correction, at least. Accuracy of dating moved to $\pm$ 9·5% with I_N included, compared with only $\pm$ 15% with supralinearity ignored.

However, recent research has indicated that the second-glow inter-cept can often be decreased by addition of laboratory radiation before the routine 500°C heating.[23] From this it is inferred that I_N is less than I_0 with the difference of intercept values depending upon the previous natural dosage. The possibility of 'calibration' of the dose dependence of I-values has been considered and a linear correlation shown to be quite successful.[24]

1j ANOMALOUS FADING IN FINE-GRAIN DATING

Kinetic theory predicts stability of energy storage in the 350°C to 500°C region of the glow-curve at 10^6 to 10^9 years, which would seem to exclude any significant TL loss over archaeological periods. However, there are a few instances where it is clear that such a theory is being flaunted (Fig. 5.8). In this illustration storage of an irradiated fine-grain disc for only two months results in an almost uniform drop of

5.1 The Lunt at Baginton (near Coventry, England): a reconstruction of the Roman fort which stood there around A.D. 70. (Photograph: courtesy of Dr B. Hobley.)

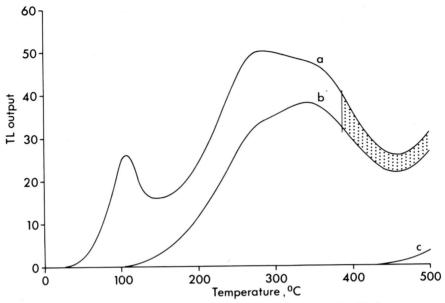

Fig. 5.8 a. Glow-curve taken immediately after laboratory irradiation.
 b. Glow-curve taken after two months storage of a laboratory irradiated sample.
 c. Background incandescence
 (references 24 and 25).

16% in the TL output between 380°C to 500°C. This loss, as it is virtually temperature-independent, is called 'anomalous' fading.

This effect has been observed frequently amongst several geological minerals, particularly in feldspars of volcanic origin and in zircon and fluorapatite, while quartz and limestone have been exonerated.[25] However, amongst pottery examples there is nothing to suggest that differences in mineralogy can account for the presence of fading.

There is another distinctive feature of anomalous fading which hints at a possible way to overcome its adverse effects. As a rule, about half of the first month's TL signal loss occurs within the first day of storage, indicating the fading mechanism has a multiplicity of decay modes with a wide range of loss rates. It is likely that any anomalous components still in the sample after a few months have a half-life approaching the 10^5 years acceptable in terms of archaeological stability. A laboratory procedure by which all irradiations are stored some months before glow-curve measurement, in an attempt to allow any unstable TL to decay away, has yielded good results amongst material from a Neolithic level of Knossos and a fourteenth century Thai site, at Kok Moh.

$1k$ ACCURACY OF TL DATING
To draw into routine TL analysis the various complicating factors discussed above the age equation (5.2) is usually re-written as

$$\tau = \frac{Q + I_0}{(\alpha + \beta) + (\gamma + \text{cosmic})} \tag{5.7}$$

where the annual dose-rate is divided into its two gross components, internal (as $\alpha + \beta$) and external (as $\gamma + \text{cosmic}$). Here 'α' is the 'effective' α-radiation dose-rate, after introduction of the efficiency parameter, k.

In the quartz inclusion technique use of the 'parallel-slope' criterion for supralinearity correction seems extremely reliable. But reduction of the effective α-radiation component in the annual dose-rate to almost a negligible level puts a heavier burden on the γ-radiation contribution and its associated problems of seasonal fluctuations of water uptake and radon mobility in the soil. In the absence of *in situ* phosphor dosimetry (see section 1*h*), as would occur when a season's digging involves complete site clearance, it is unlikely that dating accuracy can be improved beyond the $\pm 7\%$ (1 σ, standard deviation).

Errors in the fine-grain technique have been assessed in detail,[26] with the exception of the influence of dose-dependent supralinearity. This technique's greater dependence upon internal dosimetry factors should ultimately permit an accuracy close to $\pm 5\%$. However, several extra complications have been mooted but, as yet, not investigated which may make this error figure over optimistic. For example some very low TL age estimates have been tentatively attributed to defect creation induced during vice crushing. Also the introduction of extraneous contaminants, particularly calcite, carried by percolating ground water is a constant fear.

2 GENERAL DATING APPLICATIONS

The various sites to which TL dating has been applied have usually been selected to offer information where the radiocarbon dating method is either not practical, through lack of organic remains, or carries some question-mark related to possible contamination. This group includes a hearth unearthed beneath York Minster (now established as of early ninth century AD origin),[27] a Thai site of Tha Muang (c. AD 950) and an Iranian site, Zarand (c. 1700 BC)[28] and a burial at Bellan Bandi Palassa in Ceylon which was surrounded by quartz chips fractured by fire.[29] Also an interesting Iron Age/Saxon dichotomy in pottery decoration at Glen Parva in Leicestershire, England, was resolved in favour of the former. Recently, seemingly internally consistent radiocarbon dates for the Colombian site of Moralba were shown to be wildly in error, with TL dates grouping around AD 1100, in keeping with stylistic dating for wares from that region.[30]

Preliminary results in the dating of African Iron Age material is typified by the age of 2570 ± 260 years (640 BC) obtained for a powerfully-modelled sculpture found in the alluvium of a tin mine in

5.2 The Jemaa Head (H. 23·5 cm). (Photograph: courtesy of Dr B. E. B. Fagg.)

the hills close to the Jos Plateau in Nigeria (Plate 5.2).[31] The terracotta, known as the Jemaa Head, is an important example of the Nok Culture, but deposits at Nok itself, which yielded many fine figurines, carry only sketchy radiocarbon dates ranging from 3625 BC to AD 200.[32]

It is generally accepted that long-term uncertainties in the radiocarbon dating method relate to changes in the cosmic-ray flux reaching the upper atmosphere (where ^{14}C-production occurs). It is valuable to realize that the impact of such a change, even by a factor of two, would introduce a correction of only about 2% in TL age determination, as the cosmic-ray contribution to the annual dose-rate is so small. Thus dates for the Central European Neolithic sites of Stein (5350 BC), Bylany (5330 BC) and Hienheim (4610 BC), all related to the so-called *Bandkeramik* pottery style, are regarded as major contributions.[33] At that time period corrections to ^{14}C-dates are approaching 800 years (see Fig. 3.5).

At a similar time in the Old World it now appears that a bronze tradition was already emerging in northern Thailand which well precedes that of the better-known Shang Dynasty in China (c. 1500 BC).[34] Associated pottery wares with red and white decoration also akin to the Neolithic material in China have been excavated at Ban Chiang and dated to around 3600 BC.

Even earlier ceramic traditions have been established in Japan, at

Fukuie Cave, where so-called Early Jomon ware has yielded a TL age of 12000 BC. This remarkable antiquity is supported by some associated radiocarbon dates but may well be controversial as some archaeological opinions are unwilling to place these wares further back in time than the middle of the third millennium BC.

The range of application of TL dating is somewhat uncertain, but may be more than 0·2 million years, on the evidence of analysis of burnt flint extracted from fire-place debris.[35] (The limiting factor is the saturation of TL radiation response which may set in for doses ranging from 2 to 100 kilorads.) Thus the method covers an important time period from about 30,000 years onwards, when radiocarbon dating is hazardous in the face of possible sample contamination. Cases in point are the well-known, fired-clay animal and human figurines of Dolni Vestonice, in Czechoslovakia (c. 33000 BC).[36]

Unquestionably the greatest impact of the TL method has been felt in the art world in relation to authenticity investigations amongst wares of many civilizations. Such investigations include forgery during the past decade of squat female figurines from the Neolithic site of Hacilar in Turkey [37] and of wall paintings on terracotta slabs originally used for decoration of Etruscan tombs.[38] The current high prices of Chinese ceramics, particularly of the T'ang Dynasty (AD 618–906), have high-lighted TL evidence of prolific imitation of such material during the early part of this century. Use of original piece moulds excavated at that time enabled local artisans to mass produce many impeccable wares that are visibly indistinguishable from their ancient prototypes.[39]

Though bronze itself, as a metal, does not have the capacity to store TL energy, many can now be dated by their ceramic-like casting core. This broadening of application covers early Chinese bronzes of the Chou and Han Dynasties of the first millennium BC, Roman and Greek statuary and sculpture, deity figures from the Nigerian kingdom of Benin and Buddhist statuary from Nepal, Cambodia and Thailand from various periods during the past two millennia.[40] Frequently metal corrosion exposes such cores so that sampling can be generous. Other-wise many sections of decorative relief carry usable material in recesses even though the bulk of a core may have been scraped away im-mediately after manufacture.

Besides the standard TL methods a new technique is under develop-ment whereby highly radioactive zircon grains (usually containing more than 100 ppm of uranium) are separated from the pottery fabric.[41] These grains give quite high TL outputs because they suffer large internal α-radiation doses (roughly 30 kilorads per millennium of age). They are negligibly influenced by external dosage from γ-radia-tion and thus unaffected by any seasonal fluctuations of this parameter. This 'radioactive inclusion' approach has already been successfully used to authenticate a bronze horse of classic Greek style, now in the Metropolitan Museum of Art in New York.

5.3 *Saint John.* Life-size terracotta sculpture attributed to Benedetto da Majano (1442–97). (Photograph: courtesy of Sammlung Thyssen Bornemisza, Villa Favorita, Switzerland.)

3 A SPECIALIZED DATING APPLICATION

3a PRINCIPLES OF THE 'SUBTRACTION' TL DATING TECHNIQUE
The dosimetry features of the 'fine-grain' and 'inclusion' techniques of
section 1c-e can be combined conveniently in some cases to allow an
age to be determined that is independent of knowledge of the environmental dose-rate. The difference between the archaeological doses
obtained from each technique can be attributed almost entirely to the
TL energy built up by alpha radiation alone. This is clear from the
following simultaneous equations where α, β and γ represent the annual
dose-rates from each form of radiation and τ is the age. The subscripts,
f = fine-grain and i = inclusion, indicate the method employed and the
factor, a, takes account of any beta dose attenuation due to grain size:

$$(\alpha + \beta + \gamma)\,\tau = Q_f + I_f \tag{5.8a}$$

$$(a\beta + \gamma)\,\tau = Q_i + I_i \tag{5.8b}$$

In solving these equations the γ-component is subtracted out and the
β-component reduced to minor importance (as a = 0·88, for 90 micron
quartz grains usually used). A new age equation emerges:

$$\tau = \frac{(Q_f + I_f) - (Q_i + I_i)}{\alpha + (1 - a)\beta} \tag{5.9}$$

This 'subtraction' technique has a major role to play in dating
terracottas of museum origin and some pottery collected from archaeological contexts without associated burial media. An accuracy of about

5.4 Egyptian Bronze Cat
(H. 37·5 cm) of the XXVI
Dynasty (664–525 BC). This
animal, sacred to the god-
dess Bastet of Bubastis,
wears finely-engraved orna-
ments, including a broad,
beaded collar holding the
Knot of Isis amulet on the
nape of the neck, and the
Eye of Horus suspended on
the chest from a neck cord.
(Photograph: courtesy of
Sotheby Parke Bernet, New
York. *Antiquities* sale 3635,
lot number 198: May 4th
1974.)

± 13% is possible once allowance is made for the main source of random error that comes from the combination of individual errors in the measurements of Q and I (remembering that the *difference* of the archaeological dose values is usually smaller than either independent value). However, when the uranium and thorium content of the pottery fabric is low or on occasions where a low k-value keeps the effective α-dose component quite small much poorer quality of dating is inevitable.

3*b* TWO EXAMPLES OF 'SUBTRACTION' DATING

To illustrate the significance of various TL parameters in this technique, two quite different objects have been chosen:

(i) a Renaissance terracotta of Saint John attributed to Benedetto da Majano (1442–97) (Plate 5.3),[42]

(ii) an Egyptian bronze *Seated Cat* stylistically dated to between the seventh and fourth century BC (Plate 5.4). (Core sample from the shoulder.)

Both are assumed to have been dry throughout their history. The value of a was 0·95 in each case.

Annual dose-rate evaluation (rads per year)	*Saint John*	*Bronze Cat*
k-value	0·181	0·192
α-radiation	0·553	0·108
β-radiation	0·243	0·095
Evaluation of archaeological dose (rads)		
Q_f	280	890
I_f	0	0
Q_i	130	505
I_i	0	105
Subtraction Age (using equation 5·9)	470 years (AD 1505)	2495 years (520 BC)
Estimated error (1 σ, standard-deviation)	± 70 years	± 320 years

The Bronze Cat's data is indicative of the need for accurate supra-linearity assessment as I_i contributes about 37% of the fine-grain/inclusion archaeological dose difference. The subtraction technique is also extremely valuable in authenticity analysis as an absence of a sensible level of archaeological dose difference would suggest that an object had been exposed to an artificial source of external radiation (like ^{60}Co γ-radiation, for example) perhaps in an attempt to simulate a TL response fraudulently.

Chapter 6

Fission Track Dating

1 BASIC DATING PRINCIPLES

1a SPONTANEOUS FISSION AND THE FORMATION OF TRACKS

The natural radioisotope of uranium (^{238}U) is extremely massive in terms of the size of its atomic nucleus. This nucleus is also somewhat unstable and tends to break down, physically releasing small amounts of energy through the release of familiar radioactivity products, α, β and γ-radiation. Appreciably less frequently the breakdown process is much more violent with a complete division of the atom.[1] The resulting lighter fragments move away with a high velocity and large amounts of energy, only coming to a halt after the creation of extreme material damage along their path. This phenomenon is known as 'spontaneous fission' and the track produced, though very localized and short (typically around 20 microns in minerals of interest) is directly observable using an electron microscope,[2] or rendered visible by a selective chemical etching of the mineral's surface [3] (Plate 6.1).

In geological minerals the passage of time since their natural formation is marked by a build up and storage of a 'fossil' track record. For man-made glasses and fired materials this record is annealed out during heating so that any fission tracks they now contain measure the period elapsed since that heating, i.e. the archaeological age. Similar regions of damage can be created by fission products artificially by the effects of neutrons generated in a nuclear reactor, where the uranium isotope activated is ^{235}U. This 'induced fission' acts as a measure of the uranium content of the material. As the decay rate for the spontaneous reaction is constant and known (see section 1d) the number of events that would occur every year for a particular content is predictable. The fossil track concentration may then be converted into the date sought.

The range of spontaneous and induced fission fragments are very similar as are the efficiencies with which they are made visible by etching. This simplifies the dating equation used to:

$$\text{Age, } A = \frac{4\cdot2 \times 10^{-24}}{\lambda} \cdot \Phi \cdot \frac{N_i}{N_s} \qquad (6.1)[4]$$

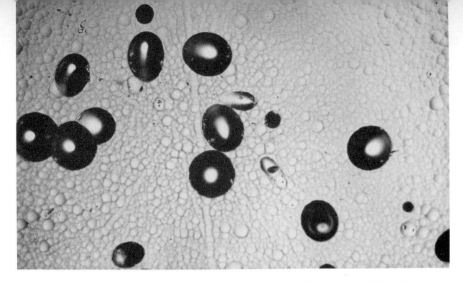

6.1 Fission track etch pits in tektite glass, viewed using epi-illumination. Spurious etch pits created by poor polishing in sample preparations are usually distinctively kidney shaped, and of incorrect dimensions. (Photograph: courtesy of Dr S. A. Durrani, Department of Physics, University of Birmingham.)

Φ is the neutron flux (often applied at a level of around 10^{15} per cm^2), λ is the spontaneous fission decay constant and N represents the track density measured. The quantity Φ, is quite difficult to assess accurately so a standard dosimeter glass of known uranium content is usually included in each reactor exposure for calibration purposes. (Fission tracks in glass are particularly simple to study—Plate 6.1). As equation (6.1) illustrates the final precision of the fission track dating method depends upon accurate knowledge of the value of λ while a low value of N_s allows only a modest accuracy in age determination.

The formation of the fission track has been likened to an 'explosion spike' that causes ejection of a huge number of electrons in the vicinity of the charged particle's path.[5] Thus a narrow cylinder is formed temporarily packed with positive ions, but, as these ions repel one another electrically, a hollow core develops, usually about 8 Å in diameter. (1 micron $= 10^{-4}$ cm, and 10^4 Angströms (Å).) The strains set up by this very localized disturbance stretch out some 40 Å further into the crystal's lattice. Factors such as low mechanical strength and a compactness of constituent atoms favour track production. Consequently mica is more sensitive than glass or zircon while olivine is highly resistive to fission damage. (This theory also correctly predicts the impossibility of track creation in metals as they have an ever-present electron density sufficient to annul ion displacement processes and cause lattice healing in the fission fragment's wake.)

1*b* CHEMICAL ETCHING PROCEDURES

The attack of a suitable acid (or alkali) etchant proceeds by preferred dissolution of material along the length of the track as the damaged region presents a highly-exposed surface compared with its surround-

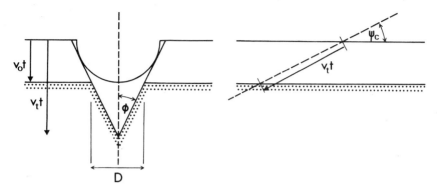

Fig. 6.1   Track etching geometry. The pit shape is determined by the ratio
V_0/V_t. When the angle of the track to the upper surface is less than
ψ_c (where $V_0 = V_t \sin \psi_c$), no preferential etching would be observed
(reference 4).

ings (Fig. 6.1). When the track direction is normal to the exposed surface a circular pit is formed in time, t, of a diameter given by,

$$D = 2v_0 t \left\{ \frac{v_t - v_0}{v_t + v_0} \right\}^{\frac{1}{2}} \tag{1.2}^4$$

Though a greater track etching rate produces a larger pit diameter,
there is a limiting value of $D = 2v_0 t$.

When the track's incidence is not normal the pit formed is elliptical
(Plate 6.1). But there is a critical angle, ψ_c, given by

$$v_0 = v_t \sin \psi_c \tag{1.3}$$

which defines the most oblique angle of track direction for its observation in etching. Thus only a fraction of the tracks cutting the original
surface will be subsequently detected.

The final portions of the fission fragment's path are less readily
seen as the lattice disturbance there is mainly through direct atomic
displacement. In etching, the value of v_t gradually tends towards v_0 in
such regions, so that the effective value of ψ_c will depend upon where
the original surface cuts the axis of the damage core. The etch pit
diameters tend to be quite variable in these conditions.

This simple geometric model describes the behaviour of glasses both
man-made and natural (in the form of obsidian and tektite). Other
minerals often present more complex patterns that relate to a crystal
orientation property. Clove-shaped pits are produced in orthoclase
(an alkali feldspar), while pyramidal pits characterize quartz. In
gypsum, dissolution is anisotropic so that normal etching produces a
series of parallel grooves. The fission tracks create short tunnels,
randomly orientated, which end at the centre of such a groove.

The research into optimization of etching processes has been extensive and the recipes for treatment are reviewed in the literature. The temperature of the etchant plays an important role, as exampled by the response of the natural resin, amber.[6] The value of v_t relative to v_0 increases with a raising of temperature, ψ_c varying from 38° to complete track absence for 28°C and 90°C, respectively. Though the etching rate is slow at the lower temperature a better track registration is achieved. Some of the preferred treatments for minerals of interest in the archaeological context are listed here:

(i) The various forms of glasses studied by this technique include uranium-enriched soda glass (the heavy element acting as a colorant), volcanic *obsidian* and *tektites*, all of which are treated with a solution of 48% hydrofluoric acid (HF) for 5 to 60 seconds at 23°C.[7] The highly-porous, finer volcanic *pumice* is usually treated with a more dilute acid solution.

(ii) *Apatite*, chemically Ca_5 (F, Cl) $(PO_4)_3$, is a common accessory mineral in igneous rocks. It has been studied in detail in this subject for its track-fading characteristics (section 1e). A brief 25 second exposure, at 23°C, to concentrated nitric acid produces the etch pattern illustrated in Plate 6.2.[8]

(iii) *Mica* (muscovite), 15% (HF) for 20 minutes at 50°C.[9]
Zircon ($ZrSiO_4$), aqueous solution of sodium hydroxide for some hours, at 220°C.[10]
Hornblende, 48% HF, for time ranging up to a minute and temperatures, at 23°C–60°C.[11]

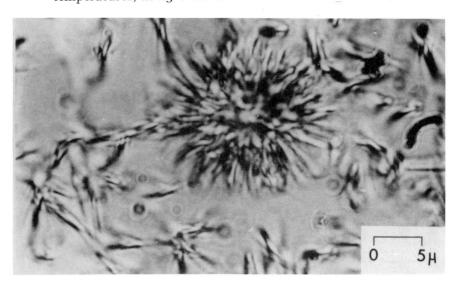

6.2 The 'sunflower' effect produced by a high density of fission track channels created around a uranium inclusion in apatite. (Photograph: courtesy of Dr N. Bhandari, Tata Institute of Fundamental research, Bombay.)

Sphene (CaTiSiO₅), concentrated hydrochloric acid, 1 hour at
   90°C.[12]

This group of minerals have all proved important in geological dating
and will be referred to again in the discussion of measurement of the
decay constant, λ (section 1*d*).

   The etching treatment sometimes adds problems to the dating
technique by the production of etch pits unrelated to fission damage.
Most of these pits correlate to some crystal defects and are distinguishable from track pits by virtue of their ordered positioning and orientation. In glasses these 'spurious' etch pits can usually be discarded on
the grounds of size, not matching the expected channel lengths of
5–20 microns and pit diameter of about 9 microns.[13] However, the
polishing of the sample's surface during sample preparation may cause
'kidney'-shaped pits to appear in subsequent etching which are not so
readily recognizable as false. One remedy that has had some success is
the annealing out of the fission-induced pits at a temperature selected
to leave the spurious regions undisturbed and measurable.[14]

1*c* MINERAL SUITABILITY FOR FISSION TRACK ANALYSIS
Once a suitable etching procedure has been established two other
factors come into play in determination of mineral choice for dating
purposes. First, the internal uranium concentration will control the rate
of build up of a number of tracks sufficient to be conveniently counted in
the laboratory. Only artificial glasses deliberately enriched with
uranium (sometimes to the 1% concentration, by weight), zircon
(containing around 0·01–0·1% uranium, by weight) and obsidian
(which rarely carries more than 6 ppm of uranium) find application in
archaeology over the past 10,000 years. The earlier periods of hominid
development, which reach back some five million years to our present
knowledge, is covered only by a few examples of analysis amongst the
natural glasses (obsidian, tektites and pumice). Sadly there have been
no zircon finds in that time period though this mineral would be ideal
for fission track dating at that stage. The spectrum of application is
far wider during geological periods covering more than a billion years
of the Earth's existence. The choice of minerals includes several
zircons, mica, apatite (usually in conjunction with sphene) and a very
old hornblende from Llano, Texas, while some submarine glasses
(probably ash layers windblown after continental volcanic activity)
supplement this list of materials. The only long-term limit set on
dating feasibility occurs when the spontaneous fission tracks become
overcrowded and difficult to separate. Many of the applications in the
literature are presented in Fig. 6.2, when an alternative dating method
is available for comparison purposes, albeit stylistic attribution of
glazes on a Japanese pottery bowl or a radioactive decay technique like
potassium-argon (K-Ar) (see Chapter 4). (This data is covered in
references 15–33, as quoted in the Figure caption.)

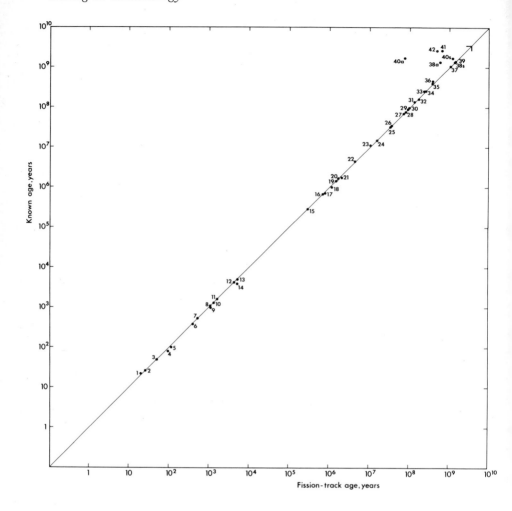

Fig. 6.2 Range of application of fission track dating.

1. Experimental glass, rich in uranium, prepared at Corning Glass Works in December, 1943.[3]
2. Commercial glass tubing coloured light yellow by the addition of 1·19% U_3O_8. Made by Osram in Berlin, before January, 1939.[3]
3. Steuben 'Topaz' wine glass made between 1925 and 1928. Now in the Scientific Department, The Corning Museum of Glass.[3]
4. Footed Beaker (French or Bohemian), last quarter of nineteenth century. Science Department, The Corning Museum of Glass.[3]
5. Candlestick (AD 1850–60). Probably made in the Boston and Sandwich Glass Co. Factory.[3]
6. Glaze on a bowl from Izumi, Japan.[15]
7. Glaze on a bowl fragment from the kilns (called *Tsubaki-gama*) at Seto City, Japan.[16] Dated, stylistically, to the Muromachi era (AD 1330–1570) or slightly earlier.

8. Obsidian arrowhead from a fire-razed dwelling pit at Onnemoto, Japan.[16] Dated by associated Okhotsk style pottery in Hokkaido Province, covering the period AD 960–530.
9. Kangavar glass from Iran (archaeological date, c. AD 1000).[17]
10. Zircon extracted from baked earth excavated at Iwasaki, Japan.[15] Archaeological date, close to AD 670.
11. Zircon extracted from baked earth excavated at Hisai, Japan.[15] Archaeological date, close to AD 470.
12. Zircon extracted from baked earth excavated at Shar-i Sokhta, Iran.[17] Archaeological date for phase IV, 2200–1800 BC.
13. Zircon extracted from pottery excavated at Shar-i Sokhta, Iran.[17] Archaeological date for phase I, 2700–3200 BC.
14. Obsidian spearhead found embedded in a pottery vase in a dwelling pit at Tosamporo, Japan.[16] Dated by related radiocarbon ages 1950–1290 BC.
15. Basaltic glass from the Mid-Atlantic Ridge.[18] Related K-Ar age: 0·29 m.y.
16. Australian tektites, related to K-Ar ages, clustering around 0·7 m.y.[19]
17. Tektite from the Philippines.[20] Related to K-Ar age: 0·68–0·76 m.y.[21]
18. Tektite from the Ivory Coast.[19] Related K-Ar age: 1·15 m.y.
19. Volcanic glass sherd in marine sediments.[22] Sample V21–145, K-Ar age: 1·45 m.y.
20. Volcanic glass sherd in marine sediments.[22] Sample V21–173, K-Ar age: 1·62 m.y.
21. Pumice from Olduvai Gorge.[23] Related K-Ar age: 1·75 m.y.[24]
22. Obsidian (Macusanite) from Peru.[11] Related K-Ar age: 4·5 m.y.[25]
23. Volcanic glass sherd in marine sediments.[22] Sample EM 8–13: 11·4 m.y.
24. Bohemian tektite from Stripi.[20] Related K-Ar age: 14·5–15·0 m.y.
25. Muscovite mica (Arizona).[26] Related K-Ar age: 32·7 m.y.[27]
26. Tektite from Lee County, Texas.[20] Related K-Ar age: 34·5 m.y.[21]
27. Apatite and sphene from Bryan Mountain, Colorado.[28] Related K-Ar age: 54 m.y., and related Rb-Sr age: 63 m.y.[29]
28. Zircon from Elkhorn Mountains, Montana.[30] Related K-Ar age: 76 m.y., on associated biotite.
29. Apatite and sphene from Magnet Cove, Arkansas.[28] Related K-Ar and Rb-Sr age: 95 m.y.[31]
30. Muscovite mica from Oregon.[26] Related K-Ar age: 97·5 m.y.
31. Zircon from Chaone Mountain, south Nyasaland.[30] Related K-Ar age: 138 m.y.
32. Apatite and sphene from Mount Ascutney, Vermont.[12] Related K-Ar age: 131 m.y., and Pb-α age of 186 m.y.[32]
33, 34. Apatites from New Hampshire.[12] Related K-Ar age: 250 m.y.[32]
35. Muscovite mica from Baltimore.[26] Geological age estimate: 425 m.y.
36. Apatite from West Victoria Islands.[12] Related K-Ar age: 455 m.y.
37. Hornblende from Llano, Texas.[25] Related Rb-Sr age: 1075 m.y.[31]
38. Apatite (a) and sphene (s) from Tishomingo, Oklahoma.[28] Related Rb-Sr age: 1350 m.y.
39. Lepidolite mica from Colorado.[26] Related K-Ar age: 1400 m.y.[33]
40. Apatite (a) and sphene (s) from Boulder Creek, Colorado.[28] Related Rb-Sr age: 1700 m.y.
41, 42. Lepidolite micas from Pope's Claim and Salisbury, southern Rhodesia.[26] Geological age estimate: 2650 m.y.

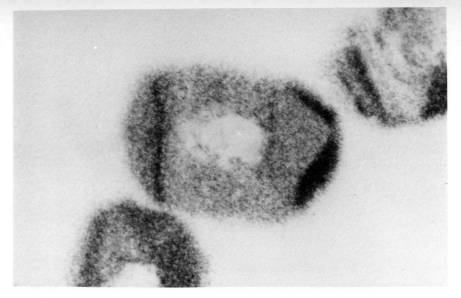

6.3 Fission-track patterns in detrital zircon grains revealing the internal distribution of uranium. Even within a single crystal variations in uranium content can vary by more than an order of magnitude between the core and surface regions. (Photograph: courtesy of Dr B. Grauert, Eidgenössiche Technische Hochschule, Zurich.)

In practice the measured uranium content can vary throughout the bulk of a crystal, most notably in zircon where order of magnitude variations of radioactivity between the core and rim of single crystals have been observed (Plate 6.3).[34] Thus the age equation (6.1) could, in principle, only yield accurate ages if the induced tracks were measured at the same surface as that used for measurement of the fossil track density. The usual procedure employed is to etch an original surface for natural track counting and then move into the crystal about 25 microns further, by re-polishing, to expose a fresh surface suitable for neutron irradiation, thereby reducing any radioactivity uncertainties to very localized variations only.

A second important consideration is the possibility of long-term instability of fission tracks in certain minerals, whereby the crystal lattice attempts to reverse the fission fragment's disturbance and recover structural continuity. Elevation of temperature speeds up this recovery process, but there is appreciable variation between minerals in the resistance they offer to this track annealing. For example, in one amber, from Gdansk, Poland, complete track erasure was obtained over a period of an hour at 115°C. For a similar effect in zircon an annealing temperature of 700°C is required.

Quantitatively, laboratory analysis allows an estimation of the kinetics of the gradual track erasure or 'fading'. To obtain a particular track density reduction in an irradiated sample annealing can either be for a short time at high temperature or over a long period at a lower temperature. A graphical solution, with τ as the annealing time

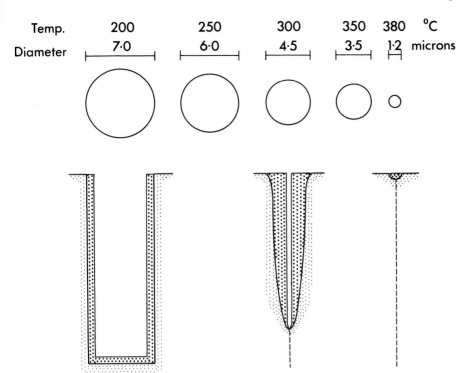

| Temp. | 200 | 250 | 300 | 350 | 380 | °C |
| Diameter | 7·0 | 6·0 | 4·5 | 3·5 | 1·2 | microns |

Fig. 6.3   Temperature dependence of fission track structure in glass, etched for two minutes in 5% hydrofluoric acid (reference 36).

plotted against (temperature)$^{-1}$ yields a value for the 'activation energy' of the recovery process, E, through the relation:

$$\tau = \text{constant . exp} \left\{ -\frac{E}{kT} \right\} \qquad (6.4)$$

(k is the Boltzmann constant, $8 \cdot 62 \times 10^{-5}$ electron volts per degree Kelvin.)

For a tektite from Indochina, the parameters $E = 2 \cdot 51$ eV and constant $= 10^{-13}$ have been measured, predicting great stability of fission tracks. Partial fading over 10^8 years would require a steady annealing temperature of 170°C over all that time. The data of Fig. 6.2 draws attention to the materials with good track retention capacity: zircon, mica, hornblende and sphene. The last of these minerals often occurs alongside apatite which has a comparatively low activation energy (between 0·74 and 1·4 eV).[35] These apatite-sphene 'pairs' act as reliable geothermal indicators. For example, at Boulder Creek, Colorado, the apatite fission track is low by nearly a factor of fourteen compared with associated sphene date and related K-Ar date of 1,070 million years. The mica from Pope's Claim and Salisbury, southern Rhodesia, also records elevated temperatures in the past with fission track ages well below their accepted geological age.

The mechanism of track fading is illustrated in Fig. 6.3. The highly-disturbed crystal portions that surround the hollow core of the track separate away from the sound regions of the bulk mineral. The narrowing of the central core and an inhibiting effect of etching waste products slows the rate of chemical attack.[36] Etch pits are smaller in the faded material, so the gradual decrease in track density is accompanied by a similar reduction of the mean pit diameter. Fig. 6.4 illustrates this for a tektite glass.[37] If the etch pit diameter distribution for spontaneous fission has a mean value one half of that due to induced fission the observed natural tracks represent only 25% of all those created in the past. The measured fission track date is then too low by a factor of four. A similar approach is possible by study of tracks within the bulk of the crystal when the etchant reaches the internal damage via cleavage planes. In some cases a cluster of tracks surrounding a uranium inclusion gives an attractive sunflower pattern (Plate 6.2).[38]

Glasses seem to require particular care as their annealing characteristics depend upon composition, with higher instability matching richness in alkali elements. Also in volcanic obsidian, track fading is accelerated by the presence of internal water.[39]

1d   THE DECAY CONSTANT FOR SPONTANEOUS FISSION

A survey of many attempts to measure the decay constant for spontaneous fission, λ, reveals a large degree of scatter of results, ranging over $5\cdot3$–$16\cdot0 \times 10^{-17}$ yr^{-1}. Segrè's early work [40] using electroplating techniques for radioactivity deposition and concentration, indicated relative fission rates for uranium isotopes as $\lambda_{238} : \lambda_{235} = 23 : 1$ and relative abundances of 141:1. (Thus the spontaneous breakdown of ^{235}U plays no significant role in the dating method.) A value of $\lambda = 8\cdot6 \times 10^{-17}$ yr^{-1} was evaluated.

More recently a similar value of $\lambda = 8\cdot2 \times 10^{-17}$ yr^{-1} has been obtained by counting the gamma radiation emitted by molybdenum (^{99}Mo) present in uranyl nitrate.[41] The molybdenum is one of the yield products of the uranium spontaneous division and radioactive in its

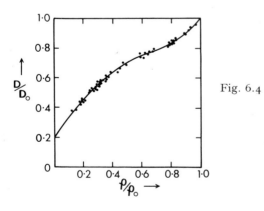

Fig. 6.4   Dependence of the mean diameter of fission track etch pits on track density when thermally annealed. The response illustrated is that of the mineral, bediasite, treated with 48% hydrofluoric acid for 23 seconds at 23°C (reference 37).

own right. A quite different approach utilizes a technique primarily developed for counting very low levels of neutron fluxes.[42] Centrifuging creates negative pressures in a liquid (alcohol, in this case) and causes metastable bubbles to form. These bubbles will nucleate in the presence of a fission event creating a visible (and audible) effect that can be counted. Using this technique, $\lambda = 8 \cdot 42 \times 10^{-17}$ yr^{-1} was obtained.

Despite good agreement between these two recent λ-estimates a somewhat lower value derived in 1964 by two of the initiators of the dating technique, Fleischer and Price, has gained most general recognition.[43] An empiricial approach sought to optimize the correlation between several fission track results and the related ages for the same material estimated by other radioactive techniques for geological minerals (specifically, tektite samples 17, 24 and 26; mica samples 25, 30, 35 and 39; an obsidian sample, 22; hornblende sample, 37, in Fig. 6.2) and by historical records for recent glasses (samples 1–5 in Fig. 6.2). Additionally an independent experiment was included where a synthetic mica sheet was placed adjacent to a sheet of natural uranium. The mica-uranium sandwich was divided in two and one part stored for half a year (to gather spontaneous tracks in the mica) while the other part was exposed in a reactor to measure the sensitivity of the mica detector in response to induced fission events. A value of $\lambda = 6 \cdot 85 \times 10^{-17}$ yr^{-1} was evaluated, with an error of about 3%. Unless otherwise stated the applications discussed below use this last value.

2   GENERAL DATING APPLICATIONS

2a   INTRODUCTION

The major application of the fission track dating method has been in geological problems and many of the papers covering more recent material seek only to illustrate the potential of the technique while studying material for which there is a satisfactory date already available from other sources. For example several recent man-made glasses have been analysed as uranium has been used as a colorant since the beginning of the nineteenth century, the glass itself being datable stylistically or through historic records (see Fig. 6.2; samples 1–5, and reference 3). However, further back in time the glasses seem to have been far purer. At Uji, Japan, a green glass ball is believed to owe its colour to the presence of 21 ppm of uranium in its constitution but there is no evidence that this element was included as an additive. Although an example of uranium-rich *tessara* has been reported in a mosaic at the Imperial Villa at Cape Posilipo, Naples,[44] this material seems to have disappeared some thirty years ago. Similar glass tessarae from Pompeii contain only minor levels of radioactivity. In Japan, despite the tedious counting involved to observe a statistically-significant number of tracks, satisfactory dates have been obtained for glass-rich kiln slag (*tatara*) and a couple of ceramic glazes (Fig. 6.2, samples 6 and 7). Also in Iran the fission track method has served to confirm archaeological evidence in the dating of glass from Kangavar. However, a glass specimen found in Landberg Fort, on the northern coast of Scotland, proved not to be of Iron Age origin as first suggested but only around 300 years old.[45]

2b ARCHAEOLOGICAL OBSIDIANS AND ZIRCONS
The beginnings of a man-made glass history is the time of its manufacture, but the natural glass created by volcanic activity, obsidian, is of geological origin. Obsidian found many uses in ancient civilizations as a large glass core could be fractured and chipped to produce many varieties of weapons and tools. These items all retain a fossil track record of their geological history except in rare instances when a chance heating annealed out that record. Such a heating reset the fission track 'clock' to zero so that any spontaneous events detected today relate to an *archaeological* incident in the past.

Three notable examples of this approach to dating are known:

(i) An arrowhead and a flake tool were heated sufficiently strongly in the destruction of a dwelling pit at Onnemoto in Hokkaido, Japan, during the eleventh century AD, or a little earlier, to cause the obsidian to bend out of shape. (Fig. 6.2: sample 8).

(ii) A vase excavated from a dwelling pit at Tosamporo, Japan, contained a small spearhead in its fabric, presumably incorporated by chance at the time of the pottery manufacture. While radiocarbon ages for the area reach back to 1950 BC, the osbidian's fission track age of 5080 ± 400 years suggests an even earlier occupation of the site (Fig. 6.2: sample 14).

(iii) A knife blade fashioned in Mesolithic times was re-softened by heat from an overlying hearth at Gamble's Cave II, Elmenteita, a site in the Rift Valley of Kenya excavated by Dr L. S. B. Leakey in 1927. A fission track age of 3700 ± 900 years suggests the hearth was used during a brief Neolithic occupation of the area. There is no direct chronological information for this site: a radiocarbon date for a cremation at the neighbouring site, Njoro River Rock Shelter, marked the Neolithic period of the region.

In a similar manner firing of zircon will remove the geological track record though this mineral is quite resistive, with an activation energy, $E = 3 \cdot 6$ eV and a full track annealing in an hour requiring as much as 700°C. Hearth material in Japan and at Shar-i Sokhta, Iran, has supplied sufficient baked earth to allow zircon extraction, with satisfactory dating results.

2c IDENTIFICATION OF OBSIDIAN SOURCES
Even in an unfired condition obsidian can offer archaeological data

with the age of the volcanic formation and the uranium content acting as identifiers of regional source of the natural glass for ancient man's use. In the archaeological deposits of the Mesolithic phase of Franchthi Cave, in southern Greece, obsidian tools were analysed originally for distinctive features in trace element chemical composition, but with only partial success. This composition matched that of a general pattern for geological volcanic flows that stretched over a distance of some 1,300 km, from the Cycladic island of Melos to Acigöl in central Anatolia. However, the uranium content of close to 4·8 ppm (by weight) and a fission track age of about 8·6 million years for the geological material at Melos proved to be the same as that of the Cave finds.[46]

Thus it appears that the cave inhabitants had begun navigation long before the Melian obsidian source was exploited by other civilizations in Crete, Thessaly and Macedonia. Radiocarbon dating of large fish bones at the site indicates that this seafaring in the eighth millennium BC was related to fuller exploitation of marine food at that time. Also this marine transport of obsidian in Mesolithic times pre-dates any other example in the world by some 1,500 years: the earliest Neolithic evidence marks the route from Anatolia to Cyprus.

3 A SPECIALIZED DATING APPLICATION

3a HOMINID ORIGINS IN EAST AFRICA

The relationship of a variety of scientific dating techniques to the establishment of time marker points in hominoid evolution is a recurring theme in this book. The Rift Valley region of Kenya and Tanzania has acted as a rare encapsulation of many episodes in man's development, stimulating vital anthropological analysis and research in palaeomagnetism and the potassium-argon (K-Ar) dating principles with far-reaching consequences (see Chapters 8 and 4). Fission track dating, too, has found its applications in this area.

The unearthing of fossil remains of our very distant past remains a matter of chance, often requiring the coming together of many natural forces with some interplay of human agencies. For example, in the vicinity of Lake Rudolf, Kenya, there are many areas of high-rising strata, gathered by past sedimentation from Ethiopian rivers, which now overlay any record of early man and put it beyond reach. However, 400 miles to the south lies Olduvai Gorge (Plate 6.4) where seasonal rains have cut their way deep into sediment layers that have formed an otherwise flat plain over vast stretches of the region. These sediments themselves act as a gradually-accrued filling to a lake contour now some two million years old.

It was the deposits of Bed 1 at Olduvai that first yielded up in-context evidence of the important early varieties of man. *Zinjanthropus* [47] and

6.4   Olduvai Gorge to-day. (Photograph: courtesy of the National Geographic Society.)

Homo Habilis,[48] plus a host of associated remains unearthed in recent years like the recent-assembled cranium of Hominid 24.[49] The survival of this material has been aided by preservation effects of a tuffaceous clay layer that overlies a basalt stratum, one of many markers of volcanic activity in the area. This basalt has given a K-Ar age determination of 1·9 million years.[50] The tuff of Bed I divides into three fractions, two minerals (anorthite and augite) and a porous natural glass, pumice, only the last of which proved of value for fission track work.

The pumice creates its own peculiar problems during etching treatment as the acid attack on pore walls gradually eroded the surface area available for ultimate analysis. To overcome this difficulty a resin-mounted section of the glassy fragments was photographed in detail after the fossil tracks had been revealed. Those same areas were located after subsequent neutron exposure and fresh etching. The additional induced fission tracks were counted in the surviving pumice surface which had been reduced in area by close to 58%, in practice. Taking this area loss into account a fission track age of 2·03 ± 0·28 million years resulted.

The volcanic activity of the Valley, while inevitably destructive at the time of eruptions has enriched an otherwise desolate terrain to allow some support for vegetation. Particularly, near the side of Lake Rudolf itself there is no lack of waterside dwelling and animal domestication, though the lake itself has changed its natural boundaries frequently in its 4·5 million year lifetime. On the evidence of a skull found lying on an exposed outcrop at nearby Koobi Fora, hominid occupation of the area stretches back at least 2·6 million years [51] (see also Chapter 4). The K-Ar analyses for tuff horizons in the sedimentary basin have been closely questioned and it is now believed that the ratio of the two isotopes has been disturbed repeatedly by successive eruptions. This results in a partial or complete 'overprinting' of each context's age, one of the most widespread of which occurred around 1·75 million years ago.[52]

Fission track analysis has been used to confirm this geothermal event.[53] A vitric tuff from the upper part of the Kubi Algi Formation (south-east of the East Rudolf Basin) yielded an age of 1·8 million years, even though it lies stratigraphically *below* the most firmly dated horizon of the region, the 2·6 million year KBS tuff in the middle of the sedimentary sequence.[54] Comparison of spontaneous and induced etch pit diameters showed that no significant track fading had occurred in recent times that could yield an anomalously low age. Thus, at the time of isotope overprinting a total annealing of earlier fossil tracks occurred, erasing a large portion of the tuffaceous glass's earlier history.

Chapter 7

Obsidian Hydration Rim Dating

I BASIC DATING PRINCIPLES

Ia INTRODUCTION

In the previous chapter, some reference was made to the role played by the natural glass, obsidian, in ancient society as a raw material for tools and weapons. Obsidian's most attractive feature, a natural strength, arises from its formation mechanism. As the molten lava oozes from its source volcano it is rapidly cooled by contact with the atmosphere, a quenching process that denies the main constituent of the lava, silica, a chance to crystallize. The viscous, cooling glass tends to form outcrops near the volcanic extrusion area [1] which can be open-mined readily although natural erosion often allowed easy surface collection of river-worn cobbles.[2] In ancient times each raw nodule would be fashioned into a cylindrical core which, in turn, was fractured by percussion into hundreds of prismatic blades. Each blade, with its razor-sharp edges, could be used without further treatment as a cutting tool or weapon point. Alternatively it served as a versatile blank for a host of more sophisticated implements. This process of glass fracture opens up fresh surfaces which will undergo some chemical change through hydration. The growth of a hydrated layer on the obsidian artefact with time supplies the basis of the *hydration rim* dating method.

Ib THE HYDRATION PROCESS

During its formation from the magma any obsidian will retain some 'pristine' water (usually about 0·3% of the glass' weight) but, during the hydration process the glass lattice undergoes a subtle alteration to form the associated mineral, perlite. The perlite matrix retains a water concentration of around 3 per cent by weight.[3] There are some parallels drawn between this process and the phenomenon of patination of flint except that the latter involves the activity of chemical agencies besides water.[4] Contrast should be made with devitrification which represents a gradual crystallization, probably aided by the internal water. That effect will create layering of only about 0·05 micron thickness over a million years and so is only of importance in the geological study of natural glass. Here we are dealing with hydration rim growth rates of

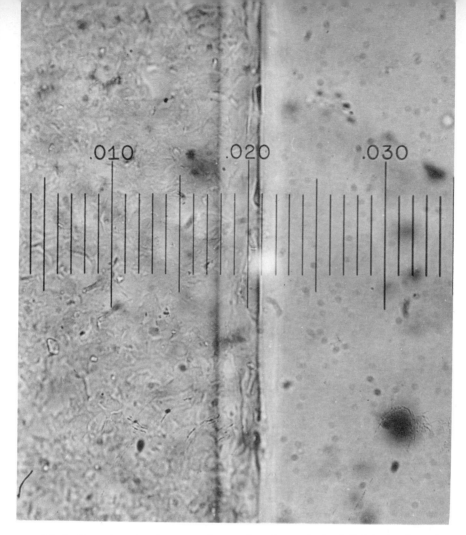

.010   .020   .030

7.1 Hydration rim structure as observed under polarized light stands out through the birefringence caused by strain in the glassy lattice when water is included. (Photograph: courtesy of Dr I. Friedman, US Geological Survey, Denver, Colorado.)

around 2 microns in a millennium of burial exposure to atmospheric and soil moisture.

On a microscopic scale the mechanism of water uptake is one of inward diffusion with a constant replenishment of moisture stock at the surface by formation of a molecular covering film. The strong affinity for water that obsidian exhibits means that the necessary external supply is comfortably maintained even in near-arid conditions: variations in local humidity have no effect upon the hydration process. The hydrated zone gradually swells behind the diffusion front and the hydrated zone is soon characterized by a series of microfractures the formation of which ease internal mechanical strains to some degree.[5]

1c MEASUREMENT OF HYDRATION RIM THICKNESS

The swollen and damaged region of the artefact refracts light to a different extent compared with the unaltered glass portion beyond the diffusion front. When viewed as a mineralogical thin section in polarized light the hydrated zone is distinct and luminescent because of the occurrence of strain birefringence (Plate 7.1). This optical distinction in the microscope is heightened by the fine line of greater intensity seen near the leading edge of the diffusion front. This line probably represents the smearing out of the optical disturbance created by new microfractures developing in the unhydrated glass and ending in that region.

Conventional microscope techniques have so far proved the most popular in this dating method but some consideration has recently been given to use of a new nuclear technique to define the hydration profile.[6] A monoenergetic beam of fluorine (^{19}F) ions will penetrate into the perlite region until they have been sufficiently slowed (by electronic collisions) to resonate in a reaction with the hydrogen present because of the water uptake. The resonance energy used is 16·45 MeV. The depth of penetration can be readily estimated from range v. energy tables read off at the difference between this energy and that of the incident beam. A change of incident energy leads to a change in the region of the obsidian where resonance occurs. The hydrogen concentration in each region is indicated by the intensity of gamma radiation produced in the nuclear reaction. This approach is ideally suited to narrower rim measurements (<2 microns) with a high resolution of 0·02 micron (which is an order of magnitude better than seems possible using optical techniques [7]), this limit being set by the finite slope of the diffusion front rather than by difficulties in the detection process itself.

1d AGE CALCULATION AND DATING LIMITATIONS

At a given temperature the hydration rate of obsidian follows the equation,

$$x^n = kt \qquad (7.1)^8$$

for penetration depth of x microns, an exposure time of t years and a *diffusion rate constant* of k. The index n is usually taken as 2, though lower power laws, even a linear relationship, have been suggested for certain sites in Arizona [9] and western Mexico.[10] Support for this figure comes mainly from direct laboratory study. A freshly-chipped obsidian taken from Tres Piedras in the Jermez Mountains of New Mexico was subjected to laboratory hydration at 100°C for nearly four years, with the hydration depth being measured at intervals over that time. The rim thickness grew according as equation (7.1) with $n = 2$ and $k = 10,000$ micron^2/millennium (for brevity $\mu^2/10^3$ yr).

In the absence of any variation of k with time, which will be considered later, the accuracy of the dating method is mainly limited by the definition of the diffusion's extent. As the total rim thickness is a function of both the k and t, the error in age determination, ε, also varies with these two quantities. For optical observation the lowest measurement error reported is 0·07 micron (reference 2). Then, for an ε-value of 10% antiquity of at least 500 years is necessary for a slow diffusion at 1 $\mu^2/10^3$ yr while a similar accuracy is possible for only fifty year-old obsidian when the diffusion rate is an order of magnitude greater. For a less extreme diffusion rate, $k = 5\mu^2/10^3$ yr, dating accuracy of better than 2% is predicted for material of the pre-Christian era.

The long-term limitation of the method lies at around half a million years that corresponds to a rim thickness of about 50 microns. At this thickness the swelling of the hydrated zone tends to create excessive mechanical strain and the rim breaks away or *spalls* along the dividing line of the diffusion front. The inner obsidian core is then re-attacked until the spalling strain is reached once more: in geological perlite the resulting 'onion-skin' effect is common enough. However, man's history of obsidian use does not seem to begin until around 25,000 years ago.

1e FACTORS INFLUENCING THE DIFFUSION RATE CONSTANT

(i) *Temperature variation* has a direct influence upon the hydration process. In the relation

$$k = A \exp\left(-\frac{E}{kT}\right) \qquad (7.2)$$

A is a constant, E is the activation energy (in kcal/mole), R is the gas constant (in these units, 1·99 calories/°C.mole) and T is the absolute temperature. For the more common obsidian form, termed *rhyolitic*, E has been estimated as close to 20 kcal/mole. The somewhat rarer *trachytic* form (of much higher alkalinity) probably has a lower activation energy (by about 3 kcal/mole) [11,12] which partially explains observations on Egyptian obsidians of both kinds side by side in the same burial medium. There, k (rhylotic) $= 8·1 \ \mu^2/10^3$ yr and k (trachytic) $= 14·0 \ \mu^2/10^3$ yr. The worldwide dependence upon temperature is supported in general terms by the very much lower values of k reported for the Arctic regions (0·36) and coastal Alaska (0·90) compared with equatorial sites on the coast of Ecuador (11·0), while the estimated 'effective' temperatures for these regions are 1°, 5° and 30°C respectively. Indeed, an equation relating hydration rate and temperature has been suggested:

$$\text{Log}_{10} k = -\frac{3877}{°K} + 13·83 \qquad (7.3)^{[13]}$$

(In this equation °K $=$ °Kelvin: °K $= 273 + $°C.) In the light of other effects below, however, this simple correlation seems somewhat remarkable.

Some difficulties arise in definition of effective temperature as the true value to be used is that of the soil in which the obsidian is buried. This soil temperature will only partially follow any fluctuations of air temperature above ground level. At depths of a metre or so the burial context is about 2°C warmer than the surface and can be quite well insulated. But the soil will follow the general climate trend throughout the year so that, strictly speaking, there is a seasonal variation of k to be taken into account. A study of this made at Maebashi, in Japan, is illustrative of this point (Fig. 7.1). While the mean soil temperature at the site over the whole year was 15·1°C, the mean k-value would be 2·66 $\mu^2/10^3$ yr (using equation 6.3) equivalent to an *effective* temperature over the year of 16·2°C. This correction of 1·1°C would appear in age determination as a 6% error.

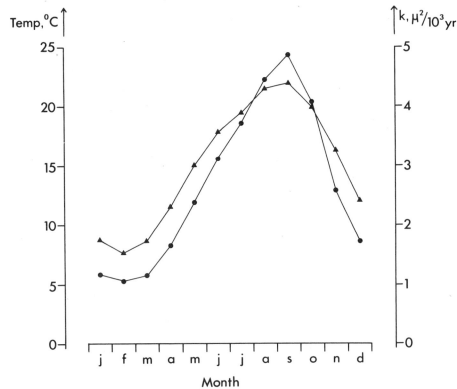

Fig. 7.1   Correlation between the monthly variation of soil temperature (solid triangles) and the diffusion coefficient (k) of hydrating obsidian. k is calculated according to the formula:

$$\log k = -\frac{3877}{°K} + 13·83$$

as applicable for Kanto, Japan (reference 13).

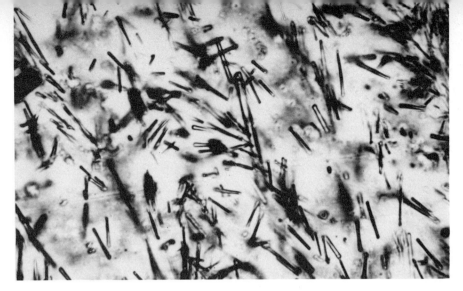

7.2 Lath-crystal microlites together with some globulite, a glassy macro-structure typical of obsidian originating from Kamitaga, at the coast in Kanto, Japan. (Photograph: courtesy of Professor M. Suzuki, Faculty of Science, University of Tokyo.)

For surface finds we may anticipate a different problem, that of direct solar heating. Hydration rim ages from Hohokam, in Arizona, are believed to be in error for this reason. This effect may also cause premature spallation. Also, at the Lorenzan site, Modoc County, abnormal rim growth has been attributed to the presence of hot springs, but this is an isolated report.

Equally problematical are the long-term palaeotemperature variations which are now confidently established by isotope studies in deep-sea sediments and fauna records in recent soil deposits.[14] The Maebashi data of Fig. 7.1 indicate a typical k-variation with temperature of 10% per °C, so that changes in the hydration rate of 1·6 to 2·0 $\mu^2/10^3$ yr in the past 4,000 years in Japan are not surprising.[15] Indeed tropical sea temperatures are believed to have been as much as 6°C lower in Late Pleistocene times, around 15,000 years ago, than they are today. An estimate of the integrated effect of the warming of the climate since that time has indicated that an obsidian freshly flaked that long ago would yield an age of about 13,600 years, somewhat more than a millennium too young due to initially low hydration rim growth.

(ii) *Soil chemistry*: At present the only indication of an influence of the burial strata of the hydration rim growth is that the presence of calcium compounds (most obviously, chalk and shell) act as a catalyst to accelerate the process.[16]

(iii) *Microcrystalline structure* contributes, in part, to the general appearance of an obsidian and their nature probably reflects the nature of the original magma cooling process. Minute particulates of partially crystallized materials may create fern-shaped patterns (scopulites) or 'knotted-hair clusters (trichites). Some fully-developed crystal inclusions may also 'litter' the bulk obsidian. These are called micro-lites, some of which have been identified as felspathic needles, magnetic fragments,[17] pyroxenes and various mica structures (Plate 7.2). No critical differences in rim thickness have been observed in glassy and microlite-rich regions of the same specimen.[18] Irregularities in the hydration band only localize around partially-collapsed vesicles that cut across the path of the diffusion front.

(iv) *Macrochemical composition variations*: While temperature acts as the major external controlling factor in obsidian hydration, in-fluencing rim growth of all artefacts gathered in a context, any general scatter or discontinuity of rim thickness is mainly due to variation of chemical composition in the group. The cause of these variations is the use of more than one obsidian source. This was illustrated at an early stage in the development of this dating method for the visually distinct green and grey obsidian tools found at Classic and Aztec sites of the Valley of Mexico.[19] The green form, which originates from mines and quarries in the Pachuca range and on Cerrade las Navajas, hydrates with a high rate constant of $11{\cdot}45\ \mu^2/10^3$ yr. The grey form, which occurs in many natural veins in the Otumba area, hydrates more slowly, at $4{\cdot}5\ \mu^2/10^3$ yr. Similar sharp variations have been found amongst archaeological material from south Kanto in Shinsu province of Japan, discussed more fully in section 3. Much less distinct discontinuities at

Fig. 7.2   Profile of water content at the hydrated edge of obsidian. The hydrated layer, now in the form of perlite (p) is separated from non-hydrated obsidian (o) by the very steep diffusion front (d) which shows up clearly as a dark band in a micrograph (see Plate 7.1) (reference 17).

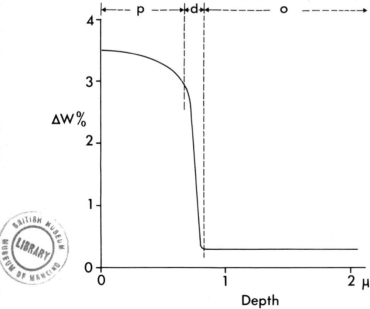

some American sites have required computer analysis of source chemical compositions and clustering of associated implements to sort them out,[20] particularly in coverage of the well-known Warner Valley cache found in central Oregon.[21] There a fine suite of tools (mainly, fashioned ovates) were stacked neatly in two piles in a recess lined with pumice fragments at the sides and a slab of yellow ochre at the bottom. The two outcrops at Beatty's Butte and Glass Mountain were fixed as the obsidian source for this group.

These rim variations due to factors internal to the obsidian have stimulated extensive and detailed research into the mechanism of water movement and bonding in the glassy lattice structure. Only some general conclusions have emerged that can be swiftly summarized here. The mobile elements derived from the surface moisture, whether water molecules or hydroxyl groups, seem to move partly by an autocatalytic process, as a reaction with the bulk structure enhances the diffusion rate.[22] Also to explain the sharpness of the observed hydration edge a diffusion mechanism with a diffusion constant that increases with rising water concentration has to be invoked (Fig. 7.2). (The maximum optical density then matches the region of highest rate of change of the water concentration profile.[23]) Thus the hydration process is likely to be influenced by the potential saturation level of uptake in the rim zone. This, in turn, appears to be greater for higher levels of original, pristine water in the glass bulk and pushes up the diffusion constant sharply.

Of the structural elements the only positive link established so far seems to be the enhancement of diffusion caused by the presence of aluminium (which usually occurs at 10–15% concentration in rhyolitic obsidian). However, the mechanisms involved are quite complex: Al-bonding in the lattice can enhance the number of free hydroxils at the cost of bonded ones and modify the movement of other impurities.[24] One model suggested is an ionic-exchange mechanism with hydroxyls replacing outward-diffusing sodium, but a nuclear resonance approach, like that described in section 1c for H-profile recognition, now using ^{23}Na ions for bombardment,[25] indicated no significant variation of that element throughout the glass. The obsidian flows that supply the raw material are all likely to differ from one another in these features of internal chemistry so that it is essential to subdivide any particular context's artefacts according to source and search for group clustering of rim widths if the dating method is to be treated as absolute.

These various parameters, internal and external, could well account for the deviation of many of the empirical 'on-site' age equations developed (see references 9 and 10, for example) from the pure *square-law* form appropriate to a diffusion process, if k is also a function of the penetration depth, x, in equation (7.1).

Quite separately an interesting empirical time scale has been developed for basaltic glass in the Hawaiian Islands where the hydration rind that forms is palagonite.[26] The thickness growth is *linear* with time for material ranging in age from AD 500–1850. Rate constants have been determined of $7 \ \mu/10^3$ yr for artefacts submerged in fresh water (at an average temperature of 17°C) and $11 \ \mu/10^3$ yr for Island sites (at around 24°C, on average). However, for the palagonite, the mechanism of formation seems to be quite distinctive. An immobile layer punctuated with tubular microchannels builds up between the glass and the water. These channels allow fresh attack to continue while the water concentration grows behind. Eventually iron and manganese oxides remobilize leaving a stable palagonite layer at the surface. It is not yet clear if there are any lessons to be learnt from this glass chemistry in interpretation of perlite formation.

1*f* ARTEFACT RE-USE

Irrespective of all the earlier considerations of variation of the hydration phenomenon in any specific context, 'rogues' still appear in most of the obsidian collections with rims in excess of their burial partners. Although some of these may be attributable to heirloom hoarding it is far more likely that economy dictated re-use and partial re-working of older implements. In some cases three hydration rims may be detectable; (i) a very thick one that corresponds to the *geological* age of the original outcrop that grew almost to its present thickness even before man fashioned the obsidian for his own benefits, (ii) a fragmented layer related to the first use of the obsidian implement and (iii) adjacent regions with the thinnest layer (mainly around the working edges) marking the material's re-use in a later culture.

This custom seems particularly prevalent in California, Mexico, Ecuador and amongst aboriginal tools found on Easter Island in the eastern Pacific.[27] Although the presence of at least the two archaeological rims matching each phase of use is the most direct indicator (as on the *mataa* in Fig. 7.3) there is no reason to exclude cleaning of the implement before re-working. One archaeological problem created here is that one portion of the record of an earlier occupation of the site has been erased. To detect this loss of information a statistical technique has been developed whereby gaps in a trend pattern of rim thickness increase with context depth are sought.[28] The context matching this gap often contains a few artefacts with rim widths below the expected value, thus emphasizing an act of plundering of its obsidian stock during a later phase.

The site of Chorrera, in Ecuador, is often quoted as an example of this confusing effect. During the Tejar phase (AD 460–710) implements were systematically gathered and re-fashioned in preference to fresh manufacture. With the knowledge that obsidian always rated as an important trading commodity, such behaviour may be used as evidence of a breakdown in commercial links at that time. However, the alternative and, possibly, more obvious reason for the absence of a particular rim thickness range in a sequence should not be overlooked; that of temporary site abandonment. In the case of a building sequence at Maunga Auhepa, on Easter Island, a recognized gap in occupation in the eighteenth century could be limited to a span of no more than thirty years by obsidian hydration studies.

2 GENERAL DATING APPLICATIONS

In archaeological studies the hydration rim method is generally used in a 'relative' mode with a time scale attached by control markers set up at intervals by some other dating evidence. For example, chronicles of the Spanish conquest of the Aztec civilization would set a terminal date for the primary occupation of Chiconautla at close to AD 1518. The tight clustering of hydration rim values for that site defines a minimum thickness of 2·27 microns for green obsidian artefacts. Thus $k = 11·45 \ \mu^2/10^3$ yr. Otherwise associated radiocarbon dates set the pattern as in the case of Mostin in northern California, where burial bones from a grave of the ninth millennium BC were grouped with seven obsidian implements.[29] (The presence of the latter indicate surprisingly early settlement in that area.)

The scale of obsidian sampling for this technique is quite overwhelming with more than 300 sites analysed by 1967 covering 3,500 pieces from the Valley of Mexico alone and some 2,000 dates calculated for the Kaminaljuyu site in Guatemala, for example.[30] However, a full appreciation of the severity of effect of internal parameters on diffusion rate is quite a recent feature in this field and could account for the limited early success of phase distinction at sites like Chorrera in Ecuador, where a general k-value of $11 \ \mu^2/10^3$ yr was used for all the material.[31]

The importance of obsidian as a raw material in antiquity is nowhere better illustrated than at the numerous sites scattered along the Valley of Mexico, a natural basin of the central highlands at some 7,000 feet above sea level. The post-Aztec or 'Colonial' era has been brought to life as a highly-active period in rural Indian life, in contrast to literary evidence that suggests a cessation of the obsidian industry after the sixteenth-century conquest. Dated sites have been divided according to the composition of their artefact assemblages, into residential (such as Maquixco, Teacalco and Chiconautla mentioned earlier), food-gathering centres (Cuanalan) and agricultural (Mixcuyo). (Rasp flakes will have been used for pulp removal from *maguey* cactus leaves to leave fibre for cloth and netting manufacture, notched points were used for hunting deer and spear fishing, and much-serrated knife blades probably served as fish-gutting equipment.) At the same time some rather thick hydration rims detected in artefacts mixed with Aztec material have prompted a search for earlier occupation in the Valley parallel to that recognized in the other highland valleys of

Oaxaca and Tehuacan. Activity before 1500 BC covered a cultural movement from hunting to organized agricultual efforts.

In Japan emphasis has been laid upon the very early horizons of human activity covering the first ceramic phases that produced Jomon wares and earlier. The remarkable antiquity of Jomon pottery has been established by radiocarbon[32] and thermoluminescence analysis[33] of Fukuie Cave material which dates to the eleventh millennium BC. However, hydration rim studies of the pre-ceramic era indicate, in the worldwide sense, an equally startling early development of obsidian-working skills reaching back to 18,000 BC in the Hokkaido region and to 23,000 BC in the south Kanto district (see section 3.2 below). Indeed at the site of Shirataki, Hokkaido, a complete chronology has been set up for the series of five terraces of occupation that overlook the river Yubetsu and lie beneath an obsidian outcrop of Pliocene origin. Amongst the obsidians there was much evidence of frequent technological change, each one of which now carries a time marker. Similar analysis of the rich point-tool culture of Uenodaira (on the southern slopes of the Kirigamine volcano in Nagano Prefectory), place the site at the boundary of initial ceramic development.[34]

Looking at the future, studies in progress include a systematic study of New Zealand's obsidian sources in connexion with composition detail [35] and the dating of many Maori and Polynesian settler sites in that region.[36] Similarly, confirmation is sought of early dating for sea transportation of obsidian around the south-west Pacific from source locations like Talasea in New Britain, to New Guinea and Reef Islands in the Santa Cruz group some 2,000 km away.[37] Radioacarbon dates associated to flake artefacts in these areas suggest the beginning of the first millennium BC as the time for this activity.

3 SPECIALIZED DATING APPLICATIONS

3.1 ABORIGINAL ARCHAEOLOGY AT EASTER ISLAND

European traders in the east Pacific first 'discovered' Easter Island in AD 1722 and found an active community of indigenous natives eager to bargain for all manner of goods. This phase of the Island's history is clearly identified by finds of imported blue beads throughout the settlements. The main documentation for the Island is to be found in missionary records which indicate abandonment of earlier tribal customs in AD 1868, a date which matches the final use of a ceremonial site at Orongo. But the local aboriginal tribes had their own history some of which they were able to recall and recount to the new arrivals. Vivid memories of the elders would describe the many wars between the two main tribes that culminated in the battle of Poike Ditch close to AD 1676. But what of earlier times? Here modern archaeologists only conject that this famous battle divided a Middle and Late Period and suggest an Early Period pre-dating the twelfth century.

Obsidian dating thus has three time markers upon which to build a chronology and confident source identification, the Island itself bearing two volcanic regions, Orito cone and Rano Kao tuffs. The narrowest rims measured of close to one micron taken in conjunction with the terminal phase of Orongo yields a hydration rate of $11 \ \mu^2/10^3$ yr. Rim thicknesses could be listed of 1·6 microns for trade bead appearance and 1·75 microns for Poike Ditch.

Two dwelling sites yielded valuable results. A stone house on the side of Rano Raraku crater was built early in the nineteenth century re-using earlier foundation materials as stone carving in the local quarry had long ceased. This dating was indicated by a lance-head of *mataa* (Fig. 7.3) with a narrow hydration rim of 1·2 microns thickness. On this same artefact a rim of 2·1 microns thickness indicated its original usage around the middle of the sixteenth century. It seems possible that this obsidian came to the surface once more during the recent building hiatus. Meanwhile a more comprehensive study of a large group of obsidian chips from Maunga Auhepa indicated a succession of three building phases broken by a brief abandonment around the middle of the eighteenth century and final dereliction around 1850. This sequence of events was established despite some distinct disturbance of the site's deposits throughout its history.

An important feature of this dating work is its high resolution on the time scale. A practical measurement accuracy of 0·1 micron together with such a high diffusion constant (no doubt related to the tropical climate) converts to a narrow time span of about thirty-five years or better over the Island's historical period. For such young material radiocarbon dating could not rival this, particularly in the light of the short-term fluctuations of ^{14}C-activity known in recent times (the de

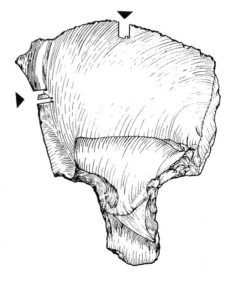

Fig. 7.3 *Mataa* lancehead from a nineteenth-century stone house on the side of Rano Raraku crater on Easter Island in the Pacific. Specimens taken from the natural eroded regions of the implement bore a hydration rim 2·1 microns thick, in contrast with the 1·2 micron rim on the worked edge (reference 27).

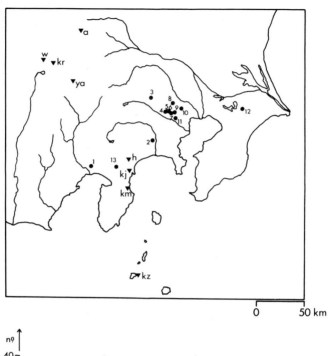

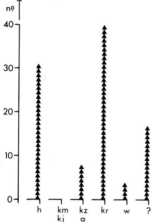

Fig. 7.4 *Map* of the key sites for the pre-ceramic period in Kanto, Japan, together with principal sources of obsidian raw material:
1. Yasumiba, 2. Tsukimono, 3. Sayama, 4. Heidaizaka, 5. Nishinodai, 6. Musashinokoen, 7. I.C.U. 8. Bikunibashi, 9. Nogawa, 10. Moro, 11. Sengawa, 12. Sanrizuka, 13. Hatsunegahara, kz: Kozujima, km: Kamitaga, kj: Kajika, h: Hakone, ya: Yatsugatake, kr: Kirigamine, w: Wadatoge, a: Asama

Inset: Obsidian sources utilized by tool makers at Sanrizuka, as identified by composition, fission track and hydration rim studies. Out of a total number of a hundred artefacts more than 70% could be attributed to the widely-separated sources Hakone and Kirigamine (reference 13).

Vries effect of Chapter 3, section 1*h*) which introduces errors of about eighty years.

3.2   PREHISTORIC ACTIVITY IN KANTO, JAPAN

As a comprehensive archaeological study using scientific techniques the recent work of Dr M Suzuki on obsidian from Kanto district, in Japan, is outstanding. In hydration rim analysis it examples most of the details discussed in section 1, notably seasonal soil temperature fluctuation (Fig. 7.1) and obsidian source identification as illustrated here in Fig. 7.4. Key sites of the south Kanto region gather around the valley of rivers that flow down from hills rich in obsidian outcrops. In the Tokai district sites are generally quite close to obsidian sources at the coast. Out beyond the confines of a sweeping bay the Izu Islands (amongst them the important obsidian source of Kozujima) stretch some 100 km out into the Pacific.

Discrete clustering of rim thicknesses at many of the sites gave the first clear signs of a multiplicity in obsidian supplies. The breakdown of artefacts at Sanrizuka (illustrated in Fig. 7.4, site 12 in the map), allotted 83% of the pieces to their source material. For this purpose each outcrop was initially studied for peculiarities in microlite content: inclusions of globulite characterized the Kirigamine (Kr) source while a thick density of lath crystals specified Kamitaga (Km) and Kajika (Kj) coastal material (Plate 7.2). Then other regions were distinguished by their geological ages, as measured by the fission track dating method (see Chapter 6) together with a record of variation of uranium content between the various outcrops. For example, the inland sources of Asama and Wadatoge could not be confused as the former is recent (0·02 million years) and of low U-content (1·2 ppm) while the latter is far older (0·85 million years) and the richest in U-content (6·8 ppm) in the whole area. The only problematical division lay between Asama and Kozujima obsidian but a difference in potassium content (2·3% and 3·6% respectively) offered a chemical solution.

To set up a time scale some isolated pieces of burnt obsidian were dated by the fission track method (Table 7.1) to the exclusion of the radiocarbon data available. (This is understandable for this very early material that pre-dates any bristlecone pine calibration of the kind discussed in Chapters 2 and 3.) The relative rates of hydration for different obsidian sources were obtained by comparison of rim widths of the various clustered groups within each site. For example, the Sanrizuka context yielded forty implements made from Kirigamine obsidian and thirty-one contemporary implements made from Hakone obsidian. The mean rim thicknesses of 6·14 and 1·34 microns respectively indicate relative hydration rates of 18·5:1. The complete sequence of hydration rates for this region lists as follows (all quoted in $\mu^2/10^3$ yr): Hakone (0·28); Kajiya and Kamitaga (0·98); Kozujima and Asama (2·67); Kirigamine (5·13); Wadatoge (7·92).

Table 7.1: Hydration rim and fission track data used in chronology building in Kanto

Site*	Obsidian source*	Rim thickness (μ)	Fission track age (yr)	$k(\mu^2/10^3yr)$
Sanrizuka (12)	Kirigamine (Kr)	6·14	7,400 ± 300	5·10
Yasumiba (1)	Kozujima (Kz)	5·49	11,100 ± 300	2·71
ICU, Loc. 15(7)	Wadatoge (W)	10·95	15,200 ± 300	7·88
	Kirigamine (Kr)	8·83	15,200 ± 300	5·12

*Data in brackets refer to location points on the map of Fig. 7.4.

From a chronology soundly based upon the detailed understanding of obsidian hydration processes in that region, the movement of this raw material throughout the Kanto district (including the northern region in the hills) was traced both spatially and through time.[38] Some of the information is summarized here. The occupants of Heidaizaka (site 4 in Fig. 7.4) were already 'importing' obsidian from the Kamitaga source to the south some 25,000 years ago. At Tsukimino, 20,700 years ago, sea transport of Kozujima obsidian is indicated even though the nearby source of Hakone was known. Indeed there seems to have been a general preference throughout pre-ceramic and Jomon times for the glassy-textured obsidians from the regions away from the Hakone group, the rougher texture of which may not have been so well suited to minute chipping and elaborate flaking. Even Tokai sites, like Hatsunegahara (site 13 in Fig. 7.4) utilized Kirigamine material extensively while *only* sea-imported obsidian could be found at Yasumiba (site 1 in Fig. 7.4) in the final pre-ceramic phases about 11,000 years ago.

This study has also raised at least one major archaeological question, for, in the Izu Islands there is little evidence of settlement until the ceramic era begins, though they lie in the path of the Kozujima mainland trade routes. Even then, artefacts fashioned not only from Kozujima obsidian but also from an inland form from Tsumetayama appear. This latter source seems scarcely to have been used locally so what induced its usage hundreds of kilometres away across the water remains a mystery.

Chapter 8

Archaeomagnetic Dating

INTRODUCTION: THE EARTH'S MAGNETIC FIELD

We live on the surface of a planet which, in its inner depths, some 3,000 km beneath our feet, has a molten core rich in iron and nickel and constrained under huge pressure. The very heart of the Earth is solid, over a diameter of approximately 2,400 km. The molten region can gather energy from various sources including heat generated by radioactivity in the interior, convection effects caused by the planet's cooling at the surface and some mechanical torques due to precession of the Earth's axis.[1] A dynamo effect results in which a complex system of electrical currents flow throughout the liquid core. In turn these currents give rise to the Earth's magnetic field.

In measurement at the surface this magnetic field looks, for the most part, like that due to a bar magnet located at the Earth's centre but tilted at an angle of about 11° to the axis of rotation.[2] This so-called 'dipole-field' that defines the basic notion of 'north' and 'south' has some additional components (the 'non-dipole field') superimposed upon it which can contribute up to 20 per cent of the total field in some regions. It is thought that this secondary component arises from irregularities in the current pattern of the core generated at protrusions on the inner surface of the solid mantle.[3]

The non-dipole field appears to change its orientation with time when viewed from one specific point, as the mantle rotates more quickly than the core material. Over the past 400 years the direction of movement has been westward in several parts of the world at times at as high a rate as 0·23° of longitude per year.[4,5] But the mantle/core interface irregularities and their associated magnetic fields have only a limited lifetime and change every few centuries. This is evident in magnetic pole position data obtained for medieval times when the drift was *eastward* instead (Fig. 8.1).[6]

On a worldwide scale the non-dipole field makes the total field's orientation and its variation with time look quite different from continent to continent. Thus for dating using magnetic field *direction* it is necessary to build up local calibration curves, each of which are treated as reliable over a region of about a 500 mile radius.

Magnetic field *intensity*, F, is also a quantity that varies with time.

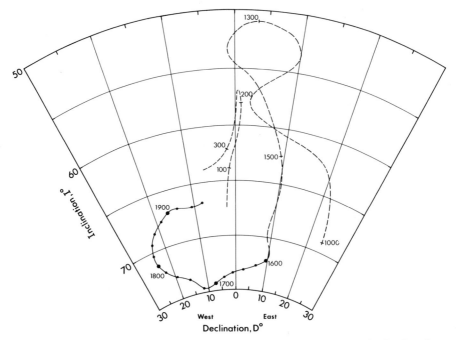

Fig. 8.1   The secular variation of declination (D) and inclination (I) for London.
Before AD 1580 the data is archaeomagnetic, after that date and up to
present day the data is derived from official documentation (reference
4).

From an observer's viewpoint this may be an artificial and localized
effect caused by a tilt of the magnetic dipole axis as a new north-south
direction is defined or there could be an absolute change in the magnitude of the dipole's magnetic moment (M) matching a change in strength
of the core's main electrical current system. There will also be regional
variations in F due to restricted current circulations near the core
surface, producing localized non-dipole field contributions.[7] Intensity
investigations have recently assumed a much increased significance
following the recent re-appraisal of the radiocarbon dating method for
prehistoric times (see Chapter 3) and a much closer scrutiny of climate
changes in the past.[8] Also there is now clear evidence of longer-term
complete field direction reversals caused by collapse of the main
dipole and its regrowth in the opposite direction (see section 8.3 below
and Fig. 8.6).[9] It is possible that the worldwide synchronism of these
reversals can act as a relative dating tool.

I   FIELD DIRECTION STUDIES

1a   THE FOSSIL RECORD OF FIELD ORIENTATION
Much of our knowledge of the direction of the Earth's magnetic field

over the past four centuries has been gleaned from direct documentation. The definitive parameters are 'declination' (D) and angle of dip, or 'inclination' (I). (Declination, D, is the angle between magnetic North—as located by a compass needle rotating freely in a horizontal plane—and geographic, or true, North. Inclination, I, is the angle between the magnetic field direction and the horizontal plane. I varies with latitude. The dipole nature of the Earth's field results in the links of force being vertical to the surface at the magnetic poles ($I = 90°$) and parallel to the surface at the magnetic equator ($I = 0°$).) The London Observatory recorded D and I using suspended magnetized needles for the past four centuries [10] while, in Japan, some data points are derived also from ship's diaries (initially during the voyage of the British ship, *Clove*, in those parts in 1613) and even a 'celestial glove' on which the geomagnetic meridian was marked. [11] The vital role of magnetism as a navigation aid and the pendantry of scientific reporting of the sixteenth and seventeenth century supply adequate reasons for confidence in this early material.

Aside from written records similar information is to be found 'locked-up' in the magnetism of baked clay objects that cover the time over which man has had knowledge of fire; not only in pottery, but hearths, kilns and cooking ovens as well. Once clay in any of these forms has been fired to about 700°C or more it is responsive to storage of a so-called 'thermoremanent' magnetism (*TRM*). This TRM is gathered during the fabric's cooling and is characterized by a direction of magnetization which is the same as that of the Earth's field at that time and at that locality. Subsequently, unless there is a fresh firing, that TRM remains almost entirely unaffected by any field direction changes that might occur over the centuries. This 'fossil record' can also be expressed in terms of the parameters, D and I, introduced earlier.

The changes in D and I that occur with time define the 'secular variation' appropriate to the observation point. (Though this definition should also include a measure of field intensity it is rarely included as written information of the magnitude of F is only available over the past two centuries.) Two methods of data display are often employed in this work, that already illustrated in Fig. 8.1 for London[4] and the system of Fig. 8.2 for the Kinki District of south-west Japan.[12] Similar reference curves can be found in the literature for the Ukraine[13] (for time period of the third to fourteenth centuries AD), for fire-pits in pre-Columbian Indian villages of Arizona,[14] for France,[15] Iran,[16] Egypt,[17] the USSR, [18] Bulgaria,[19] Greece,[20] and Australia.[21] (The last of these looks at D and I-variations during the remote period of 25,000 to 30,000 years ago, rather than more recent archaeological times covered by the other papers.) Also there is a separate reference curve for the Arita region of Japan, at the north-west corner of the island of Kyushu.

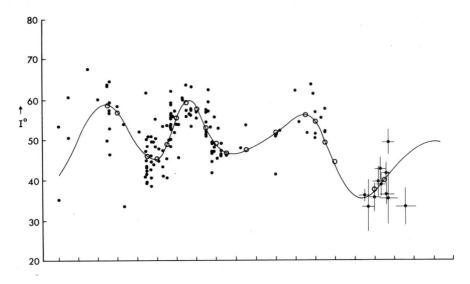

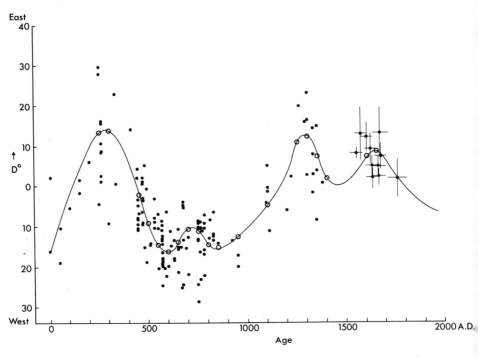

Fig. 8.2 Secular variation of inclination (I) and declination (D) in south-west Japan. Individual data points are plotted as solid circles and average values for every fifty years, where practical, are recorded in open circles. A guideline on the typical level of errors association with each analysis is given to the right of the figure (reference 12).

Though this region about 1° east in latitude from the Kinki District, there seem to be significant differences in the trough and peak positions of the D and I reference curves.

1b THE PHYSICAL PRINCIPLES OF TRM

An understanding of the methods by which TRM is measured in the laboratory calls for an outline of the physical causes of TRM in baked materials or, more specifically, the haematite (α-Fe_2O_3) and magnetite (Fe_3O_4) within them.

On an atomic scale there is a coupling of magnetic moments that causes their parallel alignment within a small volume of the mineral, called a 'domain'. Thus, within each domain there is a 'spontaneous' magnetization in a uniform direction. In haematite a domain may be as much as 0·15 cm across and thereby occupy the entire mineral grain volume. In magnetite domain dimensions are far smaller (typically, 0·03 micron) so that each grain comprises of a whole cluster of magnetized regions. These grains will not exhibit an overall spontaneous magnetization as the domains will orientate so that the magnetic flux lines form closed loops within the mineral. The behaviour of these two iron oxides is termed 'ferromagnetic'.

The magnetization of raw clay is almost zero as the domains are randomly orientated. What field alignment there is at normal ground temperatures is far below the level that can be induced by heating to a few hundred degrees celsius. As the domains take up thermal energy the atomic couplings are disrupted and each atomic magnetic moment

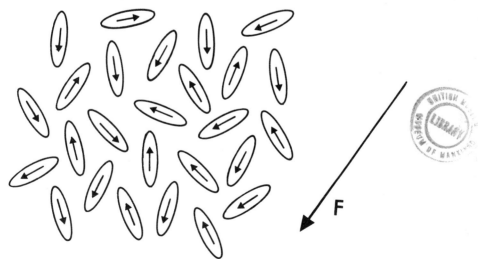

Fig. 8.3   Spontaneous magnetization arising from preferential orientation of magnetic domains along the direction of the field, F (references 7 and 22).

contributes individually to a net magnetic alignment parallel to the Earth's field.[22] (This is termed 'paramagnetic' behaviour.) On cooling the domain structure re-forms but some of the high temperature preferential orientation is 'frozen' into the material, as TRM.

This is not due to a change of spontaneous magnetization intensity within each domain, but rather because there is a greater number of domains with their magnetization pointing in one direction than any other. This is illustrated in two dimensions (Fig. 8.3) for haematite which attains its TRM by magnetization along 'easy' directions in the grain volume defined by shape and crystal anisotropy. (For model purposes ellipsoidal grains are shown. Their 'easy' direction would follow the major axis.) The multi-domain grains of magnetite behave somewhat differently.[23] There it is a matter of domain wall movement with regions aligned with the field swelling at the expense of those of opposite sense.

It requires appreciably greater effort to coerce alignment out of haematite than magnetite so that the TRM associated with the former is regarded as extremely stable or 'hard'. However, the specific magnetization (gauss. cc/g) of magnetite is some three orders of magnitude greater than that of haematite. It is possible to roughly predict the magnetization of a sample cooling in the field of present day at around 10^{-1} to 10^{-4} gauss. cc/g, depending upon the firing temperature, the firing condition (an oxidizing atmosphere producing reddened clay with haematite in the matrix: a reducing atmosphere produced grey clay with magnetite) and iron oxide content in the bulk clay (1–10% concentration).

The limit of TRM build up with temperature occurs at the 'Curie point' on the mineral: (565°C for magnetite, 675°C for haematite) at which stage all co-operative alignment of atomic moments in domains has been destroyed. In fact the field-biased paramagnetic behaviour sets in at a somewhat earlier stage, at the so-called 'blocking temperature', T_B. Once the sample has cooled below T_B, even by only a few degrees, sensitivity to the external magnetic field all but vanishes. The value of T_B for a particular haematite grain is largely controlled by its size, as crystals of dimensions less than that required to set up a complete domain structure will have weaker atomic interactions in operation. For example a grain only 150 microns across will have $T_B \simeq 20°C$. Consequently the magnetization curve of a clay during baking will be smoothly increasing as each grain size range is effected rather than a sharp switch that a single domain/single blocking temperature model would predict.[24] This behaviour is of appreciable importance in demagnetization analysis discussed later (Fig. 8.4).

1C ADDITIONAL SOURCES OF REMANENT MAGNETISM

There is little likelihood of the TRM of well-baked clay being affected by external factors other than chance re-firing. It would require an extremely strong field of several hundred oersteds or more to re-align magnetite domains and appreciably more to alter the 'hard' TRM of the haematite. Only lightning strikes are considered to create such a difficulty. Chemical alteration can result in a magnetic mineral formation that carries magnetization with a direction matching that of the prevailing Earth's field. This 'CRM' possesses all the stability properties of TRM and is indistinguishable experimentally. The main causes of CRM creation are thought to be excessive weathering and prolonged hydration, the effects of which are visually recognizable.

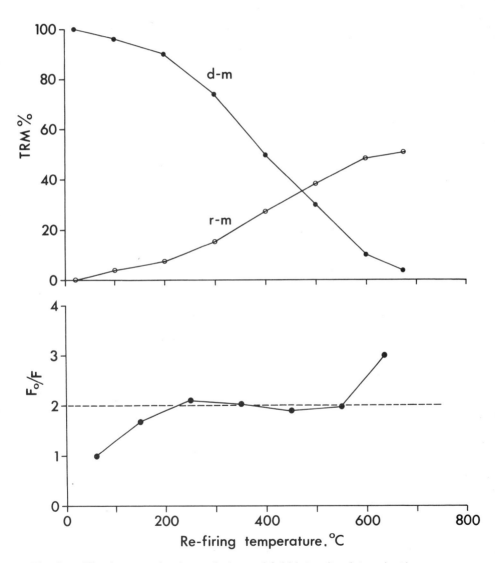

Fig. 8.4   The demagnetization technique of field intensity determination.

A more serious hazard lies internally: that of 'viscous' remanent magnetism (*VRM*). For grains with a blocking temperature close to ambient ground values even seasonal warmth can force some domains into a paramagnetic state for a brief while. The TRM of these grains will change from year to year. Such orientation 'flipping' will also occur for larger grains though with decreasing likelihood for higher and higher T_B-values. The VRM signal gradually grows with time of exposure to an external field as more and more domains make this transition.

The viscous aspect of this effect becomes apparent when the external field is annulled. In zero field conditions some traces of remanent magnetism may still hang on over a matter of weeks. But on theoretical grounds it is possible to predict that even a two week treatment of this nature will reduce the archaeological VRM signal by more than a third, even for 50,000 year-old material. Sample pretreatment either by 100°C heating in zero field or demagnetization in an oscillating field has been recommended for VRM removal.

1d SAMPLE COLLECTION AND MEASUREMENT

For field direction studies in hearths and kilns reliable results can only be obtained if the position of the constructional clay has remained undisturbed. Often this requirement limits sampling to well-fired flat floors, a feature only commonly found in medieval structures and some Roman–British kilns. Irregular subsidence and some break up of the surface by frost cause some inevitable scatter in I and D-values. Kiln walls are susceptible to a 'fall-out' effect of about 3° as they tend to tilt uniformly outwards after the kiln falls into disuse (usually coupled to some arching of the floor, as well).[25] These problems are well illustrated by data for walls of the English medieval kiln at Grimston,[26] where I-values ranged from 59° to 71° and D-values ranged from 7°W to 44°E. By comparison the floor of a kiln from West Cowick of the same period gave I-values of 57° to 64°, and D-values of 2°E to 12°E.

There is also evidence of a distortion of the ambient field direction by the kiln structure's own magnetism.[27] This will cause the I-values for floor samples to read slightly shallow and for wall samples to read slightly steep, in each case by about 2°. The TRM declination in floor material will not be effected by any systematic magnetic distortion of this nature.

Satisfactory data for I can be obtained from some specific kiln products of which we can say that we know the position they were in during firing. Stacking of tiles and bricks would require one face or edge to be horizontal while glazed wares would be baked in an upright position. However, it is clear from kiln debris that the production of more mundane pottery wares involved quite random heaping of pieces rather with a view to maximum output per firing than tidy arrangement.

Kiln or hearth sampling involves the removal of various portions of the structure, each sealed up in a rigid casing of plaster of paris or foaming polystyrene. The surface of the encasing material is levelled and marked with a line that is related to geographic north by on-site theodolite measurements. Often the process of cutting around each kiln portion, so that it stands free to be framed before plaster addition, and general 'handling' in setting up the encasing stage causes a slight sample displacement. Thus each plaster 'box' carries markings of any tilt of man-made origin, checked just before the whole block is undercut and carried away.

Two types of magnetometers are currently used to measure TRM directional features. The 'astatic' system involves placing the sample beneath two rigidly-linked magnets of equal strength but opposite polarity, suspended on the end of a quartz or phosphor-bronze fibre. (This equipment is particularly well illustrated in reference 14). A mirror is mounted on the magnet-linking bar so that fibre rotations can be recorded optically via change of incident angle of a fixed fine light beam. The antiparallel magnet alignment prevents the pervading Earth's magnetic field creating any torque on the fibre, unlike the archaeological sample itself which effects the magnet nearest to it to a greater degree.

Of course, the TRM field in the sample is orientated in a three-dimensional space as a vector of particular field strength, so that three different measurements have to be taken, shifting the sample into a different perpendicular plane each time. Then geometrical calculations yield I and D, while the intensity of magnetization can be estimated from the equipment's calibrated sensitivity. In principle an astatic system is capable of detecting 10^{-7} gauss, but this is rarely attained in practice, partly because of some non-uniformity in the shape and magnetization of some samples.

A bulkier sample is better treated using a 'spinner' system.[28] As it is rotated slowly within the volume of a large coil system the baked clay's magnetic moment induces a small alternating voltage. Compensating coils connected in the opposite sense to the detection system serve to annul any external sources of interference. Recent developments in this system include replacement of pick-up coils by fluxgate detectors (most useful for smaller samples)[29] and direct computer interpretation of the output signal.[30]

The mean values of I and D obtained define a preferred vector direction for the magnetization. Statistically the scatter of readings obtained from several samples from the same locality is quoted as a 'Fisher index', v_{95}, whereby there is a 95% probability that the true magnetization vector lies within the cone defined by v coaxial about the preferred direction. A reasonably accurate v_{95} value is given by,

$$v_{95} = 0 \cdot 75 \, (E_I + E_D \cos \bar{I}) \tag{8.1}$$

where E_I and E_D are the standard errors for the laboratory measurements and I is the average value of the inclination. Typical good data like that obtained for a Roman kiln at Carthage [31] of I = 49° 45′ to 52° 0′ and D = 3° 45′ W to 1° 45′ E, yielded ν_{95} = 0·8°.

1e   DATING RESULTS

Much effort has gone into development of the necessarily regional D and I reference curves and only recently have some 'magnetic dates' begun to appear in the literature. The English data of Fig. 8.1 is

8.1   Kilns unearthed between 1965 and 1968 at Tengudani valley, Arita, in north-west Kyushu, Japan. An alignment of firing-chambers on the right form a kiln which dates to 1603–27, and is thought to have produced the earliest porcelain in Japan. (Photograph: courtesy of Professor N. Watanabe, University of Tokyo.)

amongst the most firmly established and most used. Unfortunately during the Roman era in that area, D is an insensitive parameter while I only oscillated a little, so secular variation has little dating value then. However, the reference curve's movement is more 'active' and unambiguous during the sixteenth century. Consequently a glass furnace at Bagot's Park has been dated to AD 1535 with less than a quarter of a century's uncertainty, contrary to original archaeological opinion which placed the structure about fifty years later.[32] Several other analyses have served a valuable purpose of confirming independent documentary evidence.[33]

In Japan magnetic studies in kilns at Arita have confirmed the timing of the beginnings of porcelain manufacture in that country. Historically Korean potters arrived in that district at the beginning of the seventeenth century and one, traditionally named Sanbe Kanagae, recognized the quality of the local clay, and set to work. However, the very existence of Kanagae as other than legend remained in doubt until the past decade when his name was found on the local Ryusenji Temple and eventually his tomb was unearthed on the nearby hillside. Now, from one kiln chamber amongst a great number at that site (some of which are of nineteenth-century origin) (Plate 8.1) his activities have been extricated and dated to AD 1603–27, and a general ordering of the manufacturing history of that region has been defined.

Similar work in Arizona has firmly fixed a date of 300 BC for one of the earliest Hohokam Indian fire-places in Arizona. This work has carried some major implications for that region's archaeology, notably suggesting that those people were the first organized irrigationists in the United States and of a cultural development level well in advance of their cliff dwelling neighbours to the north by as early as 700 BC.

As far as future results are concerned the recent preliminary study of fire-places in north Peru are of some interest.[34] Though they suggest an I-variation of only about 1·5° per century only, between 800 BC and AD 600, cultures of that region are notoriously difficult to date, so the study is being pursued.

2 FIELD INTENSITY STUDIES

2a BASIC PRINCIPLES OF ANALYSIS

There is an immediate advantage to be gained from measurement of TRM intensity rather than its directional properties: knowledge of a sample's original position can be dispensed with. This appreciably widens the choice of artefacts that can be used for analysis to include pottery fragments taken from any section of a vessel and even figurines in baked clay, some of which have an archaeological history in Europe stretching back more than 30,000 years. However, there is a fabric difficulty that creates different restraints of material suitability. For field strength evaluation a sample has to be repeatedly re-heated. This is not an acceptable treatment in the case of grey or black magnetite-rich material as transitions to oxides of the Fe_2O_3 series will result during the first high temperature exposure thus invalidating subsequent analysis.[35]

Demagnetization techniques used in this work may be explained as follows. A heating to a temperature, T, will free all domains for which $T \geqslant T_B$ of their record of ancient TRM. If subsequent cooling was carried out in zero field conditions the sample would still retain the ancient TRM in domains for which $T < T_B$, as a magnetization, M_0 (T: 675°C). That is to say, incremental portions of the magnetization curve are additive.

The total and residual magnetization levels are proportional to the ancient field intensity, F_0. If the zero field condition in the experiment described above was removed the grains with lower blocking temperatures would respond to the ambient field, F, as the sample cooled. Thus,

$$\frac{M_0 \, (20°C : T)}{M \, (20°C : T)} = \frac{F_0}{F} \qquad (8.2)$$

In practice F can be a laboratory field of known strength.

In this condition the sample contains two magnetization vectors of which we would only see the composite effect, M_1. But an 'antiphase' condition can readily be arranged by repeating the experiment with the direction of F reversed, giving a composite magnetization, M_2. The difference $(M_1 - M_2)$ acts as a measure of F (as F_0 cancels out in subtraction) while $(M_1 + M_2)$ measures F_0.

Thus ancient and fresh laboratory TRM levels can be generated for a sequence of T-values, as illustrated in Fig. 8.4. The ancient TRM loss during demagnetization can be compared with the laboratory TRM induced by *re*magnetization for successive temperature intervals. Thus in the example illustrated while 24·5% of the total ancient TRM signal is removed in the 300°–400°C interval only 12% is restored in a similar heating in the present-day laboratory field. Thus the ratio F_0/F is a little over 2.

In a practical run the field ratio will often be close to a steady level only over the middle temperature range. Below 200°C there may be interference from VRM while a high field ratio between 600°C and the Curie point is probably due to mineralogical changes occurring during refiring.

Intensity results which have been obtained for the past 4,000 years for Czechoslovakia [36] and the Indian settlement regions of Mexico and Arizona [37] are illustrated in Fig. 8.5. In each case two intensity maxima are in evidence, indicating a westward drift of the non-dipole component of the Earth's field by about 120° of longitude in 600 years. This behaviour is detectable, though rather less obviously in a visual sense, in archaeomagnetic data from Japan [38] and South America.[39]

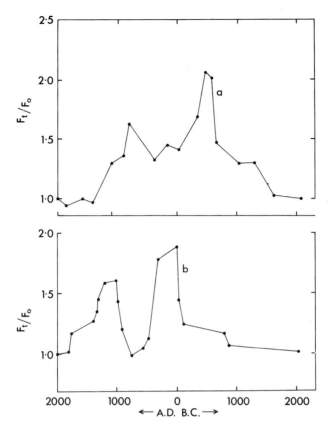

Fig. 8.5   Field intensity changes over the past four millennia as measured in Czechoslovakia (at Prague) and in central America (Mexico and Arizona). (F_0 is the present day field intensity) (references 36 and 37.)

2*b*   APPLICATIONS OF INTENSITY ANALYSIS

The sharpness of short-term variations in intensity and the risk of ambiguity caused by a single field intensity matching several historical dates has largely excluded any direct dating applications using reference curves like those of Fig. 8.5. However, on occasions when directional data are ambiguous excessive strength or weakness of F could resolve matters to advantage.

But study of all three secular variation components in various world regions has been used to evaluate, in absolute terms, the strength of the Earth's dipole field and its tilts compared with the axis of rotation.[7] A near-sinusoidal change of geomagnetic moment with time is apparent which has already been linked to radiocarbon concentration variations on the Earth over the past 8,000 years (see Chapter 3, section 1*h*, and Fig. 3.6 particularly).

It is interesting to record some recent correlations made between the northern hemisphere's atmospheric pressure distribution in the troposphere and the magnetic field strength contours of the same region.[40] The former is characterized by 'dumb-bell' shaped low pressure regions at high latitudes with winter 'focal points' at 80°W and 130°E in longitude. The same structure is evidenced in the magnetic plots except that the dumb-bell axis appears to be rotated, relatively, about 25° West. Also there is evidence of a westward drift of the pressure system during recent decades that would match geomagnetic data, at least qualitatively. This work carries many implications with respect to the ill-understood mechanisms by which solar energy effects the vast mass of the lower atmosphere and, thereby, influences the climate and the ^{14}C-reservoir of our planet.

3 PALAEOMAGNETIC STUDIES

3a FIELD POLARITY DEFINITIONS

Secular variation studies over geological times have revealed a remarkable phenomenon, that of complete switch about of the Earth's magnetic field in comparatively short times of the order of 10,000 years, perhaps sometimes even more rapidly. The recognition of these reversals, mainly from analysis of deep-sea sediments cored to great depths, has lead to the development of a convention of their description, the basic details of which are illustrated in Fig. 8.6. An 'epoch' is defined as a period during which the Earth's field, having rotated through 180°, has held a specific polarity for more than 0·5 million years. Some fifteen epochs have been identified and looked at in some detail covering a time period of about 13·5 million years. The most recent, to which reasonably accurate K-Ar dates have been attached in definition of their boundaries, carry titles as follows: *Brunhes* (today–0·69 million years), *Matuyama* (0·69–2·43 million years), *Gauss* (2·43–3·32 million years) and *Gilbert* (3·32–5·10 million years).

Superimposed upon the main directional changes are some equally complete direction reversals of much shorter duration (10^5 years or less), termed 'events'. These too carry titles, such as *Blake*, *V*.*3*, *Jaramillo*, *Gilsá*, *Olduvai*, *Reunion*, *Kaena*, *Mammoth*, *Chociti*, *Nunivak*, C_1 and C_2 events.[41-48]. The absence of the Reunion event in sediment cores has led to its existence being questioned though its infrequent detection may be due to a brevity of duration (less than 50,000 years). Also the Gilsá event has often been included in the more extensive Olduvai event nearby, but this is probably unjustified.[49]

'Excursions' represent a field deviation of more than 40° from the prevalent epoch direction but no complete 180° switch that could be described as stable. Those of the Bruhnes epoch are of particular interest as they occurred during the period of evolution of modern man.

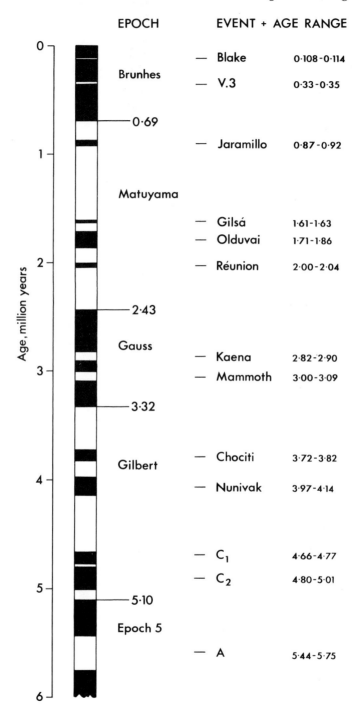

Fig. 8.6   Chronology of epochs and events in magnetic field reversals that occurred over the past six million years (references 41–48).

The *Laschamp* excursion probably dates close to 12,500 years ago if the data from its frequent observation in many parts of the world are brought together [50] and probably encompass the so-called *Gothenburg* event of the same time.[51] For the latter the description as an 'event' is extremely tenuous as a complete flip over of the field has been claimed for only one sample.

Another recent excursion, that at Mungo Lake in Australia (Plate 8.2), was detected in the fabric of aboriginal fire-places estimated to be about 30,000 years old.[52] This represents the only definite polarity variation so far detected in archaeological remains though there are archive records of the research of G. Folgheraiter who claims to have detected a field reversal in eighth century BC Attic and Etruscan vases.[53]

Physical explanation of these reversal phenomena naturally centres about interpretation of the behaviour of the Earth's dynamo core described in the introduction of this chapter. It is currently thought that the main dipole field can drop in strength quite rapidly to a low but non-zero value, allowing the non-dipole component to pre-dominate.[54] (Consistently, during the reversal transition the weakened total field tends to 'wander' particularly violently.) Then the dipole quickly turns over and begins to regain its strength in the opposite

8.2　The desert regions around Lake Mungo, one of a chain of lakes in the south-western regions of New South Wales, Australia. Aboriginal fire-places exposed here were in use by ancient man more than 30,000 years ago. Recent studies of bone remains suggest the local inhabitants at that time were an archaic form of *Homo erectus*. (Photograph: courtesy of Dr J. M. Bowler, Australian National University, Canberra.)

direction, eventually supplying the major component of the Earth's field once more.

Understandably there has been extensive pondering on the impact of a field reversal on our natural habitat. The Earth's fossil record has shown a great number of catastrophic extinctions of floral and faunal species, like the disappearance of most families of *trilobites* (a now extinct marine invertebrate) close to the beginning of the Silurian geological era.[55] Until now it has not been possible to offer any reasons for such extinctions which have occurred in every major fossil group over the past 0·5 billion years. However, the level of correlation between many faunal extinctions (and, in some cases, appearance of a new species) in ocean-core studies seems so high as to outweigh pure chance.[56] Some are briefly listed here.[57]

(i) *Foraminifera species*: *Sphaeroidinella dehiscens* becomes the dominant species in this fossil group at the beginning of the Kaena event, yet sharply declines at the Matuyama-Brunhes boundary. *Globorotalia margaritae* becomes extinct at the Gilbert-Gauss boundary. *Globorotalia nepenthes* has only a protracted history, bracketing the C and Chocita events only. *Pulleniatina* species changes its coiling direction abruptly just above the Chociti event.

(ii) *Radiolaria species*: *Panarium penultimum* makes an evolutionary transition to *Penartus tetrathalamus* just above the Gilbert C event, with a gradual decrease in the size of polar columns. In Pacific sediments two significant extinctions occur, that of *Pterocanium prismatium* just above the Olduvai event and that of *Eucyrtidium elongatum peregrinum* just above the Kaena event. In Antartic sediments several species vanish abruptly at the Matuyama-Brunhes boundary, including *Saturnulas planetes*, *Pterocanium trilobum* and *Prunopyle tetrapila*.[58]

(iii) The *silicoflagellate*, *Mesocena elliptica* has a short history that just brackets the Jaramillo event. The *diatom*, *Rhizosolenia praebergonii*, emerges at the end of the Mammoth event but vanishes just above the Olduvai event.

Earlier theories for extinction and mutation mechanisms were somewhat drastic, invoking a spill over of radiation from Van Allen belts on to the Earth's atmosphere and direct impact of the solar wind on the planet's surface at a time of much reduced field intensity.[59] But even the most pessimistic dose-rate estimates do not offer a realistic support for such notions [60] for which the human race itself should be thankful. Change in temperature may well be a contributing factor but extinction of some species of marine invertebrates, notably the radiolaria, *Eucyrtidium calvertense* and *Clathrocyclas bicornis* cannot be explained in this way.[61] Direct influence of magnetic field strength upon an organism is now regarded as a reality [62] though no evidence pertinent to species discussed here is yet available. However, it is impossible to ignore the one obvious stumbling block of all these theories: why should any species, like *Pterocanium prismatium*, for example, live without disturbance through several events in two earlier epochs only to decline just after the Olduvai event?

Other violent happenings on the Earth similarly correlate to field reversal and add possible explanations for its causes. Glassy tektites and microtektites are strewn throughout the sediments of the Indian Ocean and the South Pacific and attest to an impact of a massive cosmic collision of intensity, in terms of energy release, orders of magnitude greater than the Krakatoa volcanic eruption in 1883. Whatever cosmic body produced this catastrophic explosion, comet or giant meteorite, it may well have effected a change in the Earth's magnetic dynamo.[63] And indeed, microtektite dating of the main Australasian microtektites by the fission track [64] and K-Ar methods [65] has yielded an age of 0·7 million years, matching well with the Matuyama-Brunhes boundary. Comet landfall could also provide a mechanism for faunal extinction and modification as gases like frozen ammonia and methane in cometary nuclei could well have extensive ecological effects when introduced rapidly into the atmosphere and oceans. Some organisms actually thrive on these compounds.

The ultimate test of such a 'cosmic impact' notion will be evidence of correlation of similar field reversal events with the other major tektite falls of the past, in Czechoslovakia about fifteen million years ago and in Libya about thirty-five million years ago.

Strong correlation has been detected between the timing of the Earth's peak volcanic activities and that of geomagnetic events, again most obviously at the Matuyama-Brunhes boundary.[66] A powerful earthquake may well have the capacity to cause a wobble in the Earth's spin axis and so a period of prolonged volcanism could supply the necessary impetus for a geomagnetic field flip.[67] This notion too carries ecological implications in that volcanic ash, when held in the atmosphere for a long time (particularly at high latitudes) shields the planet's surface from solar radiation. Distinct worldwide cooling, as indeed seems to have occurred near the beginning of the present Brunhes epoch, would result and faunal changes could follow. It is also tempting to see similar links between times of magnetic events and glacial high-spots.[68]

Many of the topics of this section are, at present, largely peripheral to the main theme of chronology in archaeology. However, the potential of this work is already apparent from the successful cross-linkage of fossiliferous horizons at Lake Rudolf, Kenya, that magnetic reversal stratigraphy has made possible.[69] Because of the worldwide effect of changes defined as epochs and events it may well be practical to reliably connect context to context across continents and build up a very broad picture of hominoid development during the past thirty million years.

Chapter 9

Chemical Methods of Dating Bone

INTRODUCTION

The first indications that chemical changes in bone structure could offer dating information came in 1844 when Middleton observed that trace levels of fluorine in ground water were gradually absorbed in fossil bones and teeth, at the cost of hydroxyl ions in the constituent mineral, hydroxyapatite.[1] It is now recognized that uranium incorporates in that mineral matrix in a similar manner except that is now calcium ions that are replaced.[2] At the same time some fossilization effects are degradative like the loss of protein (collagen) which occupies pores in the phosphatic mineral network. Now it is the loss of the element, nitrogen, that marks the passage of time.[3]

Unfortunately all of these changes occur at a rate that is strongly controlled by the environment of burial so none offer absolute age determination. However, the sections that follow do offer several examples of relative dating amongst bone remains from a similar matrix. But a recent advance in amino-acid research may prove valuable. In a living organism the molecular architecture of each amino acid is asymmetric. However, after that organism dies a re-alignment begins to produce an opposite symmetry. This transfer, termed *racemization*, is only completed in about a million years so that the intermediate molecular 'order', as an age indicator, covers an important period of hominid development (section 9.2).[4] As this method is still in its infancy it is difficult to predict its potential accuracy.

1a FLUORINE DATING: BASIC PRINCIPLES

The rate of fluorine uptake by fossil bone varies from site to site, dependent upon climate, amount of the element in circulation and hydrological conditions of the burial medium. Alluvial sand or gravel deposits with good drainage properties are most suitable while cave deposits are of little use as calcite seams prevent ground water percolation. Even with a quite uniform bone-bearing deposit a specimen's fluorine content will depend somewhat on its texture. Spongy regions absorb fluorine at slightly higher rates than compact regions. The former are also more susceptible to contamination from intrusive silts which then act as a weight in the sample that is unrelated to true hydroxyapatite content. To eliminate this problem the ratio, $100 \times \%F/\%P_2O_5$, is measured. Fresh bone carries a 42% content of P_2O_5 while complete conversion of the bone structure to fluorapatite, $Ca_5(PO_4)_3F$, means the introduction of close to 3·8% fluorine.[5] The maximum theoretical ratio value of 9 is approached even in some Upper Palaeolithic material (Fig. 9.1).[6]

Fluorine determination can be measured in a variety of ways, chemically. Apart from the conventional distillation methods in the literature [7] a diffusion technique [8] or separation of an ion exchange resin [9] can be conveniently used to determine low concentrations of the element. Physical determinations include the use of X-ray diffraction [10] and photon-activation analysis.[11] Each F or OH ion is surrounded by three calcium ions at one level while Ca-O columns are linked with PO_4 groups to form a hexagonal network. The different sizes of the monovalent anions cause variation in cell parameters, primarily in the F interspacing, designated *a*. For hydroxyapatite, $a = 9·41$ Å, for fluorapatite $a = 9·35$ Å. For an ancient bone the lines of the X-ray diffraction pattern vary in separation according to the amount of fluorine incorporated. Resolution of about 0·06% in fluorine content is possible by this method.[12]

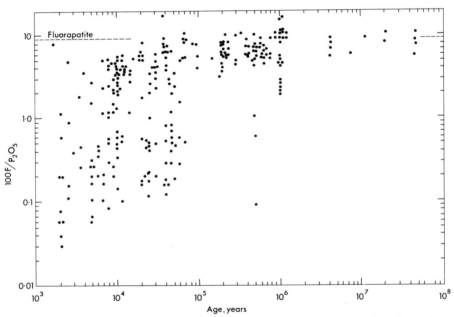

Fig. 9.1   Measured variation of the fluorine/phosphate ratio with time for bone fossils. Complete apatite-fluorapatite conversion marks the theoretical limit of this ratio (reference 6).

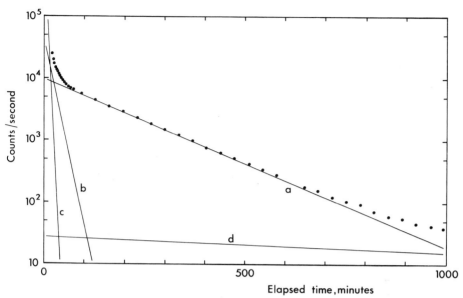

Fig. 9.2 Decay curve for the peak intensity of 511 keV radiation in the gamma spectrum of a photon-activated reindeer tibia. The fossil comes from Gewande in North Brabant (Netherlands). The various decay curves are: a. fluorine (^{18}F, $t_{\frac{1}{2}} = 110$ minutes), b. nitrogen (^{13}N, $t_{\frac{1}{2}} = 10\cdot0$ minutes), c. oxygen + phosphorus (^{15}O + ^{30}P, $t_{\frac{1}{2}} = 2\cdot3$ minutes), and d. potassium (^{43}K, $t_{\frac{1}{2}} = 22$ hours) (reference 11).

The bombardment of bone with high energy photons (up to 18 Mev) activates all the elements in the bone structure by reactions of the form, ^{19}F$(\gamma, n)^{18}$F, in conventional nomenclature. The neutron release of all these reactions is accompanied by low energy gamma-ray emission (0·511 MeV). The activity of the N, O and P contents rapidly decays away but the half-life of the fluorine reaction is around 110 minutes so that it is soon the dominant contributor to the gamma signal (Fig. 9.2). The fluorine content can be measured with an accuracy of about 10% in this way.

The X-ray diffraction approach has been heavily criticized on the grounds that the interplanar spacing, *a*, is partly dependent upon the amount of calcium present (sometimes as much as 10%) but there is no stoichiometric amount of carbonate substituting for phosphate.[13] Instead there is a crystalline phase present as an isomorphic apatite intermediate which contains carbon dioxide. Changes in *a* then arise not only from recrystallization and a change of fluorine content but also from change in carbon dioxide concentration, increase in chlorine content and replacement of calcium by similar ions like sodium and potassium. It is worth noting that the fluorine-phosphorus ratio used in chemical analysis is also affected by carbonate variation with time as the phosphate concentration is diluted by that impure phase in the

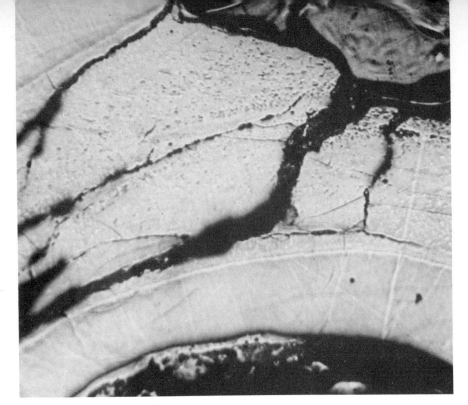

9.1 a. Section of epoxy-mounted bovid tooth from Olduvai Gorge. The tooth dentine is the porous region above the curved enamel in the lower portion of the photograph.

    b. Fission track map of the uranium content of the same bovid tooth, as recorded in a mica sheet laid on the section prior to neutron-activation of the ^{235}U-content. The dentine is rich in uranium (approx. 700 ppm) compared with the enamel (20 ppm). (Photograph: courtesy of Dr M. Seitz, Geophysical Laboratory, Carnegie Institution of Washington.)

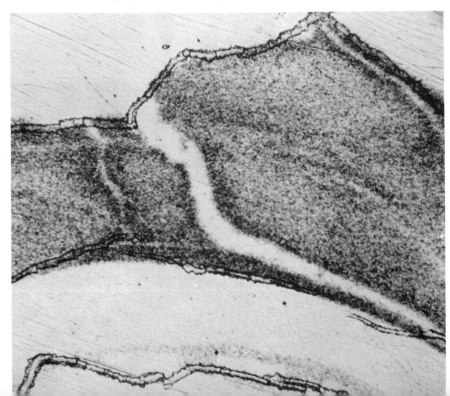

fresh apatite structure. This could well account for ratio values of 9·3 to 15·6 measured at Olduvai Gorge that exceed the theoretical value for fluorapatite alone (Fig. 9.1).

1*b* URANIUM BUILD UP IN BONE

The factors that control uranium uptake in fossil bone are essentially the same as those discussed above for fluorine, except that the initial build up is relatively slow. Radiometric assay (usually expressed in terms of U_3O_8 ppm) is rarely of much use in relative dating of post-glacial bone deposits but the daughter elements that are generated by the absorbed uranium parent cause a steep rise in activity in Pleistocene material. Thus a concentration of as much as 600 ppm in million year-old teeth correctly contrasts with modern human canine values of 0·02 ppm and less.[14]

Tooth enamel does not appear to take up uranium (or indeed fluorine) in a particularly systematic fashion and that which is gathered is found in filaments of high concentration around exposed edges and interior crevices (Plate 9.1a, b). Underlying dentine carries a much more uniform uranium distribution but there is now strong evidence that the uptake of radioactivity has only limited stability. The uranium in ground water is probably in a high oxidation state as this is its most soluble form. Within the tooth, decaying organic material will create a reducing environment conducive to uranium precipitation. However, there will come a time when internal decomposition is complete so that re-oxidation may occur and the uranium content begin to fall once more as leaching proceeds. The turnover point is likely to depend strongly on climate and this stage noted in Olduvai Gorge bovine material, at about 1·5 million years, is probably well above average as those fossil beds were deposited in quite dry conditions. There seems evidence of a similar model of uranium uptake in highly-active bones from Mongolia with the added complication that partial loss of the gaseous decay product, radon, may cause errors in total U_3O_8 assay.[15]

Techniques of uranium analysis include fission track mapping of sectioned bone [16] (which also indicates details of inhomogeneity) and semi-quantitative, but non-destructive determination using direct Geiger counting at a specimen's surface.

Despite the broader similarities in the mechanisms of fluorine and uranium uptake there seems to be no strict correlation between their concentrations in fossil skeletal material [17] (see Table 9.1). In contrast with fluorine analysis, uranium is considered to offer a reliable relative dating method in volcanic areas under tropical conditions.[18]

1*c* NITROGEN LOSS FROM BONE

Fresh bone contains about 5% nitrogen, concentrated in its collagen constituent. During burial the inner regions of the bone structure are quickly opened up by removal of marrow and osteocyte cells attacked

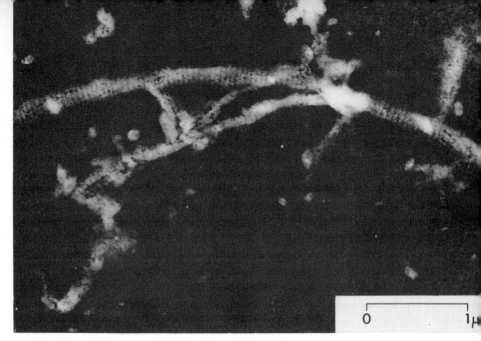

9.2   Collagen fibres in fossil bone. The periodicity of the fibres is almost completely retained, indicating fossil good preservation. (Photograph: courtesy of Dr K. P. Oakley, British Museum, Natural History, London.)

by internally-activated intracellular enzymes.[19] (In teeth the parallel process is that of odontoblast removal to leave fine channels in the dentine structure.) The osteocyte cells separated the bundles of collagen fibres (Plate 9.2) held together by an osteomucoid cement so the latter is now open to nature's attack. Each amino-acid component of the collagen offers a different level of resistance to leaching, depending mainly upon local moisture conditions.[20] (The ambient ground temperature and the bone fragment's size itself will also have some influence as the leaching process is diffusion controlled.[21]) However, in temperate climates it would be unusual to find anything more than trace levels of nitrogen in bone more than a quarter of a million years old.

The limitations of this degradation process as a dating method are only too well underlined by several examples of unfossilized material in geological strata. A tusk of the early elephant genus, *Elephas primigenius*, found in the frozen mud of Siberia contained collagen fibrils with perfect periodicity in its banded structure, even though it was some 15,000 years old.[22] A humerus from a woolly rhinoceros excavated from Pleistocene clay in London contained all the amino-acid components of a modern bone, while a few could still be traced in fossil fish bones embedded in hard shales of Ohio which are almost 300 million years old. We also know that many civilizations sought deliberately to preserve their dead, not only by direct embalming as in the case of the Egyptians but also by careful and elaborate tomb sealing as evidenced by the Marquis of Tai burial (Han Dynasty, 206 BC–AD 24) recently unearthed at Changsha in China.[23] Such human agencies would produce an inertia effect upon ultimate protein decay and make any scientific dating quite unrealistic.

186

Nitrogen content is usually assessed using a standard micro-Kjeldahl apparatus that requires no more than 100 mg of material though this is often preceded by a paper-chromatography study to check on the extent of protein breakdown in the fossil. Some pre-treatment may be necessary to remove nitrogenous contaminants introduced by conservation of the more brittle bone finds. Detectability of 0·01% nitrogen content is practical. Within a single context it is probably reasonable to expect a clustering of no better than 0·2% around an average of 1·0%, say, a variable partly dependent upon the diversity of fauna present.

1*d* DATING APPLICATIONS

Over the past two decades some important data has been gathered amongst European and African fossils, usually using fluorine, uranium and nitrogen analysis in tandem. Those pertinent to the discussion below are summarized in Table 9.1. Elsewhere studies of note include an attempt to build up a fluorine calibration curve for the interglacial intervals of the Pleistocene era in West Germany,[24] ranging back over 1·5 million years and a study of several Californian fossil horizons.[25]

The English group that ranges over the past 0·25 million years,

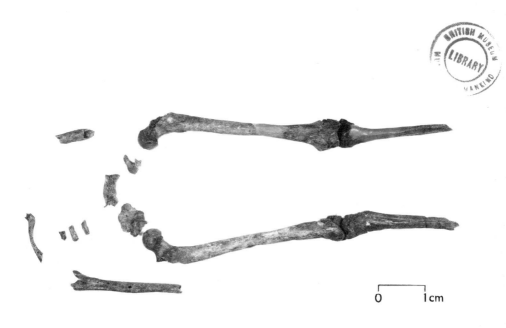

0   1 cm

9.3   Fossil post-cranial bones of Galley Hill Man, found in the Swanscombe Gravels in 1888. Fluorine and nitrogen analyses indicate that this skeleton was an intrusive, post-Pleistocene burial, less than 10,000 years old. (Photograph: courtesy of the Trustees of the British Museum, Natural History, London.)

Table 9.1: Examples of fluorine, uranium and nitrogen analyses amongst fossils*

Location and nature of fossil find	$\dfrac{100\ F\%}{P_2O_5\%}$	Equivalent U_3O_8 (ppm)	$N\%$
(i) European group			
Northfleet (England). Human post-cranial remains. Anglo-Saxon	0·2	—	2·0
Galley Hill (England). Human post-cranial remains. (Radiocarbon date, 3310 ± 150 yr.**)	0·5	—	1·6
Coldrum (England). Skull, Neolithic	0·7	—	1·9
Ebbsfleet (England). *Mammathus* incisor. Upper Pleistocene	4·6	6	0·2
Swanscombe (England). 'Shell bed'. *Trogontherium* incisor. Middle Pleistocene	5·5	15	nil
Swanscombe (England). Gravel beds. Skull, *homo* genus. Middle Pleistocene	6·1	27	0·18
Associated mammal remains of various species	5·7–6·8	10–32	≤0·09
Cresswell Crags (England). Cave site *Epimachairodus* canine. Palaeolithic?	0·8	<1	2·1
Doveholes (England). Fissure deposit. *Epimachairodus* canine. Early Pleistocene	8·6	68	nil
Mount Perrier (France). Alluvial deposits. *Epimachairodus* canine. Early Pleistocene	6·3	30	nil
Val d'Arno (Italy). Alluvial deposits *Epimachairodus* canine. Early Pleistocene	5·3	35	0·2
La Denise (France). Findspot uncertain Skull fragment, *Homo* genus.	0·19	—	1·68
La Denise (France). Quaternary deposits *Rhinoceros* species, occipital skull fragment.	4·89	—	0·74
(ii) African group			
Makapansgat (South Africa). Cave breccia.	2·2	7	—

*Where analyses were not undertaken by one technique or another, a blank (−) is recorded.

**See Barker, H., Mackay, J., 1961: *Radiocarbon, 3*, 41.

Location and nature of fossil find	$\dfrac{100\ F\%}{P_2O_5\%}$	Equivalent U_3O_8 (ppm)	N%
Bone (type unspecified). Pliocene Sterkfontein (South Africa). Cave breccia.	1·1	7	—
Bone (type unspecified). Pliocene Swartkrans (South Africa). Cave breccia	2·3	6	—
Bone (type unspecified). Plio-Pleistocene. Tuang (South Africa). Lower breccia	3·8	21	—
Bone (type unspecified). Middle Pleistocene Tuang (South Africa). Upper breccia	3·8	6	0·1
Bone (type unspecified). Middle Stone Age. Saldanha (South Africa). Surface collection.	5·9	20	0·2
Skull, *Homo* genus. Middle Pleistocene Associated faunal remains (Including *Palaeoloxodon Mesochoerus*)	5·9–7·8	13–25	—

to Swanscombe skull, illustrates the correct general trend of the three elements' changes with time. The Galley Hill post-cranial remains (Plate 9.3) is an important example in that it was found in the Swanscombe Gravels in 1888, along with several Lower Palaeolithic hand-axes and remains of an extinct elephant. Such a findspot, though well above the level of excavation of the Swanscombe skull, was expected to be of an age in excess of 0·1 million years. This pre-dates Neanderthal Man yet the skeleton itself had several traits we attribute to modern man. The fluorine and nitrogen analysis indicates clearly that this burial is intrusive and suggests a Neolithic rather than Palaeolithic age, a conclusion that has since been confirmed by radiocarbon dating. The Swanscombe fauna also indicates the typical level of scatter in concentrations that might be encountered within a context.

When, in 1876, a canine tooth of the 'sabre-tooth tiger', *Epimachairodus*, was found in a cave at Cresswell Crags in an Upper Palaeolithic level its very authenticity was questioned. This genus is common enough in Early Pleistocene deposits in Europe and indeed occurs in a nearby site, Doveholes. An argument was advanced that this fossil, like several others that we know of, was treasured by a Stone Age man who carried it far from its original location. However, comparison of F%, N% and U_3O_8 content of the Cresswell Crags specimen with that of three early sites clearly indicates its comparative youthfulness.

In contrast, human remains claimed to have come from ancient Quaternary deposits at La Denise (near Puy-en-Velay, in France) are clearly very much younger than the true fauna of that context, as illustrated by parallel analysis of a bone specimen from a species of rhinoceros.[26]

For purposes of discussion the African fossils are presented in reverse to the European group, starting with the oldest material from Makapansgat, in South Africa. As discussed in Chapter 4 (section 1*f*) the South African fossils are not yet reliably dated although a recent study of valley erosion that causes the opening up of these cave sites in the hillside has ordered the sites in relative antiquity as listed in Table 9.1: Makapansgat, Sterkfontein, Swartkrans and Taung.[27] The faunal evidence of the first two of these sites suggests an age for their renowned skull finds of about three million years while Swartkrans is only about two million years old and Taung, much younger, perhaps 0·8 million years. The fluorine and uranium data show no similar sequence. Indeed, the Taung lower breccia (a rock consisting of sharp fragments embedded in a fine-grained matrix) would seem to be by far the oldest amongst these sites according to U_3O_8 content. Equally alarmingly the fluorine content fails to distinguish at all between the cave opening date, perhaps 0·9 million years, and the Middle Stone Age date of the upper breccia, perhaps only 0·09 million years. On this evidence it would seem sensible to regard the dolomite and chert horizons that constitute these caverns as quite unsuitable for this form of study.

The Saldanha skull, found in 1953 on the ground surface at Elandsfontein in South Africa, was accompanied by an extensive faunal series including many extinct mammals including a short-necked giraffe (*Libytherium*) and an unusually large baboon (*Simopithecus*). This skull, together with a similar specimen found during lead mining at Broken Hill (now in Zambia) surrounded by a similar faunal array, became the centre of a controversy that has only recently been resolved. Coon, in his book, *The Origin of Races*,[28] cited these fossils as evidence for the late development of the Negro race, suggesting a *Homo erectus/sapiens* transition time as recent as 40,000 years ago. In contrast the White race was considered to cross this threshold about 250,000 years ago, on the evidence of the skull structure of Swanscombe and Steinheim Man. A rebuke of this argument has partly hinged on whether the skull remains and fauna at Elandsfontein were truly contemporaneous, in view of their origin as surface finds. Fluorine and uranium analysis strongly support this assumption.[29] With this uncertainty resolved and a re-calibration of the Stone Age eras of South Africa, based on radiocarbon dating, the Saldanha and Broken Hill skulls have now been transferred to the later part of the Middle Pleistocene, more than 125,000 years ago.[30]

1e THE PILTDOWN AFFAIR

Knowledge of these chemical 'dating' techniques amongst the lay population largely stems from publicity, in 1950, of the faking of a fossil skull, called *Dawn Man*, unearthed in gravel deposits at Piltdown in south-east England some thirty-eight years earlier.[31] A discussion of this hoax is almost obligatory in any review of the scientific techniques. However, fresh evidence has recently emerged that quite firmly points the accusing finger at Charles Dawson as perpetrator of the fraud, a suggestion frequently resisted in the extensive literature now available on this subject.

Unravelling the Piltdown affair depends mainly on an appreciation of the time-table of the various events that relate to it plus a catalogue of the fossil finds involved in the scientific investigation and age attribution (Table 9.2). Dawson first presented the controversial fossils at a meeting of the Geological Society of London in December 1912, in conjunction with Smith Woodward (then Keeper of Geology at the Natural History Museum) whose aid had been enlisted in excavation some months before. Critics of Dawson had to face a convincing argument from Woodward who maintained that there was every indication the cranial bones and jaw used to reconstruct the skull were contemporary (Plate 9.4).[32] The remains were very close together in burial and both parts were of similar colour and degree of fossilization. Though Woodward admitted the jaw was extremely ape-like he noted the flat wear on the molars could only have arisen in the eating style of humans.

It is worth noting at this point that the prevailing atmosphere in the anthropological community was ripe for the appearance of such a man/ape skull. In 1891 Dubois had found what is still recognized as one of the earliest fossil hominids, *Pithecanthropus Erectus*, in the

Table 9.2: Chemical analyses of the Piltdown remains and related fauna

Location and nature of fossil find	$\dfrac{100\ F\%}{P_2O_5\%}$	Equivalent U_3O_8 (ppm)	N%
(i) Piltdown gravel deposits			
Jawbone	⩽0·03	0	3·9
Cranium	0·1	1	1·4
Molar (hippopotamus)	⩽0·1	3	<0·1
Molar (*Elephas*)	2·7	610	nil
(ii) Early Pleistocene fauna			
Red Crag (Suffolk). *Mastodon* molar	1·9	46	trace
Doveholes (Derbyshire). *Mastodon* molar	—	75	—
Ichkeul (Tunisia). *Elephas* molar	2·7	580	trace

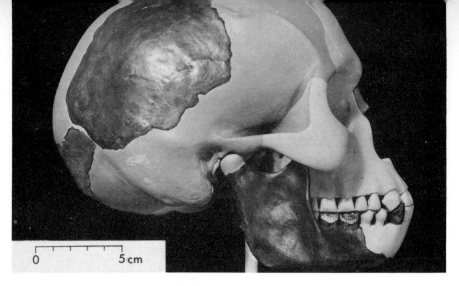

9.4   The Piltdown Skull, *Eoanthropus Dawsoni*. (Photograph: courtesy of the Trustees of the British Museum, Natural History, London.)

volcanic sediments of Java. Heidelberg Man emerged in 1907 from early diluvial layers of the river Neckar to produce the first example of man's presence in Europe more than 0·3 million years ago; then Neanderthal Man was unearthed in Dordogne in 1908. The fossil sequence of the Lower Palaeolithic in Europe was established (Heidelberg →Swanscombe →Neanderthal) with Java Man exhibiting rather more primitive traits and consequently somewhat older, perhaps 0·7 million years. The Piltdown find, *Eoanthropus Dawsoni*, served as an admirable ancestor to all these species.

The doubters of this fossil's integrity were duly impressed when, in July 1913, a canine tooth was found by a young man, Teilhard de Chardin, at the same site. Its structure was exactly that predicted by Woodward some months before, ape-like but worn in a way alien to modern ape species. In 1915, Dawson claimed a second fossil skull find only two miles away.

In hindsight we can reconstruct quite accurately the way in which the bones were given their antique appearance and detect the large number of errors made by the faker. Both the cranium and mandible have some archaeological age, perhaps 600 years according to radio-carbon analysis,[33] but the former is human while the latter comes from an orang-utan. A dark brown colouring was required to match the gravel in which it was found, so the bones were stained with iron sulphate solution and then oxidation accelerated by use of a dichromate solution. Both chromium and iron have been detected spectrochemically and the formation of gypsum crystals that resulted from the attack of the sulphate solution on the bone mineral was anomalous. The later canine tooth find had been coated rather less imaginatively with oil paint, Vandyke brown.

The additional chemical analyses listed in Table 9.2 not only indicate that the Piltdown skull parts resemble modern bone much more than

192

their Early Pleistocene faunal counterparts elsewhere in England but even the additional elephant and hippopotamus teeth extracted from the same gravels are not original, though certainly very old. The degraded hippopotamus molar contains a very low fluorine content more in keeping with cave sites in Mediterranean islands while the elephant's molar (maybe from an extinct species) has a huge uranium content of 610 ppm, a level only otherwise encountered so far in fossils from Ichkeul in Tunisia.

The flatness of the molars can be attributed to deliberate filing down. This should really have been evident to the original investigators as natural wear would first remove portions of enamel and then produce hollows in the softer underlying dentine. In the Piltdown molars the exposed dentine was flush with adjacent enamel.

The circumstantial evidence against Dawson, apart from the obvious direct link as the bone deposit discoverer, includes his acknowledged reputation as an antiquarian and geologist which would have equipped him far better than many to attempt the skull's detailed chemical preparation. He would no doubt have been aware that several old orang-utan skulls had come to Britain late in the nineteenth century from Sarawak and many were available for study in the Natural History Museum. That this region or somewhere like it was the origin of the Piltdown mandible seems reasonable as nitrogen and fluorine data indicate a good preservation, probably on the floor of a dry cave.

The suspicions about Dawson's involvement have hardened appreciably in the last few years, in part because his signature on a fake map of eighteenth-century Sussex established his character as a hoaxer.[34] To this can be added his involvement in a second forgery scandal related to brick stamps from the Roman shore fort at Pevensey, also in Sussex.[35] The inscriptions of these stamps, HON AUG ANDRIA, have for many years been regarded as a rare reference to the Emperor Honorius and documentation of his refurbishing of sea defences in the last decade of the fourth century AD, after his victory over the Irish and Picts. In fact, thermoluminescence dating of the bricks' fired clay suggested a twentieth-century age for these artefacts. The significant feature of this forgery detection lies in the fact that Dawson exhibited the bricks at the Society of Antiquaries in London in April, 1907. De Chardin cannot be tied to this hoax as he only met Dawson a year later, so attachment of blame for the Piltdown affair to the former becomes much less acceptable.

2 AMINO-ACID DEGRADATION PROCESSES

2a THE AGEING OF PROTEINS IN FOSSILS

The breakdown of collagen, when considered in detail, requires an appreciation of the reactions that effect constituent amino acids in burial conditions, particularly the role played by temperature and moisture. Fresh collagen is characterized mainly by three amino acids, glycene, hydroxyproline and hydroxylysene, the last two of which account for the primary nitrogen loss from bone during degradation.[36] The fibre structure is generated by peptide linkage of these groups in linear sequence. In amongst these major components there are small quantities of some seventeen other amino acids, notably isoleucine, aspartic acid and alanine, which undergo similar breakdown and change with the passage of time. There are several 'ageing' processes to be considered, each following a path defined by the individual reaction rate constant (k) and an activation energy (E). In principle, with so many parameters available it is possible to define a fossil's history both in time and climate.

The breakdown of pure amino acids can be simulated by solution in water plus heating.[37] Most of these chemical reactions, like the decarboxylation of alanine (ALA), follow first-order kinetics:

$$(ALA)_t = (ALA)_0 . \exp(-kt) \tag{9.1}$$

with $k = 1.04 \times 10^{-12}$ yr^{-1} at 19°C (292°K) in this case. The variation of the reaction rate constant as a function of temperature (expressed in degrees Kelvin) is then given by,

$$k = \text{constant} \{\exp(-E/RT)\} \tag{9.2}$$

(The gas constant $R = 1.987$ calories/°K mole.) For alanine, $E = 4.40 \times 10^4$ cal/mole. The less stable amino acids include threocine and serine with E-values of 3.38×10^4 and 2.93×10^4 cal/mole, respectively (Fig. 9.3).

Unfortunately the 'water + heat' break up of the amino acids with time, termed generally as 'pyrolysis', does not yet offer the dating possibilities that the graphical data imply. There is an appreciable

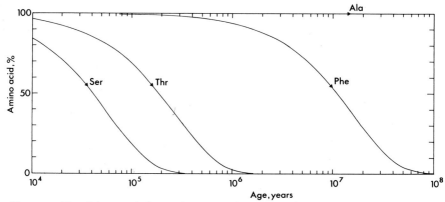

Fig. 9.3   Breakdown of the amino acids (alanine, phenylalanine, threonine and serine) with time, here evaluated at an ambient temperature of 20°C (reference 37).

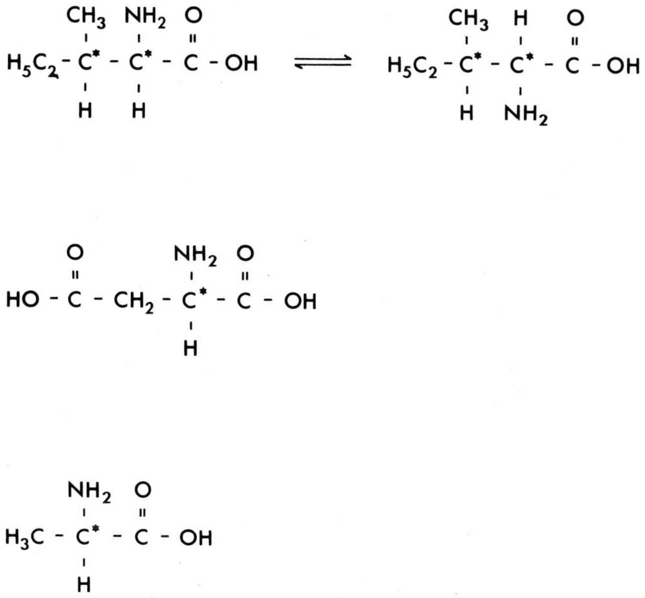

$$CH_3 \quad NH_2 \quad O$$
$$H_5C_2-\overset{\mid}{\underset{\mid}{C^*}}-\overset{\mid}{\underset{\mid}{C^*}}-\overset{\mid\mid}{C}-OH \quad \rightleftharpoons \quad H_5C_2-\overset{\mid}{\underset{\mid}{C^*}}-\overset{\mid}{\underset{\mid}{C^*}}-\overset{\mid\mid}{C}-OH$$
$$H \quad H \qquad\qquad\qquad H \quad NH_2$$

$$O \qquad NH_2 \quad O$$
$$HO-\overset{\mid\mid}{C}-CH_2-\overset{\mid}{\underset{\mid}{C^*}}-\overset{\mid\mid}{C}-OH$$
$$H$$

$$NH_2 \quad O$$
$$H_3C-\overset{\mid}{\underset{\mid}{C^*}}-\overset{\mid\mid}{C}-OH$$
$$H$$

Fig. 9.4 (i) Racemization (or, more correctly, epimerization) of L-isoleucine to D-alloisoleucine, involving a subtle reversal of rotational sense of the molecular structure.

(ii) Molecular structure of aspartic acid and alanine. Each has the molecular structure in the bonding at the active carbon atom (C*) to permit racemization between L- and D- isomers (reference 37).

number of examples of fossil materials which still carry significant quantities of some of the less stable amino acids in defiance of the simple kinetic principles presented here. Some of these anomalies are thought to be due to contamination as microorganisms flourish in the organic rich environment close to the bone. In other cases it seems likely that the original amino acid distribution in the species was quite different from that of its present-day form so that the initial concentration of any particular component before degradation is an unknown.

Besides breakdown the amino acids (with the exception of glycene) are capable of alteration by a process termed 'racemization' which involves a subtle reversal of the sense of 'rotation' of part of the molecule structure of an organism after death (Fig. 9.4). The re-aligned condition (a non-protein form labelled the 'D-isomer') is a mirror image of the original (labelled the 'L-isomer'). This process is a *reversible* first-order type that seeks an eventual equilibrium between L- and D-isomer concentrations. Expressed in a form akin to equation (9.1), a racemization age equation can be written as,

$$\ln\left[\frac{1+R}{1-K'R}\right] - \ln\left[\frac{1+R}{1-K'R}\right]_{t=0} = (1+K')\,k_L\,.\,t \qquad (9.3)[38]$$

where R is the ratio of D- to L-isomer concentrations and $K' = K_{eq}^{-1}$, the reciprocal of the equilibrium ratio of those same concentrations.

For the L-isoleucine conversion to D-alloisoleucine, $K_{eq} = 1\cdot 38$ and the logarithmic term ($t = 0$) evaluates at $0\cdot 028$, as the starting value of R is close to $0\cdot 016$. For aspartic acid,[39] $K_{eq} = 1$ and the logarithmic-term ($t = 0$) evaluates as $0\cdot 14$.

Racemization rate constants follow the same exponential variation with T quoted in equation (9.2) and share a common activation energy of $3\cdot 34 \times 10^{-4}$ cal/mole. For the isoleucine reaction kinetic studies at elevated temperatures yielded a value of $k_{iso} = 2\cdot 6 \times 10^{-6}$ yr^{-1} at 19°C. ($k_{asp} = 1\cdot 8 \times 10^{-5}$ yr^{-1} for aspartic acid at the same temperature.[40]) These rate constants indicate the range of applicability of isoleucine dating to be of the order of 0·5 million years or so (see Fig. 9.5) while aspartic-acid dating covers the era of Neanderthal Man through to the present era.

2b FACTORS EFFECTING RACEMIZATION

Breakdown of proteins, as chemical reactions, are more sensitive to

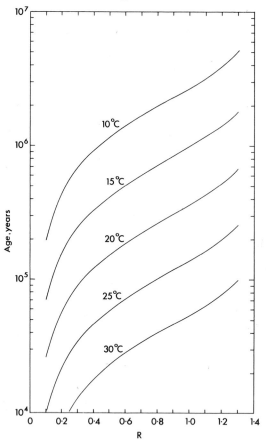

Fig. 9.5 Effect of temperature dependence of the isoleucine racemization reaction on fossil age determination. R is the ratio of the D- to L-isomer concentrations (references 38 and 41).

temperature variation than to the passage of time. The reaction rate constant varies by about 20% per °C. This is illustrated by the family of curves of·Fig. 9.5 derived for isoleucine from equation (9.3) and using an experimentally-derived (k_{iso} *versus* T) relation,

$$\text{Log}_{10}\, k_{iso}\ (\text{yr}^{-1}) = 19\cdot41 - 7304/T \qquad (9.4)\ ^{[41]}$$

Unfortunately there is no lack of evidence of temperature fluctuations of at least 1°C throughout the past million years. Variations of abundance in planktonic foraminifera [42] and oxygen isotope analyses [43] indicate changes of about 6°C in ocean temperatures during the various major glacial eras while pollen analysis [44] record in detail the short-term temperature fluctuations of the past 70,000 years including the most recent glacial retreat beginning around 18,000 years ago.[45] Dating results so far gathered seem to indicate that only cave deposits, especially those quite removed from the large continental ice sheets, offer a stable enough environment for use of isoleucine dating in its more distant range, particularly if oxygen isotope data from associated stalagmites can indicate the extent of any temperature fluctuations. A similar argument would suggest that aspartic-acid racemization will be at its most effective in the recent post-glacial era in temperate climates, though reliable data for faunal remains in warmer zones [46] have been obtained for ages up to 43,000 years.

The presence of water is essential for racemization to occur.[47] Bone internally retains about 5% water content and this is quite sufficient to support the chemical reactions involved. However, the collagen structure is also under attack by direct hydrolysis of the peptide bonds. Once these bonds have gone amino acids act as free agents and racemize much more rapidly. Thus the 'natural' situation of a fossil burial becomes complex. If the water inside the fossil is static so that a 'closed-system' model could be applied (and laboratory simulated) the observed racemization extent is the sum of two conversion levels, one related to free amino-acid content and one related to amino acids that are still protein-bound.

In contrast, if the ground water is mobile an 'open-system' model would be appropriate. If the free amino acids were completely leached then the racemization level measured would only be that of protein-bound components. This condition can also be laboratory simulated but a weight ratio (water-to-bone chips) of about 100/1 is required. A more realistic situation, involving a ratio of between 0·05/1 to 10/1, falls quite hopelessly between the two extremes. The impact of this problem can be judged from the data that bone, affected only by its indigenous water, attains an isoleucine R-value of 1·08 over three days of heating at 430°K but continuously-leached bone has $R = 0\cdot21$ for such treatment.

Because leaching is a diffusion-controlled process it depends upon temperature and will be most effective amongst smaller bone fragments and those most heavily fossilized, with open pore structures. Indeed a situation can be envisaged wherein the bone behaves increasingly as an 'open-system' structure as more and more degradation occurs. The present behaviour of a fossil may only partially indicate its initial response to environment.

There is one hazard, as yet only partially considered in protein degradation, that may contribute significantly to problems in amino-acid dating so far encountered. This involves the influence of accumulation of foreign metal ions in cavities of the collagen fibres.[48] Copper and iron are now recognized to be effective in destroying amino acids during hydrolysis and thereby accelerating collapse of collagen structure.[49] Though a technique has now been developed to prevent such suppression of amino-acid yield during laboratory analysis [50] the influence of these metallic contaminants in the long-term are difficult to assess, if only because the rate of their uptake during burial is unknown.

There are also some factors external to the fossil bone itself that are capable of modifying the L-to-D-isomer conversion rate. Though in the normal range of pH-values for soils (about 5 to 8) racemization rates of most amino acids are quite steady, in more acidic conditions (ph $\sim$ 3) and more alkaline conditions (pH $\sim$ 10) order of magnitude changes in ratio are predicted.[51] Also there are real contamination threats posed by free amino acids in the surroundings percolating into the fossil's volume, as the L-D conversion is a reversible exchange seeking an equilibrium condition without the confusion of extra components of either isomer.[52] Such problems become evident in discordant dates obtained from different amino acids within the same fossil.

2c OUTLINE OF SAMPLE PREPARATION

The detailed chemistry involved in sample preparation to put the protein in a form suitable for chromatography is given in several papers quoted in the literature (see references 36, 39, 50 and 53 particularly). The underlying principles of chromatography can be exampled by the paper/liquid technique.[54] The amino acids are hydro-lyzed and a small droplet on the resulting hydrolysate is placed at one end of a filter paper strip. When this region of the strip is immersed in a selected solvent each amino acid is drawn up the paper's length at a characteristic rate as the solvent's front advances by capillary action. Each component is then gradually separated into distinct zones on the paper column with position determined by the relative solubility of the amino acid in the cellulose-bound water associated with the filter paper. (Modifications of this technique include pre-treatment of the paper to improve resolution [55] and use of a glass column instead.[56]) Leucine rises above valine, valine above alanine and so forth. Chemical 'development' of the paper's surface (usually with *ninhydrin*) causes staining related to the amino-acid concentration.

Gas chromatography achieves a similar division of components as they are carried through a column of porous material coated with an organic liquid. Now it is the retention time of the amino acid within the column that is characteristic. Improvement in resolution for this technique has been achieved by use of extremely high pressures (around 2,000 atmospheres) in the carrier gas stream.[57]

L-isoleucine and D-alloisoleucine divide sharply in amino-acid analysis but all the other L- and D-isomers are only separable by standard chromatographic techniques after a derivative has been synthesized. For example aspartic acid has to be isolated from other bone amino acids by an ion-exchange process and then converted into a solution of dipeptides.

One interesting source of contamination is that of fingerprints which carry most of the amino acids found in bone, with the exception of cystine, and large amounts of the less stable members like serine, threonine and aspartic acid.[58] Once exposed surfaces have been removed from a specimen and bulk contaminants (like silted quartz and calcite) have been washed away, only forceps handling is possible.

2d DATING APPLICATIONS

Many earlier amino-acid dates must be treated as highly suspect as the complexity of the protein degradation process becomes more apparent. Some results for African fossils only measured recently are of interest as they relate to topics discussed elsewhere in this book.

The Broken Hill skull was mentioned in section 1*d* of this chapter in connexion with the controversy of the timing of the *Homo erectus/sapiens* transition in the Negro race. The site of Broken Hill lies only 150 km from a relatively young site, Mumbwa, which has been dated by the radiocarbon method as 19,780 ± 130 years (UCLA 1750). Racemization analysis of a bone fragment of that context yielded $k_{asp} = 4.96 \times 10^{-6}$ yr^{-1} which was then regarded as applicable to the entire region. A D-/L-aspartic acid ratio of 0·55 for a portion of the Broken Hill skull predicted an age of approximately 110,000 years. This compares reasonably well with Middle Pleistocene estimates deduced from separate faunal evidence. A similar 'calibration' procedure has been applied to Olduvai Gorge fossil strata using radiocarbon analysis of a 17,000 year-old ostrich shell to predict a k-value of 1.48×10^{-5} yr^{-1} for that site. An age of 56,000 years for the upper Ndutu Beds has been deduced. While this approach may well serve to reduce errors due to palaeoclimate uncertainties it is worth noting that fossils of different age may still lose free amino acids by leaching at quite different rates. Thus a k-value which is valid for a short time span may not hold up over periods an order of magnitude greater.

It is evident from recent papers that the future research into racemization will be concentrated upon extension of the suite of amino acids that can be used most conveniently for dating. In this direction alanine and glutamic acid are of interest since their k-values are very similar to one another and a little over twice that of isoleucine. Consequently their L-to-D-isomer conversion covers a time range between that of isoleucine and aspartic acid, at 0·1–0·2 million years, with sensitivity. However, there is no reason to believe that these other amino acids are any less susceptible to the complications outlined in section 2*b* above.

Chapter 10

New Scientific Techniques applied to Art History

INTRODUCTION

During the late Palaeolithic period, some 30,000 years ago, early man was just beginning to shake off his hunter's role and seek some stability in community life. His rock shelters were adorned with paintings and engravings of the animals with which he competed for survival or killed for food. Sturdily-built bisons and tusked mammoths depicted on the walls of caves in south-west France [1] and kangaroo sketches in early flint mines in Australia,[2] together with lively scenes of the chase, give us some insight into the way of life of those early artists. Ochre fragments extended the 'palette' beyond a monotonous manganese black. Mammoth ivory, reindeer-horn and haematite were sculpted into small figurines and deep-cut reliefs. As settlement spread, communities grew and religious beliefs crystallized into firm doctrines. An increasing amount of effort was diverted away from production of everyday domestic material towards carefully-fashioned items to be treasured with a destiny as an heirloom or to figure in ceremonial rites. Proliferation of materials, particularly pottery and metals, and some pigment experimentation has widely diversified what we might regard as an artefact in archaeological excavation.

In our own times a growth in appreciation of the technical skill, local tradition and patience that these objects engender has led to them being set apart and re-defined as 'art-objects'. The addition of a price tag has psychologically increased this separation but, in reality, art objects remain archaeological artefacts. One factor does introduce a distinction that many of us regret, that of poor recording of provenance in the art market which, in turn, has opened the door to forgery and ill-considered imitation. Consequently scientific analysis in the art world has, of necessity, found itself playing two roles, the first intended to increase our knowledge of past technology, the second directed towards solution of authenticity problems. Recurrence of the latter aspect in this chapter expresses more than just the author's personal bias. It allows a brief discussion of other scientific techniques, particularly neutron activation analysis of trace impurities, that could prove of similar value in solution of some archaeological problems of recent times. This work can serve as a supplement to other authenticity studies already reported in this book: thermoluminescence of ceramics and bronzes, lead-decay dating of lead white pigment, ^{14}C-dating of parchment and cast iron and fluorine analysis of the Piltdown skull.

For brevity, certain aspects of art work study are excluded in the following discussion as they involve use of standard scientific techniques, fully surveyed in previous literature. Among pigments this includes the quite radical changes in palette composition caused by chemical technology advances of the eighteenth century onwards. For example, the advent of *Prussian blue* can be confidently set c. 1704–7, that of *cobalt blue* to 1804 and *titanium white* to 1919 (references 3–6). (The last of these, when found in what was first regarded as an ink stain on the famous Vinland Map, has recently indicated that it is not of fifteenth-century origin as originally thought.) Among metals, where compositional information is sought, gross properties like surface plating of non-noble metals can be detected either by density determination for coins [7,8] or microscope investigation of bulk items.[9,10] Instead this chapter concentrates on the sophisticated radioactive techniques which have only been fully developed in the past decade and are only just beginning to find their potential in the art world.

1a NEUTRON ACTIVATION ANALYSIS

When an element's atomic nucleus absorbs a neutron the resulting compound nucleus is unstable and subsequently breaks down by radioactive decay. At lower energies of irradiation up to 1 eV (in the so-called 'thermal' neutron region) the main form of interaction is 'radiative capture', followed by an eventual decay with the emission of gamma radiation. In these reactions, formally denoted as (n, γ) events, the energy and half-life of decay of the resulting gamma rays characterize the element involved. For example, for copper activation data can be summarized as:

$$^{63}\text{Cu} \ (n, \gamma) \ ^{64}\text{Cu} \qquad E_\gamma\text{: 511,1340 keV} \qquad t_{\frac{1}{2}} = 0.53 \text{ days.}$$

while for chromium, we have

$$^{50}\text{Cr} \ (n, \gamma) \ ^{51}\text{Cr} \qquad E_\gamma\text{: 320 keV} \qquad t_{\frac{1}{2}} = 27\cdot8 \text{ days.}$$

At much higher neutron energies, around 14 MeV, other reactions can be induced that involve subsequent decay with emission of a variety of radiations. For example, nickel converts to cobalt and then breaks down by proton and gamma ray emission characterized as follows:

$$^{58}\text{Ni} \ (n, p) \ ^{58}\text{Co} \qquad E_\gamma\text{: 810 keV} \qquad t_{\frac{1}{2}} = 71 \text{ days.}$$

Thermal neutron activation is conveniently available at nuclear reactors. Readers who have visited a reactor station will be familiar

with the water pool that overlies the nuclear fuel for protection purposes and will remember the colourful blue glow caused by Čerenkov
radiation. This water also serves to slow the neutrons down to the
desired energy for activation analysis. High energy neutrons are usually
supplied as an external beam facility at a cyclotron unit. Their usage
has been mainly limited to metals of high copper content and a related
compositional analysis of brasses (section 1d).

The detectability of the concentration of an element in a material
depends on several factors. Not every neutron-nucleus collision leads to
capture. A capture probability is expressed by a *cross-section*, σ, by
which the number of radioactive atoms, N^*, activated in time, t
seconds by a neutron flux, is given by,

$$N^* = N_0\, \Phi\, \sigma\, t \qquad (10.1)$$

Here N_0 is the number of atoms per cc. of the studied element, Φ is
usually quoted in neutrons/cm², so the units of σ are cm². (In practice
the cross-sections are quoted in *barns*, where 1 barn $\equiv 10^{-24}$ cm².)
As σ is a function of the neutron energy to allow intercomparison of
response of different elements, it is conventional to quote only the
cross-section's value, σ_0, at $E_n = 0.025$ eV, where the major part of the
absorption of the 0 to 1 eV spectrum occurs. (A complete list of σ_0-
values of this definition are given in the standard reference work,
Handbook of Chemistry and Physics, published by the Chemical Rubber
Publishing Co.)

Thus, in principle, an element like silver could be studied in two
ways as it has two isotopic forms:

^{107}Ag (n, γ) ^{108}Ag E_γ: 118,420 and 615 keV
$t_{\frac{1}{2}} = 2.4$ mins $\sigma_0 = 44$ barns

^{109}Ag (n, γ) ^{110m}Ag E_γ: 657, 760,884 and 937 (plus others of weaker
intensity)
$t_{\frac{1}{2}} = 270$ days $\sigma_0 = 2.8$ barns.

The first of these would give the larger spectrum signals as more
^{108}Ag would have been activated and its decay would feed pulses more
rapidly into the detection system. In practice the sample transfer time
from reactor to the detector's location results in that signal's severe
depletion before measurement. Thus it is the ^{109}Ag-activation that is
usually studied even though no longer irradiation and measurement
times are necessary.

The gamma-ray spectrum itself may contain a large number of peaks
superimposed on the detection system's background and tending to
overlap to some degree (Fig. 10.1). However, as the theoretical shape
of a spectrum peak is known, computer 'stripping' techniques have
become common practice which takes out the stronger signals, one by
one so that weaker ones can be resolved more easily.[11] This approach
also enhances the minimum detectable level of several scarcer elements.

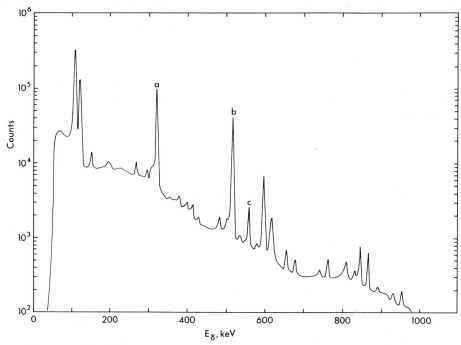

Fig. 10.1 Typical gamma-ray spectrum obtained from a neutron-activated lead white pigment specimen. Peaks marked are: a. chromium (^{51}Cr, 320 keV) b. copper (^{64}Cu, 511 keV), and c. arsenic (^{76}As, 559 keV).

The maximum signal is not only governed by the total number of a particular atom type present but also by the saturation effect where the rate of growth of N* is balanced by loss due to radioactive decay occurring at the same time.

Quantitative analysis of elemental concentrations brings in another parameter, the efficiency of the detection system at each energy value. This is measured by inclusion of a 'standard' sample of known composition in the irradiation process. (Preferably there should be some similarity in the concentration of the major constituents of the 'unknown' and the standard so that the bulk absorption features are similar). The detection system is a thallium-activated sodium iodide or lithium-activated germanium crystal connected to a multichannel pulse height analyser. Though the germanium crystal has a very high energy resolution in the gamma-ray spectrum it is also extremely expensive. Some applications where a sensitive element is being studied almost exclusively are well served by the sodium iodide alternative.

1b LEAD WHITE PIGMENT: TECHNOLOGY AND CHRONOLOGY

Lead white has played an important role in western painting for many centuries, with use as a primer (in an admixture with chalk) since the Middle Ages and as almost the only white in easel oil painting.[12] The pigment's composition is a mixture of 70% carbonate and 30%

hydrate: $2PbCO_3.Pb(OH)_2$. Chemically it interacts with linseed oil to form a 'soap', lead linoleate, which has the excellent painting properties of density and homogeneity, while it resists atmosphere degradation when coated with a thin varnish film.

From a scientist's standpoint, lead white is an attractive pigment as it was commonly used on its own over large areas (familarly, in the linen cuffs and collars of Dutch portraiture), so that problems of contamination are diminished. Also, sampling is often quite practical near the picture's edge, in a region which would be hidden by a frame when the work is on display.

To aid spectrum-peak resolution some specialized 'fast-separation' chemical techniques have been developed to recover each element individually from a sample as small as 100 microgram.[13] This results in data collection on fast-decaying elements like barium-139 and manganese-56 as well as copper-64.

Though lead carbonate occurs naturally, as the mineral *cerussite*, only the use of artificially-prepared pigment is recorded. Fortunately the methods of lead white manufacture are well documented from Roman times to present day. The similarity of the recipes mentioned by Theophrastus, Pliny and Vitruvius in early times and those to be found in sixteenth and seventeenth-century manuscripts [14] indicate that the technology changed very little until late in the eighteenth century. In all cases the starting point was the lead sulphide ore, *galena*, which was converted to the lead oxide, *litharge*, by roasting. Smelting in an oxygen-starved atmosphere yielded the simple metal. Strips of the lead (called *buckles*) were mounted over acetic acid in a batch of clay pots, and each unit was piled up in a bed of dung. The latter's fermentation produced carbon dioxide which, together with the acetic vapours, gradually converted the metal to the pigment carbonate. (In the eighteenth century output was improved by replacing the dung with waste tanner's bark to increase the heat of fermentation.)

To gather the pigment the buckles were beaten to free the white flakes. Those engaged in the work complained more and more about the associated health hazard and thus stimulated an important manufacturing change, that of squeezing the lead through brass rollers and collecting the separated pigment in a water bath below. For similar reasons hand grinding was gradually replaced by milling linked to extraction systems to keep the workshop air free of residual pigment dust. By the early part of the nineteenth century much of the lead white manufacture was mechanized.

At much the same time, cupellation, the conventional method of silver extraction from lead ore in ancient times, was replaced by the more efficient Pattinson and Parkes processes.

Both this refinement and the rolling process mentioned earlier caused some quite detectable changes in impurity contents of lead white pigment in Dutch paintings between about 1810 and 1870.

Traces of zinc from the roller brass appear, sometimes at about a 30 ppm concentration, whereas white on earlier works rarely carried more than 1 ppm of that element. Meanwhile the silver content drops from earlier levels of about 25 ppm down to about 5 ppm. Some example of these changes are illustrated in Fig. 10.2a, b. The early sixteenth-century work, *Jesus amid the Scribes* (attributed to the Antwerp Master) (Plate 10.1) and the Jacob Jordaens work of 1620, *Meleager and Atlanta*, have similar composition patterns. However, these patterns are distinct from the work of 1848, *The Gothic Hall in The Hague*, by A. Wynantsz, and post-1860 paintings by artists like J. J. Schenkel, H. W. Mesdag and A. van Welie.

At this stage three other impurities included in Fig. 10.2, copper, mercury and chromium, act as chronology indicators. The former seems to be carried along with the silver content fall, with works such as *The Butcher's Shop*, by Abraham van Hecken, dating to 1768 (Cu content, 205 ppm) contrasting sharply with post-1860 works where the Cu content is less than 60 ppm. Similar changes in mercury content are less obvious with movement from about 5 ppm to about 2 ppm occurring gradually across the first half of the nineteenth century. (However, after 1920 the Hg-level drops consistently below 1 ppm.) Of the last element, chromium, little can be said to explain a heavy decrease of impurity level from around 400 ppm prior to 1700 down to less than 40 ppm afterwards. In the absence of any innovation at present on record, we can only assume that this particular change stems from an ore source replacement.

By 1845 a new pigment, *zinc white*, was on the market in Paris and available from the firm of Hafkenscheid in Amsterdam only a decade later.[15] The cold whiteness of this pigment appealed to many artists and only its tendency to dry brittle and subsequently crack prevented its commercial dominance. Instead zinc/lead white mixtures became increasingly common. Our lead white impurity record duly responds with several examples of Zn-content in the 1,000 to 30,000 ppm content range. Smaller increases in some cases, to around the 100 ppm level probably result from contamination of grinding equipment within a factory producing both pigments.

In modern lead white pigments the Zn-content is sometimes very high (around 2,000 ppm) if the original lead was obtained by an extraction process that involves molten zinc. However, complete change in technology over the past decade, to electrolytic and precipitation processes, now give us lead whites which are virtually impurity free: in particular the Zn-content is down to about 5 ppm. Thus we reach a conclusion that a high zinc impurity level of 100 ppm or more, strongly suggests the pigment in which it occurs is modern, while a silver and copper impurity level of greater than 20 ppm and 200 ppm respectively is consistent with a pigment pre-dating 1800.

The general rules developed for lead white in Dutch paintings do not

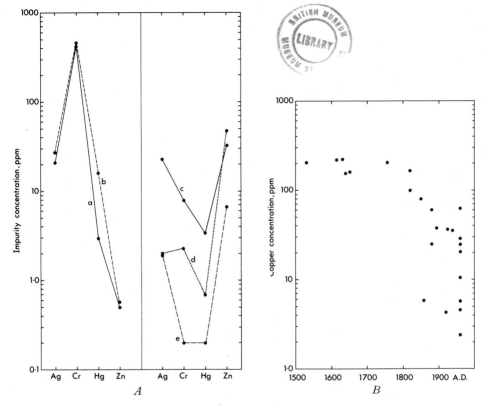

Fig. 10.2   *A*. Impurity analysis of lead white pigments:
  a. *Jesus in the midst of the Scribes*, Antwerp Master (c. 1510),
  b. *Meleager and Atalanta*. Jacob Jordaens (c. 1620),
  c. *The Gothic Hall in The Hague*. A. Wynantsz (c. 1848)
  d. A work by Q. van Houten, title unknown (c. 1881)
  e. Factory pigment from G. Greve of Utrecht (manufactured in 1961).

  B. Chronological variation of copper concentration in lead white pigments from Dutch paintings (reference 13).

hold good for early Venetian works, like those of Titian, Tintoretto and Tiepolo. The silver content amongst works of these artists are much lower (less than 10 ppm).[16] Instead the ratio, of Cu/Ag content, seems to be a sensitive indicator of lead white origin (presumably representing differences in lead ore source).[17] For example, this ratio measured for several works of Rubens lies between 0·1 and 8·2 while for works of Tintoretto the limits are 26 to 135. The element, antimony, also seems valuable in the Dutch/Venetian comparison, as illustrated by two Tiepolo works. White lead in *The Veneration of the Trinity by Pope Clement* painted in Venice in 1735 contains only 8 ppm of Sb-impurity, but *Adoration of The Kings* painted during Tiepolo's brief stay in Würzburg contains an Sb-impurity level of 191 ppm. In contrast with early works from either region of Europe, a modern forgery would be likely to carry a white pigment virtually free of antimony altogether.[18]

10.1 *Jesus in the midst of the Scribes*, attributed to the Antwerp Master (c. 1510). (Photograph: courtesy of the Royal Museum of Fine Arts, Antwerp; catalogue number 385.)

IC IMPURITY ANALYSES AMONGST OTHER PIGMENTS

Little research has been attempted amongst other colours than white as they rarely occur on their own, but, at best, occur as a single undiluted layer overlying several other pigments.[19] However, two pigments, vermilion and ultramarine, have been investigated for a specific reason. Each has a natural form (*cinnabar*, *lapis lazuli*) which has a history of usage in painting in their own right, while documentation of the natural-artificial transition is extensive in technical literature. The choice between the two forms as far as the artists themselves are concerned is less predictable in terms of chronology.

Vermilion was almost certainly first synthesized by the Chinese early in the Christian era and knowledge of it transmitted to the West by the Moors.[20] Manuscripts of the eighth century like that of the Arabic alchemist, Geber, speak of forming a red compound from the union of sulphur and mercury, while the writings of Cennino Cennini claim that the artificial form was common in Renaissance paintings of the fifteenth-century. A recently-discovered late seventeenth-century manuscript, *The Pekstov Papers*, lays down in detail the Dutch approach to vermilion manufacture, though the pigment was available well before that time.[21] All these recipes refer to the so-called 'dry-process' method of production which involves sublimation of the black amorphous mercuric sulphide that results from the melt of the component elements. This artificial form was only displaced in the late eighteenth century when the much less expensive 'wet-process' method was developed to a commercial level in Germany, whereby the black mercuric sulphide was heated in a solution of an alkali sulphide.

The 'wet-process' form of the pigment, as fine-grained precipitate, is readily distinguishable from the 'dry-process' or natural forms which appear granular and angular under a microscope. However, the natural mineral does seem to have some distinctive features in trace element analysis with arsenic, copper and antimony concentrations of more than 300 ppm. In contrast various artificial preparations are virtually free of the latter two elements and have only small amounts of arsenic (less than 50 ppm). On this basis the red in a Pieter Breughel (the Elder) work (Koninklijk Museum voor Schone Kunsten, Antwerp: catalogue no. 777), *The Sermon on the Mount*, dating to 1610, is artificial, while that of Hecken's *The Butcher's Shop* (Rijksmuseum, Amsterdam: catalogue no. 1119), dating to 1640, is clearly of natural origin.[22]

Of the ultramarine variants far less can be said at present except that the artificial product often contains far larger concentrations of caesium and thorium.[23] One of the strongest controlling factors in this pigment's usage has been availability and cost of the source mineral which came exclusively from Afghanistan until the nineteenth century. In the seventeenth century ultramarine was either used sparingly (as in the *Toilet of Venus* by Velasquez,[24] where it occurs as an intense

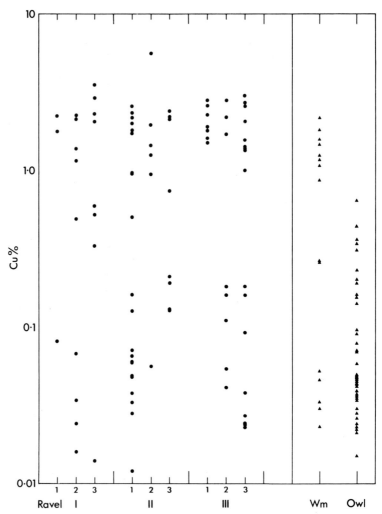

Fig. 10.3   Copper impurity concentration amongst early Greek silver coinage. To the left are Corinthian coins classified according to O. Ravel's *Les Poulains de Corinthe*; Period I (570–520 BC), Period II (520–460 BC) and Period III (460–430 BC). Each period divides into three classes but exact time markers for these are in question. To the right are Athenian coins known as 'Wappenmünzen' (c. 575–525 BC) and Early 'Owls' (c. 525–479 BC) (reference 31).

blue highlighting in Cupid's sash) or substituted with *azurite*. The synthesis of ultramarine in 1814, by the distinguished chemist Vaquelin, prompted a determined search for inexpensive manufacturing processes. In 1828, J. B. Guimet reported his success to the *Société d'Encouragement pour l'Industrie National* in Paris and stimulated a partial recovery in the pigment's popularity.

Microscope analysis has usually been promoted as the means to distinguish the natural and artificial ultramarines. The former is characterized by its angular grain shape and the common occurrence of associated minerals from the same geological source, particularly calcite, quartz and iron pyrites. In contrast the artificial pigment has small rounded particles of regular size. This means of distinction was presented as evidence of forgery of a work *The Merry Cavalier* (attributed to Frans Hals) which became the subject of a much-published court action in 1925, 'Muller & Co., *v.* de Haas'.[25] Surprisingly this rather subjective evidence appears to have carried as much weight as separate chemical evidence indicated the Cavalier's collar was painted in zinc white while the whole background was finished in the nineteenth-century pigment, *cobalt blue*.

Trace element distinctions are more likely to be valuable if they can be established amongst the natural sources as the output of the Ovalle mines of Chile and the Lake Baikhal and Transbaikhalia mines of Siberia now offer important alternative lapis lazuli sources to the original Afghanistan material.[26]

1*d* THERMAL NEUTRON ANALYSIS OF METALS

The somewhat crude ore-refining methods used in ancient and medieval times resulted in metalware and coins produced in those periods containing a wide range of impurities. Apart from a limited number of reports of gold, silver and antimony determinations in copper coinage (references 27–29), most of the neutron activation research has concentrated on the elements to be found in silver, particularly that used for coinage in the Near East.

The silver ore available to mints would inevitably carry minor levels of gold and copper (typically 0·1 to 1·0%) while other impurities, like antimony and arsenic would be introduced along with any copper deliberately added for purposes of debasement.[30] Also where silver ore refinement involved cupellation some lead contamination would have been unavoidable (see section 1*b*).

Thermal neutron activation of the complete coin allows a detection of copper and gold concentrations of 0·01% and 0·001%, respectively, in a silver matrix.[31,32] Amongst Greek coinage of the sixth and fifth century BC, copper seems to be a sensitive indicator of ore origin, as the data for Corinthian and Athenian material illustrates (Fig. 10.3). Two distinct Corinthian concentration groups can be defined (particularly in the two later periods, marked II and III, after the notation of O. Ravel in *Les Poulains de Corinthe*), one covering the range of 0·7 to 3·0% content, the other 0·01 to 0·20% content. For Athens, a general scatter of copper-content values for so-called 'wappen münzen' (which bear a variety of obverse decorations) contrasts with a consistently low impurity level in 'owls' (with the head of Athena on obverse and owl on reverse). Numismatically 'owls' are thought to

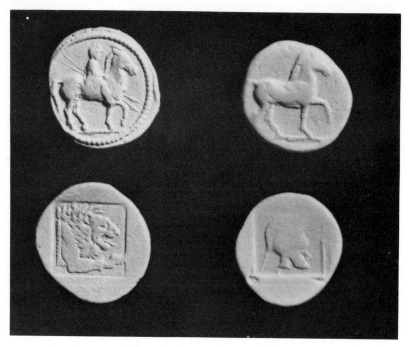

10.2 Macedonian silver tetrabols of the fifth millennium BC.
   a. Heavy tetrabol with an obverse design of an accompanied horse (Cu ⩽ 0·25%).
   b. Light tetrabol with an obverse design of a free horse (Cu, 5–24%). (Photographs: courtesy of the Heberden Coin Room, Ashmolean Museum, Oxford.)

have superseded 'wappen münzen' around 525 BC, and it is tempting to link the former's purity to the initial exploitation of the silver-laden Laurium mines, nearby.

Fifth-century coins from Macedonia group into two categories which are even more distinctly separated (Plate 10.2). Heavy *tetrabols* with an obverse design of a horse accompanied by a rider or standing figure, are all of high purity (copper content below 0·25%) while light *tetrabols* with a free horse on the observe are debased (copper content 5–24%). The former probably rated as worthy of use in foreign trading with the latter acting as token coinage for general circulation within Macedonia.

The gold impurity in the Greek coinage discussed here tends to be of much less value in the scientific sense: in general all that might be said is that there is a tendency for readings in both impurities to be high or low together. However, amongst earlier Sasanian silver coinage from Persia (AD 224–457) it would appear that quite strict limits on gold content can be set of 0·2 to 1·2%, though some much purer metal source seems to have been exploited later, around the reign of Ardashir III (AD 628–29). Certainly several fakes of coinage of Shapur I (AD 241–

72) stand out sharply by virtue of their refined composition (gold impurity, c. 0·03%). Such a distinction has also been established amongst silver artwork (primarily plates) of the same period.

The technique of sampling this coinage is particularly important. It involves rubbing a roughened quartz tube onto sound metal, after the outer regions of corrosion have been abraded away. (This corroded region would tend to be somewhat enriched in gold content as that noble metal would tend to resist leaching attack rather better than the host silver. The opposite would be the case with any copper present.) 'Streaks', as these samples are called, weigh no more than 0·1 mg.

Recently Sasanian investigations have been extended to cover several trace impurities such as iridium, iron and mercury.[33] Their detection requires drill sampling (though 100 microgram of material suffices) and sample pre-treatment, using precipitation techniques that take out the much more intense activities of copper, gold and silver itself.

Streak analysis has also been valuable in study of the fineness of silver coinage, the *dirham*, of the Mamluk rulers of Egypt and Syria (AD 1250–1517).[34] It seems clear that one ruler, Qutuz, was forced to exercise some debasement at his mints in order to raise money for his battle against the Mongols, at Ayn Jālut, in AD 1260. In contrast, even in the final stages of Mamluk dominance (c. AD 1510) the dirham currency maintained its fineness in the face of a deteriorating economic situation. This was particularly surprising as silver was scarce and copper abundant, while the gold coinage had already been debased.

1*e* ALTERNATIVE RADIATION TECHNIQUES FOR OTHER METALS

There are conflicting views about the usefulness of thermal neutron activation for silver and copper impurity analysis in a *gold* matrix. Earlier studies appear pessimistic,[35] but recent investigations of the Frankish coins from the Sutton Hoo royal burial and Merovingian (AD 580–700) coins in the British Museum's collection are in good agreement with parallel specific gravity analysis.[36] Instead charged particle irradiation, using 30 MeV protons or 26 MeV deuterons, has been recommended [37] where activation involves reactions of the form:

$$^{63}\text{Cu (p, pn) }^{62}\text{Cu} \qquad E_\gamma: 511 \text{ keV} \qquad t_{\frac{1}{2}} = 9\cdot8 \text{ minutes}$$
$$^{63}\text{Cu (p, n) }^{63}\text{Zn} \qquad E_\gamma: 511 \text{ keV} \qquad t_{\frac{1}{2}} = 38 \text{ minutes}$$
$$^{107}\text{Ag (p, pn) }^{106\text{m}}\text{Ag} \quad E_\gamma: 531 \text{ keV} \qquad t_{\frac{1}{2}} = 8\cdot3 \text{ days}$$

and matching reactions like

$$^{63}\text{Cu (d, p) }^{63}\text{Cu} \qquad E_\gamma: 511 \text{ keV} \qquad t_{\frac{1}{2}} = 38 \text{ minutes.}$$

The induction of the copper activity is achieved by a brief exposure, perhaps only a matter of minutes, followed promptly by gamma-spectrum analysis to cope with the brevity of the relevant half-lives. In the case of silver determination irradiation may take about an hour while spectrum analysis is delayed a week to allow short-term activity to fade away. Detection limits of 0·005% and 0·05% for copper and silver determination, respectively, have been reported.[37] The choice of charged particle in this work is dictated by the size of the object under study (usually coins). As the range of 26 MeV deuterons in gold is close to 0·6 mm their use is restricted to thinner coins (0·6 to 1·2 mm). The range of 30 MeV protons in gold is about 1·1 mm so this radiation is used for thicker coins and larger objects.

Application of this approach to coin analysis includes Roman material of the Republican and Imperial periods 46–38 BC and AD 85–388 respectively), together with some related forgeries. The latter included a Domitian *aureus* (Cu: 0·90%, Ag: 1·1%) and two Trojan *aurei* (Cu: 1·6%, Ag: 3·7% and Cu: 1·3%, Ag: 1·8% respectively) all of which stand out in sharp contrast to the general concentration levels over those two emperors' reigns (AD 81–85 and AD 103–117 respectively) of,

$$\text{Cu: } 0\cdot01\text{–}0\cdot07\% \text{ and Ag: } 0\cdot14\text{–}0\cdot49\%$$

Other analyses include Cyzicene electrum coins where the precious metals are alloyed in approximately 50/50% proportions plus a small copper content of between 0·1% and 4·4%, and lead determination in silver tetradrachm from Bactria which indicated a detection limit of about 0·15% impurity content. This latter work is particularly important as lead is not detectable using thermal neutron activation.

For general impurity analysis in a *copper* matrix, particularly zinc, *fast* neutron activation has been found to be effective. Typical reactions include,

$$^{66}\text{Zn (n, 2n) } ^{65}\text{Zn} \quad E: 1119 \text{ keV} \quad t_{\frac{1}{2}} = 245 \text{ days}$$
$$^{56}\text{Fe (n, p) } ^{56}\text{Mn} \quad E: 850 \text{ keV} \quad t_{\frac{1}{2}} = 2\cdot6 \text{ hours}$$
$$^{123}\text{Sb (n, 2n) } ^{122}\text{Sb} \quad E: 566 \text{ keV} \quad t_{\frac{1}{2}} = 2\cdot8 \text{ days}$$

This approach has obvious advantages in study of brasses whether truly ancient, like those of Gujarat and Kasmir (seventh to twelfth century AD in India) where the typical zinc level is about 15%, or amongst fakes of Roman bronze *sestertii* coinage. Many of the periods of the bronze-to-brass technological change in India, South-East Asia and the Far East are well established.[38]

High energy *photon* activation (around 23 MeV) can be effectively applied to nickel and cobalt determination in *iron* artefacts. Nuclear reactions include:

$$^{54}\text{Fe } (\gamma, \text{n}) \, ^{53}\text{Fe} \quad E_{\gamma}: 370, 511 \text{ keV} \quad t_{\frac{1}{2}} = 8\cdot6 \text{ minutes}$$
$$^{58}\text{Ni } (\gamma, \text{n}) \, ^{57}\text{Ni} \quad E_{\gamma}: 511, 1360, 1750, 1910 \text{ keV} \quad t_{\frac{1}{2}} = 37 \text{ hours}$$
$$^{59}\text{Co } (\gamma, \text{n}) \, ^{58}\text{Co} \quad E_{\gamma}: 511, 810 \text{ keV} \quad t_{\frac{1}{2}} = 71 \text{ days}$$

Archaeologically, if not necessarily chronologically, this approach has potential in analysis of meteoric iron objects of which there are many examples to be found in the ancient Near East, like a dagger blade from the Tomb of Tutankhamun [39] and the cutting edges added to bronze axes of the Chou Dynasty (c. 1,000 BC) in China.[40]

2a X-RAY FLUORESCENCE (XRF) SPECTROSCOPY

When a material is bombarded with X-rays of energies ranging from 0 to 130 keV its constituent atoms become excited. Each element present will settle back to stability by emission of secondary, fluorescent X-rays with a characteristic energy that permits identification and an intensity that relates to concentration. As the levels of input radiation usually employed cause no physical damage and leave no residual radioactivity this approach can provide a completely non-destructive quantitative chemical analysis of an ancient object. Unfortunately the penetration depth of X-rays (both primary and secondary) is limited so that the XRF data obtained is representative of only about a 50 micron thick portion of a specimen. This restriction creates major problems in the study of alloyed metals which are subject to elemental surface depletion after a long burial [41] while corrosion effects will cause mobility of many minor impurities (like arsenic and phosphorus in iron artefacts [42]) that result in complicating segregation and enrichment effects.

However, cleaning of an object can be confined to a small zone, perhaps only 2 mm across, and bare metal analysed using some form of point-source spectrometer. The form that such detection equipment

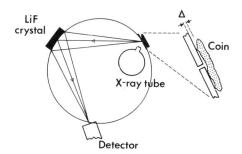

Fig. 10.4 a. X-ray fluorescence equipment known as the 'Milliprobe,' operated in a 'dispersive' mode. Johansen focusing conditions are used where the crystal is bent to an arc generated by a radius equal to the diameter of the Rowland circle, but ground to an arc generated by the Rowland circle. Inset: positioning of a coin with an uneven surface on the aperture of the milliprobe (reference 43).

b. Radioisotope - excited X-ray fluorescence. This is 'non-dispersive' (reference 45).

takes can be quite diverse but two general principles are involved.

(i) A 'dispersive' construction which directs the sample X-ray output along a specified path to the detector, usually a xenon proportional counter (Fig. 10.4a, b). This path includes a diffraction at a lithium fluoride crystal which is bent to match the so-called Johannsen focusing system.[43] Satisfaction of optimum geometry for each energy (or wavelength) of X-ray requires sophisticated electro-mechanical control but this operation mode can give an energy resolution of as low as 40 keV in the spectral analysis.

(ii) At the cost of some loss of energy resolution a 'non-dispersive' technique has been developed with the practical gain of displacement of a bulky high-power X-ray tube (plus its weighty power supply) with either small artificial radioactive sources (Fig. 10.4b) [44] or a portable low-power X-ray source (Plate 10.3).[45] In this equipment the detector is 'energy-dispersive' in that the pulse heights of its output are proportional to the energy of the X-rays producing them. A 'lithium-drifted' germanium crystal has a resolution of as low as 160 keV as long as it is continuously held at liquid nitrogen temperature and a counting efficiency of almost 100% for an X-ray of 25 keV but cannot conveniently detect elements lighter than potassium. A silicon crystal similarly doped is some 40% less efficient at 25 keV (which corresponds to tin excitation) but more effective amongst lighter elements, limiting

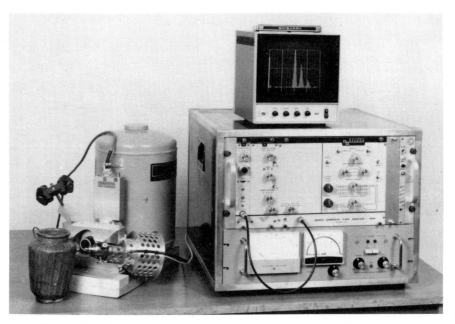

10.3 X-ray fluorescence equipment designed in the 'non-dispersive' mode, known as the Isoprobe. (Photograph: courtesy of the Research Laboratory for Archaeology and History of Art, Oxford University.)

only at sodium. Clearly the nature of the artefact largely controls the choice of instrumentation.

XRF detection limits tend to be somewhat poorer than those quoted for neutron activation analysis. Figures reported include: gold in a silver matrix, 0·05%; silver in a copper matrix, 0·01%, but such levels are usually more than adequate for the purpose of archaeological interpretation.

Two factors, in particular, control the accuracy of an XRF analysis:

(a) irregularity of a specimen's surface which upsets the geometry of the detection array (see Fig. 10.3, inset). A spacing of only $\Delta =$ 0·5 mm may cause a count-rate fall of as much as 45%, yet the contours of a coin or a bronze figure could certainly be that variation over small areas. This fall-off will affect all the constituent elements present so the usual solution to this problem in the case of a binary alloy is to measure the *ratio* of the concentrations of main constituents and evaluate absolute concentrations from calibration specimens of known composition. More complex alloys would require a detailed family of such calibration curves.

(b) The intensity of an analysis line in the X-ray energy spectrum may well be influenced by the presence of other impurities in the main matrix under study. Such 'matrix effects' can be appreciably reduced by setting up reference curves to cover the more obvious element mixtures like metal alloys but minor impurities are more difficult to deal with. For example, an unsuspected lead content of 10% in an alloy with a silver/copper weight ratio of 3/1 results in an overestimate of the silver content by more than 3%: lead atoms absorb the X-radiation from copper more readily than that from silver. A complex matrix, like brass, which may contain quite variable levels of zinc, lead and nickel, is difficult to analyse with great quantitative accuracy, except in its main components of copper and tin.

Notwithstanding these various practical difficulties XRF analysis has repeatedly proven 'competitive' with allied scientific techniques in the study of gold and silver coinage [46] while, for obvious reasons, the method has great value in glaze and gilding analyses where the interest in an object concentrates on a surface feature. The potential of the method's usage in pigment analysis amongst easel paintings and frescoes is only now under consideration.[47,48]

2b XRF STUDIES OF METALS

As with neutron activation results, by far the bulk of XRF literature concentrates on applications to coins. Chronological features centre upon periods of metal debasement in the major constituents caused either by economic necessity or monetary policy and technological changes that produce variations in minor element concentrations. In the following examples the linkage between art historical and scientific evidence is self-evident.

In the first category we may include the change over from an exclusively gold coinage to one exclusively of silver which occurred during the second half of the seventh century AD in Merovingian Gaul and the nearby kingdoms of the Anglo-Saxon Heptarchy.[49] This change has often been attributed to a growing gold-inflow limitation in the West caused by political upheaval in the Byzantine Empire. Merovingian leaders of the preceding century had aligned militarily with Byzantium in an attempt to hold off a Lombard invasion of Italy. Generous rewards and subsidies were presented in recognition of that support. However, civil wars and renewed Persian aggression drew the Imperial forces' attention to other frontiers and left the various states of Gaul very much to their own devices. The break is perhaps most obviously attested by the renunciation of allegiance to the Emperor expressed by Chlotar II, in 615, when he required the erstwhile Papal states to strike a currency in his own name.

By 630 it is likely that the gold stocks of the Merovingian realms were static but a stable political status built up by the ruler, Dagobert I, called for trading expansion without drainage of reserves. Controlled debasement has been suggested as the economic solution introduced at the time, followed by occasional revision of treasury attitudes at intervals over the following decades.[50] The XRF data indicates that coinage gold content followed a 'step-wise' decline, with alloying calculated in units of sevenths.[51] The coins were tariffed at 7 *siliquae* (a weight-standard derived from Byzantium) in gold/silver ratios of 6:2, 4:3 and so on (Plate 10.4).

Similar gold debasement has been identified in the mid-fifth century of the Visigoths and Suevi nations that settled in the Iberian peninsula at the beginning of the Dark Ages.[52] Until 575 (the reign of Leovigild) the Visigothic kings declined to put even their names of their *trientes* but preferred to retain a conventional portrait of the Byzantine Emperor, plus a blundered legend of his name. There is no indication of the time or place where these coins were struck. The XRF analysis undertaken recently offers the first detailed assay of that period's gold though dating implications based on change of alloy composition are still somewhat tenuous.

The coin information for the earlier Merovingian period (AD 580–655) has been utilized in the *terminus post quem* dating of a group of Anglo-Saxon gold jewellery.[53] The fineness of the alloys prepared in mints outside the central government area of Provençal fell well below official standards but it was this material that was used in making ornamental material like that illustrated in Plate (10.5a, b). However, this work did give some indication that the craftsmen making these delicate items limited their standards to a gold content of about 40% below which they were unwilling to go. As the seventh century wore on such fineness could only be maintained by re-melting older material (Plate 10.5b).

Amongst Anglo-Saxon *silver* coinage one quite striking feature of

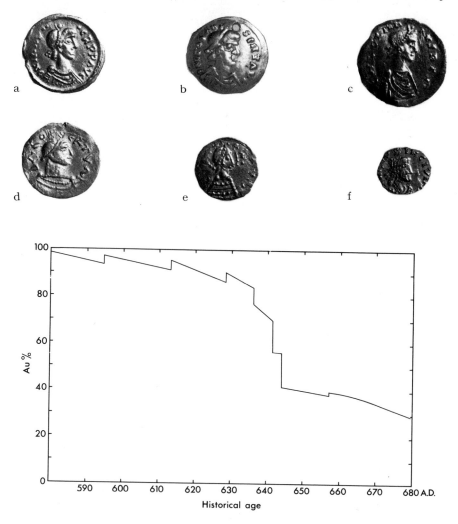

10.4 The fall in fineness of Merovingian gold coinage over the century AD 580–680, in the Provençal mints (particularly Marseilles, Arles, and Uzés). Specific analyses of some of these coins illustate the progress of this devaluation:

a. Solidus marked 'Maurice Tiberius', (c. AD 582–602) (Au: 97·3%)

b. Solidus marked 'Phocas', (c. AD 602–610) (Au: 97·2%)

c. Solidus of 'Clothaire II', (c. AD 613–627) (Au: 94·1%)

d. Solidus of 'Dagobert I', (c. AD 629–639) (Au: 88·4%)

e. Coin of Sigibert II, (c. AD 632–638) (Au: 44·8%)

The standard of coin fineness was consistently lower at mints, such as Paris, outside Provence. Coin f is an Elegius struck at Paris in the name of Dagobert I (Au: 73·0%) (compare with coin d above). This lower standard seems to have been applied in the making of Anglo-Saxon jewellery of the type illustrated in Plate 10·5. (Photographs: courtesy of Dr J. P. C. Kent, British Museum.)

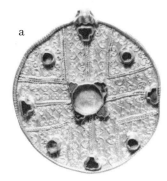

10.5   a. Jewelled bracteate set with garnets and blue glass, and filigree of beaded wire with pseudo-plaitwork. From Faversham, Kent, and datable to c. AD 600–633, stylistically.

Chemical composition, back: Au, 85%, Ag; 12·5% Cu, 2·5%.

loop: Au, 85·5%; Ag, 12·5%; Cu: 2%.

  b. Jewelled composite brooch with bronze cell walls and a gilt bronze rim: inset panels of gold filigree and bosses with gold collars. Found in a grave at Milton, Berkshire, and datable to AD 650, or a little later, stylistically.

Chemical composition, collar, central boss: Au, 58·5%; Ag, 38%; Cu, 3·5%.

Back of a filigree panel: Au, 61·5%; Ag, 37%; Cu, 1·5%.

(Photographs: courtesy of the Ashmolean Museum, Oxford; catalogue numbers, 1909.207 and 1836.59, respectively.)

technological change with time has been detected, that of deliberate introduction of zinc (in the matrix of calamine) during the alloying stage of the silver metal and the hardener, copper.[54] This seems to be a manufacturing procedure that stemmed from the progressive coinage debasement with brass-like alloy additives in preference to just more and more copper. The gradual build up of zinc content during the tenth and eleventh century is illustrated in Fig. 10.5. The reasons for this unconventional approach remain obscure.

Using a portable XRF unit, incorporating an X-ray excitation source of promethium-147 plus silicon (activation spectrum 12-45 keV), a broad survey of many massive bronzes and brasses in Italy has been undertaken including the Ephebi statue from Selinunte (fifth century BC) and the cathedral doors at Benevento (thirteenth century AD).[55] The presence of zinc (0·5–5·0%) in the medieval period is common but seems to be absent from pre-Christian metallurgy except in Roman

Fig. 10.5 Variation of zinc content in Anglo-Saxon silver coinage over the period AD 899–1016, for the reigns of Eadweard, The Elder: Aethelstan: Eadmund: Eadred: Eadwig: Eadgar and Aethelred II (reference 54).

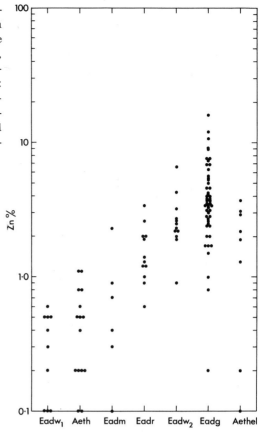

coinage and some small household goods. In sharp contrast, several recent fakes in statuary contain more than 10% zinc in their composition and thus are readily detected.

2c XRF-STUDIES OF EARLY CHINESE PORCELAINS

There is no question that the early Chinese blue-and-white porcelain of the fourteenth and fifteenth centuries hold the prime spot in the major collections around the world today. Why these wares should appeal to modern taste is not obvious but even a brief survey of porcelain styles of the past four centuries indicates that a Chinese interest in this colour scheme has been almost continuous. Indeed there are several sixteenth to eighteenth century pieces that carry imitative reign marks of emperors, like Hsüan Tê (1426–35) and Hung Wu (1368–98), of the early Ming period. Stylistically the quality of such material often defies confident dating.

Scientific interest initially has concentrated upon the cause of the wide variation in hue of the blue in the decoration, ranging from a dull greyish form (verging on black in some parts) to an almost pure

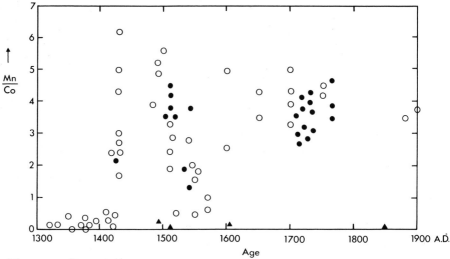

Fig. 10.6   Chronological variation of the ratio of manganese content and cobalt content in the glaze of Chinese blue-and-white porcelain (open circles) and in the blue reign marks on the bases of monochrome wares (solid circles). Analyses of four Persian wares, which presumably used local ores, are also included (solid triangles) (references 56–58).

ultramarine.[56] It was well-known that cobalt ores occur in two main forms in nature: (i) as asbolite which is much richer in manganese than cobalt and (ii) arsenic-rich, free of manganese. The asbolite form is the only one found in China while the arsenical form is common throughout Persia and the Middle East.

The evidence of XRF analysis of glazes on a large number of blue-and-white wares clearly indicates that only imported ores were used until early in the fifteenth century, prior to the Hsüan Tê period (Fig. 10.6).[57] By the middle of the sixteenth century the use of solely imported ore had ceased and was only occasionally in evidence in much-diluted form, mixed with local ores. Throughout that period no manganese-rich ore had come to light in Persia to account for the observed transition.

This work firmly dates the first exploitation of Chinese cobalt mines to the early part of the fifteenth century and refutes previous notions that imported blue was deliberately kept in stock for more refined pieces while native ores were used more freely for less sophisticated pieces. What factors control the quality of blue is still open to question but iron content [58] and firing conditions probably play their part.

3a MASS SPECTROSCOPY APPLIED TO PIGMENTS

Several elements, including sulphur, lead, carbon and oxygen, occur naturally in more than one isotopic form. Previous chapters of this book have discussed the pertinence of isotopic fractionation effects of carbon and oxygen in dating and climatology. Sulphur, too, suffers a similar fractionation though its cause is thought to be a bacterial reduction of soluble sulphates. Ordinary chemical processing, such as refining and smelting, has only a small effect upon the isotope ratios of elements in a raw ore used for pigment manufacture. Such ratios are therefore a reliable indicator of the geological source of that ore.

Chronological implications of sulphur and oxygen isotope ratios seem limited at present though very widely-used pigments, like vermilion (HgS) and the native ochres (mainly Fe_2O_3), would be involved. To begin with we have already taken note of the gradual replacement of the natural pigment, cinnabar, by its artificially-prepared equivalent, vermilion (section 1*d*). However, there are also customs records that illustrate how vermilion from China became increasingly popular amongst colour men during the second half of the eighteenth century, at the cost of Dutch manufacturers.[59] The history of ochre shows a similar 'shift of favour' amongst English artists of the post-Ramsay/ Reynolds era away from Dutch material towards Italian sienna.[60]

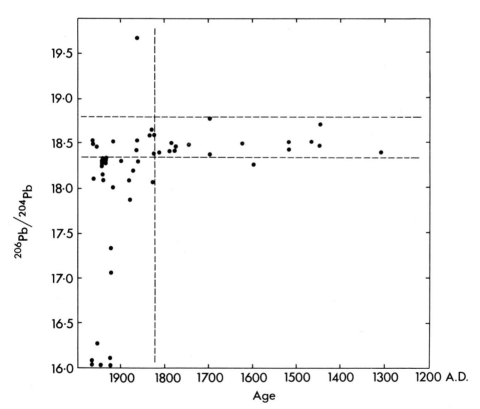

Fig. 10.7 Chronological variation of the isotope $^{206}Pb/^{204}Pb$ in lead white pigments from European paintings. The horizontal dashed lines encompass the known lead isotope ratios obtained from European ore sources (reference 26).

The possible use of $^{13}C/^{12}C$ ratio variations seems to hold far greater potential in pigment dating, particularly in unravelling the historical development of Prussian blue. This colour, which has no natural equivalent, was discovered in c. 1704–7 by the Berlin colour maker, Diesbach, when he accidentally used a contaminated potash during preparation of Florentine lake. The contaminant was blood which had calcinated with the alkali, forming a ferrocyanide. The iron vitriol in the lake recipe together with Diesbach's chance chemistry formulated KFe $[Fe(CN)_6]$, i.e. Prussian blue.

For some 170 years the pigment's manufacture from some form of animal matter derivatives was standard practice but several alternative techniques were introduced. In 1782 Scheele prepared it from ammonia and charcoal, in 1834 coal distillation products were involved and, in 1860, waste from coal gas purification provided useful calcium ferrocyanide. Then, in 1878, Geles suggested use of carbon disulphide made from charcoal while, at the beginning of this century, the pigment's source of carbon was derived from coke. Since then the use of coke has been superseded in turn by carbon monoxide and methane.

Each of the carbon sources are distinctive in their isotope ratios, as the data of Fig. 3.4 has already illustrated.[61] For example, fractionation levels for coal and methane are $\delta^{13}C = -25‰$ and $-38‰$, respectively, which are readily distinguishable in mass spectroscopy analysis.[62–64] Such differences in δ-values are a measure of technological change over a century.

In conclusion this chapter moves full circle to discuss once more properties of the most important pigment in Western art, lead white. The isotopic composition of lead changes with time due to radiogenic production from uranium and thorium decay: ^{206}Pb is the end product for the ^{238}U-chain, ^{207}Pb for the ^{235}U-chain and ^{208}Pb for the ^{232}Th-chain. There is also another stable lead isotope found in nature, ^{204}Pb, of constant abundance. Fractionation now depends upon the geological age of the raw galena ore from which the pigment was produced.

Before the middle of the nineteenth century the sources of lead in Europe were quite limited and of quite similar geological age. Correspondingly, artists' pigments of that period show only a limited isotope ratio variation (usually measured in terms of $^{206}Pb/^{204}Pb$) as illustrated in Fig. 10.7. However, after 1820, a general trade expansion led to new supplies arriving from Australia, Canada and the United States. In response to this a much wider isotope ratio scatter is observed. The obvious potential of this work is in painting authentication and even isotope 'fingerprinting' of specific artists. Sampling requirements of less than a microgram and a reproducibility of ratio determination usually better than $\pm 0.1\%$ gives lead analysis an extra appeal.

Appendix A

Chronology of Climatic Change

INTRODUCTION

Many dating applications are concerned with the timing of a transition of some sort in ancient man's life pattern. Very often these transitions are stimulated by a climatic event in a quite obvious way. For example, glacial advance could force hunters off the plains and back to a cave-dwelling existence or, as in the case of the Neanderthals some 60,000 years ago, who moved to the Mediterranean coast, cause a widescale migration. Temporary settlement could relate to a brief halt in such advance during one of the warm oscillations which so often seem to accompany the principal glacial-interglacial changes of the past.

Warmth encourages vegetation, persuades insects and larger fauna to invade fresh lands or return to old habitats, probably long before humans re-establish themselves. Consequently climate-sensitive species, in their population fluctuations in a certain region, can act as indicators of the passage of time. Then matching of similar fluctuations between regions can indicate that they and their associated archaeological artefacts are contemporaneous. This is the basis of age determination over the past 14,000 years discussed below, using either pollen horizons or mollusc fauna. Oxygen isotope analysis largely serves not only to quantify the temperature changes that the existence of these horizons imply, but also gives us an indication of detailed climatic conditions over a much longer time scale of at least 120,000 years. But first an outline of the principles of varve chronology which has supplied, along with the radiocarbon method, several of the absolute dates which pollen horizons now carry (Fig. A1).

I VARVE CHRONOLOGY

In lakes near the edge of a glacier's retreat a layer of sediment is formed with a distinctive structure. During the summer, when the melting rate is at its height, gravel, sand and clay are discharged into the lake. Coarser material promptly sinks but it may be some while after the onset of winter's cold before the much finer clay particles settle out to form a compact deposit. The following year the same process will occur all over again. Each annual layer, called a 'varve' stands out as the heavier gravels are distinctly paler in colour than the overlying lighter clay.

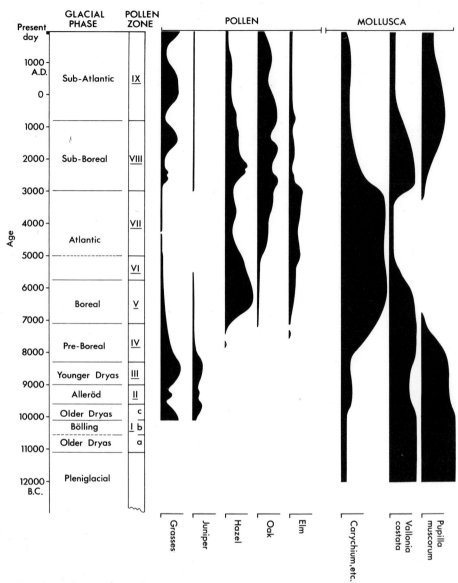

Fig. A.1 Chronology of climatic change, together with associated variations in concentration of pollen and mollusca (references 8, 11 and 25).

There is an obvious analogy here between the structure of a varve and that of an annual growth ring of wood used in dendrochronology. A hot dry summer produces a thick varve, a cold wet summer produces a thin one. By cross-linking the varve thickness patterns of adjacent regions Gerard de Geer was able to track and date the complete 3,600-year retreat of glaciers from southern Sweden and Denmark since the last Ice Age.[1] This floating sequence was then tied to similar varve patterns in river estuaries (due to rhythmic annual flooding)[2] that spans some 7,500 years through to about AD 700. In this way the beginnings of the present warm era (often called the Holocene) are reckoned to date to 10700 BC with no more than a couple of hundred years uncertainty.[3]

Glacial retreat allows arboreal advance so that comprehensive spectra of pollen contained in varves can be given time markers on a regional basis. The accurate positioning, at 6850 BC, of alder's appearance in Sweden (the so-called Å-boundary) is a good example of this principle.[4] The same pollen spectra may be found in nearby peat deposits which, unlike the varve sediments, contain archaeological assemblages. Thus the latter are dated, albeit indirectly, with the high precision that varve layer counting permits.

The broadening of varve chronology to American glacial regions has not been at all simple.[5] Wisconsin deposits have been dated to around 9350–8200 BC, by matching forest pollen spectra there with that of Scandinavia in the Stockholm and Helsinki areas, and varve sequences have been set up as far back as 17500 BC. Unfortunately these same early levels yield radiocarbon ages that are younger by some 8,000 years. The varve sequences may not be the place to look for the source of these discrepancies but the American material is complicated by evidence of simultaneous advance and retreat in different sectors of the glacier front.

Similar contradictions appear at the Lake of the Clouds, in Minnesota, where comparison has been made between the chronology of varve-like sediment layers (formed from algae microfragments) and their corresponding radiocarbon dates.[6] Some 9,530 algae-varve years matches a conventional radiocarbon date of only 8800 BP, i.e. a discrepancy of some 730 years. But this radiocarbon age ties in with only 8,700 years of Swedish clay varves. Thus we are talking of a 9 per cent difference between the two varve-counting systems at this time. It is clear that the ideal link up of continents on a varve time scale lies some way into the future.

2 POLLEN ANALYSIS

Pollen grains are the male reproductive structures produced by seed-bearing vegetation. Every year they are shed in their thousands and may travel many miles by wind or air current transportation. Nature's 'statistics' offer very few chances of female plant fertilization so the vast majority of the 'pollen rain' falls to the ground and gradually becomes an integral part of the soil structure.[7] Microbiological activity and some chemical and physical attrition soon removes mineral portions of the pollen so that only the organic grain walls are ultimately preserved in a fossil record (Plate A.1).

Predictably the best pollen records are stored in lake sediments and water-logged peat deposits where anaerobic (i.e. oxygen-starved) conditions inhibit bacterial attack of the grains.[8] But certain soil

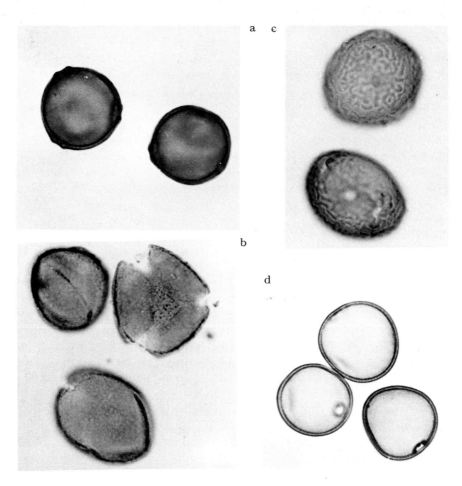

a c

b

d

A.1 Fossil pollen remains: a. Hazel (*Corylus avellana*) b. Oak (*Quercus petraea*) c. Elm (*Ulmus procera*) d. Common Bent (*Agrostis tenuis*), a grass of the type that may have formed part of the *Gramineae* of pollen zone III. (Photographs: courtesy of Professor G. W. Dimbleby, Institute of Archaeology, London.)

conditions, such as high acidity (pH value less than 5·5), aridity [9] or low temperature, allow such fossil records to exist in dry-land conditions also. The mechanism of pollen preservation and context location is then a stabilization in humic material which resists downward migration under the influence of ground water percolation.

The chronological features of a pollen record lie in the variation of concentration of a particular species with deposit depth (Fig. A1).[10] The emergence or disappearance of a tree species in a burial context can act as a time marker for relative dating purposes that is just as valuable as recognition of a new pottery or lithic style. Unfortunately the profile of a single species is usually ambiguous as it undulates with the passage of time. For example, European oak seems to have passed through four broad periods of importance in forest composition over the past 5,000 years so that, in a partial pollen record it would be difficult to 'float' a profile into its correct time slot with confidence.

However, a pollen 'spectrum' at any given level, encompassing several species all at once, can be much more informative. Some species so dominate certain periods of the past, that they can define pollen zones. Thus hazel characterizes the zones designated v and vi in Europe while the zone boundary is set by other features such as a distinct pine decline in zone v. Elm decline marks the beginning of zone viii reasonably sharply while the emergence of beech (not illustrated) is a feature that strongly marks the opening of the most recent zone, ix. Understandably as pollen spectra act as climate indicators in most circumstances this zonation system is not only numerical but also carries corresponding glacial phase names, such as 'Sub-Atlantic', with which the reader might be more familiar. (Fig. A1).[11]

Pollen analysis owes its absolute time scale to radiocarbon dating of the various zone boundaries. Thus we now speak of the zone iii to iv transition not just as the 'juniper stage' marking the swing of vegetation composition from grass-dominated open tundra, via a shrub era, to complete forestation, but as a major ecological change that occurred close to 8300 BC. Similarly, the 'elm-decline' era of the vii–viii transition is pinpointed to the quite short span of the first 400 years of the first millennium BC.

Certainly these two transitions can be correlated to climate changes that effect almost the whole of the European continent. The first ties in with the swift increase in warmth that matches the end of the last glacial period and is regarded by some as definitive of the Pleistocene-Holocene boundary (see Fig. 1.4). The second ties in with the unpleasant deterioration of weather that turned many forest regions into marshland during the Late Bronze Age of human activity and caused extensive site abandonment.

But much of recent research in this subject has indicated a far stronger, often unwitting, human agency in several of these changes. For example, blanket peat formation on Exmoor,[12] the Pennines [13] and in various upland regions of Wales [14], around 800 BC, are no longer simply attributed to an enhancement of soil acidity caused by high rainfall leaching of an originally calcareous environment. We must also take into consideration the nutrient stress created by stock grazing in the woodland so that the ecological balance is tipped as soil regeneration processes are suppressed. Similarly, while the major elm decline around the same time can also be explained by tree species dislike of acidic soils, in Ireland the process was accelerated in its later stages by man's fuller use of elm as a source of cattle fodder and for making bark bread.[15]

Several other incursions of man upon Nature's domain have been documented in this way, notably a brief deforestation in south-east England around 170,000 years ago (witnessed by a sharp hazel decline and a sudden leap in non-arboreal *Gramineae* concentration) that couples to the appearance of Palaeolithic artefacts in local archaeological levels.[16] Oscillatory features in the arboreal/non-arboreal composition of the pollen diagram often speak of the uphill battle fought by early man in his land reclamation exercises.

Pollen analysis had some swift early successes amongst the well-preserved burials of Tollund and Grauballe Man in the peat bogs of Denmark [17] and has proved invaluable in dating several items found embedded in peat deposits, such as ploughs, with little or no typological history of their own.

At the same time many aspects of farming history have been written on the basis of pollen information. Interesting in this respect is the story of ivy which, while a critical plant species for climate variations (sharply rising in concentration at the zone v/vi boundary and fading away shortly after the vii/viii transition), often appears with anomalously high concentration in pollen spectra.[18] In normal pollen rain ivy would rarely occur at more than a 1 per cent level compared with arboreal material even during its 'heyday' in the past, yet at some occupation sites it is a dominant species in the burial context. This is thought to be due to an overprinting of the normal pollen record by man's usage of this plant for animal winter fodder. Typical of this effect is the 40 per cent ivy contribution to the spectrum at the 5000 BC level of the Mesolithic rock shelter at Baulmes, in Switzerland. There faunal evidence, though admittedly sparse, suggests red deer herding.

In a quite different way certain plant species allow us to plot the diversification of agriculture. Meadowgrass, red clover and foxtail in the pollen record speak of exploitation of grazing pastures [19] while plantain and goosefoot are conclusive evidence of nearby cereal cultivation.

Outside Europe, pollen analysis is still in its infancy but encouraging results have already been obtained in Mexico [20] and Arizona,[21] tracing the origins of grain growing and early man's response to a hostile environment in that region. Pollen spectra are now available over the range AD 500–1400 and they show good agreement with tree-ring width variations over the same period, thus seeming to act as equally sensitive long-term climate indicators.[22] Most recently, pollen diagrams have been set up in both south and north Greece.[23,24] In the latter region olive pollen passes through two periods of major cultivation. The first phase covers the Middle Bronze Age to Mycenaean times (c. 1900–1300 BC) while the second phase spans the early Classical era (c. 1050–500 BC). The brief intermediate olive decline has been attributed to a discouragement of the farming community as wars ravaged their lands. Olive groves need attention and the trees themselves take some twenty years to mature.

3 LAND AND FRESHWATER MOLLUSCA ANALYSIS

Whilst acidity suits pollen preservation, neutral and alkaline conditions are needed for survival of a mollusca fossil record, as their mineral shell is made of calcium carbonate. The term 'mollusc' covers a very diverse group of fauna, including freshwater mussels and both gill-breathing and lung-breathing forms of snail. Though the latter group (notably the family *Helix*) have adapted to life on land they are still not sufficiently evolved to be able to withstand water loss so their habitat is controlled by humidity of environment. Thus remains of almost all mollusca species are concentrated in fluviatile sediments or sheltered cave deposits that could provide a moist, cool day-time habitat.

In contrast to pollen rain, mollusc distribution lacks mobility, though slopewashes and some wind scattering can provide a secondary transportation mechanism. Thus a mollusc spectrum in an archaeological deposit is strongly susceptible to local environmental factors such as density of vegetation and soil texture, rather than rainfall level.

The composition of a mollusc population alters in response to changes in environment, often in a manner closely akin to the pollen concentration changes in the same region (Fig. A.1).[25] However, mollusc population profiles often appear to be slightly displaced on the same time scale, as their rate of dispersion into fresh areas that are ecologically acceptable is slow, while, in harder times, some mollusc species show quite a prolonged resistance to displacement.[26] Also some species show a remarkable degree of adaptability. For example the land snail, *Pupilla muscorum*, was a major species in the post-glacial era around 10,000 years ago, at which time it seemed to prefer marshland conditions. Today that species has re-emerged as one preferring a drier habitat.

Spread of some species of mollusca has a human agency rather than one controlled by climate variations. Indeed these movements are usually much faster than any induced by natural forces. The best documented example of this is the transportation of the snail types used for food *Helix pomatia* and *Helix aspersa*, which were restricted to temperate regions of Europe until the last century but are now common species in the New World and in the southern hemisphere.[27] At other times the human interference with ecological conditions, mainly through forest clearance and agriculture, has accidentally opened up new habitats for mollusc dispersal.

Despite the kind of difficulties outlined here some detailed mollusc zonation as a function of time has been achieved in central Europe [28] and south-east England,[29] for the Holocene epoch. Some index species for the latter area are shown in Fig. A.1 and Plate A.2. *Pupilla muscorum* decline during the IV pollen transition matches the vegetation shift from open country to forestation, while northerly elements, such as *Carychium* and *Cochlicopa* eventually became dominant in the mollusc spectrum. *Vallonia costata* appears to have coped with forest

A.2   Important index species of land and freshwater mollusca: a. *Pupilla muscorum* (magn. ×6), b. *Cochlicopa* (magn. ×6), c. *Carychium tridentata* (magn. ×10) and d. *Vallonia costata* and *Vallonia excentrica* (magn. ×6). (Photographs: courtesy of Dr J. G. Evans, Department of Archaeology, University College, Cardiff.)

encroachment until about 6000 BC, but is as drastically reduced in population throughout the early part of pollen VII (the era of elm decline). However, the rapid recovery of this species at the time of Neolithic clearance activities make it a critical time marker. Several other species, notably *Vallonia excentrica* and *Pupilla muscorum* eventually took note of the new open conditions and dominated the mollusc spectrum during the early part of pollen zone VIII. Understandably more recent spectra contain strong elements of species introduced by man in the Roman period (such as *Helix aspersa* and *Monacha coantiana*), plus medieval additions, such as *Helicella virgata*.

Although this data now looks quite convincing, molluscan chronology remains largely untested. An exception to this is a recent study of several sites on the chalk hills of Wiltshire where the activity of prehistoric farmers is clearly detectable.[30] In the same paper a critical comparison is made between information gained from pollen and land-snail analysis, underlining several of the problems of both subjects outlined above.

4   OXYGEN ISOTOPE ANALYSIS

A quite different approach to past climatic variation is provided by fractionation effects that occur amongst the natural isotopes of oxygen. The typical abundances of these isotopes are: $^{16}O;99.76\%$: $^{17}O;0.037\%$: $^{18}O;0.204\%$, but, as with carbon, certain environmental parameters can cause very slight variations in these levels. For example, on thermodynamic grounds, the molecular oxygen isotope ratio in calcium carbonate precipitated out of water is related to the prevailing temperature (T degrees Celsius) by the equation,

$$T = 16 \cdot 5 - 4 \cdot 3 \, (\delta_c - \delta_w) + 0 \cdot 14 \, (\delta_c - \delta_w)^2 \qquad (A.1)^{31}$$

where, in usual isotope analysis nomenclature (suffix c for carbonate and suffix s for standard),

$$\delta_c(\permil) = \frac{\{^{18}O^{16}O/^{16}O_2\}_c - \{^{18}O^{16}O/^{16}O_2\}_s}{\{^{18}O^{16}O/^{16}O_2\}_s} \times 10^3 \qquad (A.2)$$

This isotope analysis shares the PDB standard (Carolina Peedee Formation belemnite) used in radiocarbon dating in much of the literature [32] but it is also common to find reference to a *SMOW* standard ('standard mean ocean water' standard quoted as conditions are in present day).[33] Unfortunately these standards differ as,

$$0\permil, \text{ PDB scale} \equiv + 0 \cdot 2\permil, \text{ SMOW scale}$$

This might seem a small quantity, but equation (A.1) indicates a difference in zero on a temperature scale which would amount to almost 1°C, using a typical δ_c of 2‰. Conventional measurement with a mass spectrometer carries an experimental error of about $\pm 0 \cdot 1\permil$, but almost an order of magnitude improvement is possible using a recently-developed fast neutron activation method.[34]

Oxygen isotope analysis would appear to have some obvious advantages over pollen or mullusca records in pre-Holocene climatic analysis as continuous sedimentation of the ocean bottom with fossil planktonic foraminifera (tiny crustaceans that shed their calcereous shells when they die) provides several million years' worth of data in long drill corings.[35] However, interpretation of foraminifera data is complicated, as δ_w-variation in the past is regarded as very much a reality, thus upsetting any simple *T versus* δ_c correlation as a fixed δ_w would allow in equation (A.1). During each interglacial the ice continents transfer appreciable amounts of their bulk into the oceans, reducing the mean δ_w-value proportionately. Temperature of the water in itself, plays only a secondary role in the fractionation process. Consequently for several years, isotope variation with time has been recognized more as a 'palaeoglaciation' rather than 'palaeotemperature' indicator.

Worse still, there are now strong indications, from analysis of various species of foraminifera collected in plankton tows with the isothermal layer of the Indian Ocean (about 50 metres below the surface), that these organisms can deposit carbonate of an isotopic composition differing slightly from the thermodynamically-predicted value.[36] For example, at one sampling station (admittedly the one with most extreme data), δ-values of $-2 \cdot 77\permil$, $-2 \cdot 50\permil$ and $-1 \cdot 98\permil$ (relative to PDB standard) were recorded for the three species, *Globigerinoides ruber*, *Globigerinoides sacculifer* and *Pulleniatina obliquiloculata*, respectively (Plate A.3, a–c). Predictions of ocean temperature could then differ by as much as 2·8°C. The future direction of this research is now in question.

In polar regions, the picture of oxygen fractionation that occurs during ice formation follows somewhat simpler rules with air temperature almost entirely controlling δ-variation.[37] There are similarities here between ice-sheet build up and the tree-ring addition mechanism of dendrochronology in that each year's snow deposition would initially carry an internal δ-profile including a summer maximum and a winter minimum. But molecular diffusion in the solid ice would have eventually obliterated these detailed oscillations. However, stepwise analysis of a mile-long core extracted at Camp Century in Greenland, using broader

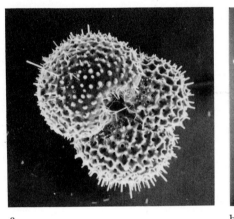
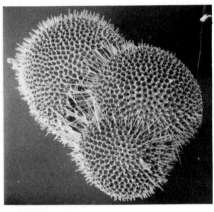

a   b

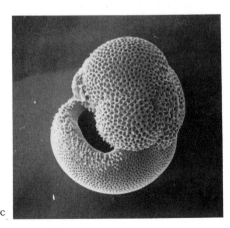

c

A.3 Foraminifera collected in plankton tows in the isothermal layer of the Indian Ocean: a. *Globigerinoides ruber*, b. *Globigerinoides sacculifer* and c. *Pulleniatina obliquiloculata* as viewed in scanning electron micrographs. (Photographs: courtesy of Mr H. A. Buckley, British Museum Natural History, London.)

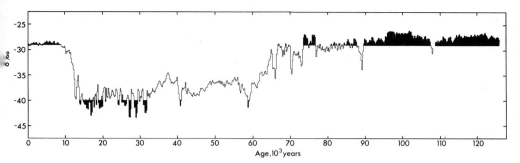

Fig. A.2   The continuous δ-record for oxygen isotope analysis in ice cores at
Camp Century, Greenland. Fitting of smooth curves to the 200 year
increment data indicates 'typical' δ-values for inter-glacial phases
(δ = −29‰) and for glacial phases (δ = −40‰) as highlighted here
by blackened data (reference 38).

10-year portions of ice deposition, has provided a remarkable picture of
climate covering a period of more than 0·12 million years, the final
section of which is shown in Fig. A.2.[38] The Pleniglacial δ-value of
close to − 40‰ is about 11‰ below the present Holocene level, a
difference equivalent to almost 14°C movement in temperature. Note
how the isotope curve is comfortably sensitive enough to detect the
well-established short-term climate fluctuations known as the Alleröd
and Bölling phases at the Pleistocene/Holocene boundary.

    There is some comparable faunal data available from a few British
sites such as Hoxne and Swanscombe but little zonation has been
possible yet within individual interglacials.[39] Little is known about
fauna of the Pleistocene cold phases but the limited number of species
would restrict its value. In contrast the decade-by-decade oxygen
isotope information provides clear evidence of several sharp climate
excursions, notably two in last interglacial at around 89,000 and 108,000
years ago.

    Even with this ice-core data any direct δ-to-temperature translation
as quoted above should be treated cautiously if only because deeper
strata originated further inland where slightly different climatic
conditions existed. Additionally we must accept that a major increase
(or decrease) of the ice-sheet's surface altitude would accompany a
general cooling (or warming) of the atmosphere. Both effects work in
the same direction to exaggerate a δ-change and it is not yet possible to
distinguish between the individual contributions.

Appendix B

Thermoluminescence Dating Using the Pre-dose Method

INTRODUCTION

In Fig. 5.6, the thermoluminescence (TL) glow-curve of quartz extracted from pottery and laboratory irradiated exhibits an intense peak at 100°C. We would not expect this peak to be of any value in dating within the concepts of TL energy storage outlined there: it would not appear in a natural TL curve because the ambient ground temperature of about 20°C in burial media would be quite sufficient to cause disruption of the electron-defect link responsible for that peak within a matter of hours.

However, this 100°C peak possesses the unusual characteristic of retaining a memory of its radiation history, despite the decay away of the electrons produced by that radiation. The memory can be 'unlocked' by a 500°C heating which activates an enhancement of the peak's radiation sensitivity quantitatively linked to the magnitude of the previous radiation dose. No enhancement can be induced by this heating in the absence of pre-irradiation of 'pre-dose'. These concepts are illustrated in Fig. B.1 for a pottery fragment from the medieval site of Nuneaton, England.[1]

When the pottery is being made the high temperatures of kiln-firing (well in excess of 500°C) violently agitate the crystal structure: impurities diffuse about the lattice and some defects are annealed out. But when the pottery has cooled down after removal from the kiln everything is stable once more. Then we expect the distribution of impurities and defects to be much more controlled by the cooling conditions of the manufacturing stage and any memory of geologically-conditioned radiation damage has been literally physically erased. (Critical temperatures in this mechanism are probably the quartz transition points at 573°C (α- to β-quartz) and 870°C (β-quartz to β-tridymite).) Brief 500°C heatings are ineffectual in lattice disruption.

In the pre-dose dating process the sensitivity of the 100°C peak of each quartz portion is measured under various conditions· of pretreatment, using a 'test dose', typically 1 rad or less (Fig. B.1).

(i) S_0 is measured prior to any heat or pre-dose treatment. It repre-

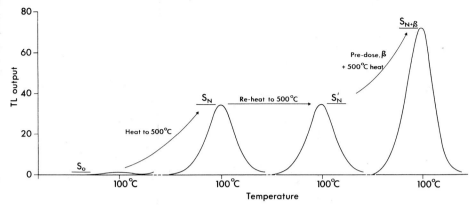

Fig. B.1   Procedure of TL sensitivity determination using the pre-dose technique (reference 1).

sents the sensitivity of the quartz immediately after its removal from the kiln.

(ii) S_N and S_N' are measured after successive 500°C heatings. That these sensitivities are, to all intents and purposes, equal indicates that *heat alone* cannot cause sensitivity enhancement in this peak.

At this point a laboratory pre-dose of β-radiation is applied and all the TL associated with it drained away by a further 500°C heating.

(iii) $S_{N+\beta}$ is measured after this treatment. The change, $S_N \rightarrow S_{N+\beta}$ quantifies the impact of the pre-dose, β.

Thus we can attribute the growth, $S_0 \rightarrow S_N$ to the impact of an archaeological pre-dose, Q, and write, on a proportionality basis:

$$Q = \frac{S_N - S_0}{S_{N+\beta} - S_N} \times \beta \text{ rads} \qquad \text{(B.1)}$$

Of course Q rads is, directly, the archaeological dose experienced by the ceramic: this sensitivity enhancement process does not suffer from any supralinearity problems as met in the more conventional high temperature methods described in Chapter 5.

For the Nuneaton example, $S_0 = 1 \cdot 2$ light units, $S_N = 34 \cdot 3$ light units, $S_N' = 34 \cdot 4$ light units and $S_{N+\beta} = 72 \cdot 0$ light units for a pre-dose, $\beta = 335$ rads. Duly Q evaluates as 295 rads.

Hereafter TL dating proceeds in much the same way as the high temperature inclusion method, utilizing the pottery fabric's internal β-dose and the burial environment's external γ-dose in combination to provide an annual dose-rate. For the study sherd, $\beta = 0 \cdot 33$ rad per year, and $\gamma = 0 \cdot 15$ rad per year (including a cosmic-ray component) yielding a TL date of AD 1360, consistent with an archaeological estimate, AD 1330–50.

Unfortunately the pre-dose technique is largely limited in application to the past millennium or so, as the 100°C peak's sensitivity cannot be

B.1 *The Penelli Sarcophagus*, in the Etruscan style. (Photograph: courtesy of the Trustees of the British Museum, London.)

B.2 *Crowned Buddha*, seated with his hands in Dhyanamudra. Khmer (Angkor Wat style), c. twelfth century AD (Photograph: courtesy of Spink & Son, Ltd, London.)

increased indefinitely with more and more pre-dose. Sensitivity enhancement (at present attributed to a process of luminescence efficiency increase with dose [2]) eventually saturates for natural pre-dose levels of around 500 rads while deviation from linearity of the enhancement *versus* pre-dose curve usually set in at 300 rads or less. But away from saturation problems, routine archaeological dating has proved to be straight forward with an accuracy of $\pm 7\%$.

The Nuneaton data, which is typical of most pottery fabrics, illustrates the most attractive feature of the new method. As the rate of sensitivity enhancement is close to 10% per rad of pre-dose applied even material less than a century old often has well-resolved S_0 and S_N values, so accurate age determination is practical. A case in point is the sarcophagus of Plate B.1, which purports to be Etruscan (c. sixth century BC) but, in fact, is a fake.[3] It was made by the Penelli brothers in 1860, using as their model the well-known Campana sarcophagus which they were responsible for restoring at the Louvre Museum some years earlier. Several other authenticity analyses of this nature have been reported.[4]

The pre-dose method has also been extremely effective in dating and authentication of many bronzes, particularly those from South-East Asia and Nigeria, using the ceramic-like casting core they contain. These cores are characteristically black in colour, rich in quartz and seem to contain appreciable amounts of charcoal fragments. For some reason this type of fabric rarely gives any significant high temperature TL but exhibits large enhancement rates in the 100°C peak, such as the 33% per rad measured for the Crowned Buddha of Plate B.2. The sand-like cores commonly found in Renaissance bronzes and those of this century (such as the products of Degas [5]) are also amenable to this approach.

Notes

I ASPECTS OF ARCHAEOLOGICAL CHRONOLOGY

1 PIGGOTT. S., 1965: *Ancient Europe* (Edinburgh).

2 CHILDE, V. G., 1939: *American Journal of Archaeology, XLIV*, 10.
CHILDE, V. G., 1949: *Antiquity, XXIII*, 129.
CHILDE, V. G., 1950: *Antiquity, XXIV*, 4.

3 RENFREW, C., 1971: *Scientific American*, 63.

4 SHEPARD, F. P., 1964: *Science, 143*, 574.
BROECKER, W. S., BENDER, M. L., 1972: in *Calibration of Hominoid Evolution*, 19 (eds. W. W. Bishop, J. A. Miller. Edinburgh).

5 PENNY, L. F., COOPE, G. R., CATT, J. A., 1969: *Nature, 224*, 65.

6 Studies of ancient man's crops include,
SCHELLENBERG, H. C., 1908: in *Explorations in Turkestan: Expedition of 1904* (Part 3), 471 (ed. R. Pumpelly).
NETOLITZKY, F., 1914: Sitzungsberichte Kaiserlichen Akademie Wissenchaften, *123, 725*.
EDMAN, G., SODERBERG, E., 1929: *Bulletin, Geological Society of China, 8*, 363.
HELBECK, H., 1959, *Archaeology, 12*, 183.
HELBECK, H., 1961; *Archaeology, 14*, 95.
WATANABE, N., 1968: *Journal of the Faculty of Science, University of Tokyo, section V, 3*, 217.

7 DIMBLEBY, G. W., 1969: in *Science in Archaeology*, 167 (ed. D. Brothwell, E. Higgs. London).
WEST, R. G., 1968: *Pleistocene Geology and Biology*, 294 (London).
MARTIN, P. S., 1963: *The Last 10,000 years: a Fossil Pollen Record of the American Southwest* (Tucson, Arizona).

8 JOHNSEN, S. J., DANSGAARD, W., CLAUSEN, H. B., LANGWAY, C. C., 1972: *Nature, 235*, 429. This is a study of climate covering the past 1.2×10^5 years while a close look at more recent times is given in by the same authors in a 1970 paper; *Nature, 227*, 482.

9 FROMM, E., 1970: in *Radiocarbon Variations and Absolute Chronology*, 163 (ed. I. U. Olsson. Stockholm) and the paper by H. Tauber that continues the discussion (p. 173).

10 COOPE, G. R., BROPHY, J. A., 1972: *Boreas, 1*(2), 97.
BUCKLAND, P. C., KENWARD, H. K., 1973: *Nature, 241*, 405.

11 EVANS, J. G., 1969: *World Archaeology, 1*(2), 170.

12 EDWARDS, I. E. S., 1970: *Philosophical Transactions, Royal Society* (London), *A 269*, 11.

13 HAYES, W. C., 1970: in *The Cambridge Ancient History, I*, 175. (Cambridge).

14 Data derived, to a large extent from Hood, S., 1973: in *Symposium über die Entstehung und Chronologie der Badener Kultur*, 111 (Slovak Academy of Science, Bratislava).

15 CASKEY, J. L., 1956: *Hesperia XXV* (2), 147.

16 GOLDMAN, H., 1956: *Tarsus II*, 238 (item 235) (Princeton).

17 SACHS, A., 1970: *Philosophical Transactions, Royal Society* (London), *A269*, 19.

18 JACOBSEN, T., 1939: *Oriental Institute of the University of Chicago, Assyriological Studies II.*

19 LANGDON, S. H., FOTHERINGHAM, J. K., 1928: *The Venus Tablets of Ammizaduqa* (Oxford).

20 BRANIGAN, K., 1968: *Studi Micenei ed Egeo-Anatolici, 5*, 12.
XANTHOUDIDES, S., 1924: *The Vaulted Tombs of Mesara* (London).

21 HALLO, W. W., BUCHANAN, B., 1965: *Studies in Honour of Bruno Landsberger*, 199 (Chicago).

22 BIBBY, G., 1958: *Antiquity, XXXII*, 243.

23 LAMBERG-KARLOVSKY, C. C., 1972: *Journal of the American Oriental Society, 92, 222.*

24 LANGDON, S., 1931: *Journal of the Royal Asiatic Society*, 295.

25 DURING-CASPERS, E. C. L., 1972: *Bulletin, Institute of Archaeology* London, *10*, 83.

26 HAVERNICK, T. E., 1965: *Jahrbuch des Romisch-Germanischen Zentral museums* (Mainz), *12*, 35.

27 HOOD, S., 1973: *World Archaeology, 5*, 187.

28 RANDSBORG, K., 1967: *Acta Archaeologica XXXVIII*, 1.

29 COOK, R. M., 1966: *Greek Painted Pottery*, 263 (London).

30 COOK, R. M., 1971: *The Journal of Hellenistic Studies, XCL*, 137.

31 CHANG, K.-C., 1968: *The Archaeology of Ancient China*, 228 and 258 (New Haven, Conn.)

32 TUNG TSO-PIN, 1945: *Yin li p'u* (Lichuang, Academica Sinica).

33 VITA-FINZI, C., 1973: *Recent Earth History*, 35 (London).

34 FLINT, R. J., 1971: *Glacial and Quarternary Geology*, 379 (New York).

35 HAMMEN, T. VAN DER, 1967: *Geologien mijnbouw, 19*, 250.

36 MÜLLER-BECK, H., 1966: *Science, 152*, 1191.

37 CERNOHOUZ, J., SOLC, I., 1966: *Nature, 212*, 806.

38 ATKINSON, I. A. E., SWINDALE, L. D., 1971: *Nature, 233*, 406.

39 HAY, R. L., JONES, B. F., 1972: *Geological Society of America Bulletin, 83*, 317.

40 REED, R., 1972: *Ancient Skins, Parchments and Leathers*, 313 (London).

41 BURTON, D., POOLE, J. B., REED, R., 1959: *Nature, 184*, 533.

42 DEL MEDICO, H. E., 1958: *The Riddle of the Scrolls* (trans. by H. Garner. London).

43 STACCIOLI, G., TAMBURINI, U., 1973: in *Application of Science in Examination of Works of Art*, 235 (Museum of Fine Arts, Boston).

2 DENDROCHRONOLOGY

1 DOUGLASS, A. E., 1928: *Carnegie Institute Washington Publ., 289* (part 2), 97.

2 DOUGLASS, A. E., 1935: *National Geographic Society, Contributed papers, Pueblo Bonito Series, 1.*

3 FRITTS, H. C., SMITH, D. G. and STOKES, M. A., 1965: *American Antiquity, 31,* 101.

4 SCHOVE, D. J., 1966: *Cycles, 12,* 271.

5 DOUGLASS, A. E., 1951: *Tree-Ring Bulletin, 17* (part 4), 31.

6 FRITTS, H. C., 1966: *Science, 154,* 973.

7 LIESE, W., 1970: in *Mitteilungen Bundesforschungsanstalt für Forst-und Holzwirtschaft,* Reinbeck, 77, 1.

8 HUBER, B., GIERTZ, V., 1970: in *Scientific Methods in Medieval Archaeology,* 201 (ed. R. Berger. Berkeley).

9 BANNISTER, B., 1969: in *Science in Archaeology,* 191 and Plate XII (ed. D. Brothwell and E. Higgs. London).

10 GLOCK, W. E., REED, E. L., SR., 1940: *Science, 91,* 98.

11 RHOADS, A. S., 1923: *U.S. Dept. Agric. Bulletin, 1131,* 1.

12 ELLING, W., 1966: *Flora, 156,* 155.

13 BAILEY, I. W., 1925: *Botanical Gazette, 80,* 93.

14 HUBER, B., GIERTZ-SIEBENLIST, V., 1969: *Sitzungberichten Österreichischen Akademie Wissenschaften* (Mathem-naturnwissen Kl.), *177,* 1 (Vienna).

15 BOWERS, N. A., 1960: *Tree-Ring Bulletin, 23,* 10.

16 SEBORG, R. M., INVERARITY, R. B., 1962: *Science, 136,* 649.

17 FLETCHER, J. M., HUGHES, J. F., 1970: *Bulletin, Faculty of Forestry* (University of British Columbia), *7,* 41.

18 FRITTS, H. C., 1971: *Quaternary Research, 1* (4), 419.

19 SCHOVE, D. J., 1955: *Weather, 10* (11), 368.

20 WHITELOCK, D., 1955: *English Historical Documents, 1,* 259.

21 SCHOVE, D. H., LOWTHER, A. W. G., 1957: *Medieval Archaeology, 1,* 78.

22 MATTHEWS, J. D., 1955: *Forestry, XXVIII* (2), 107.

23 HOLLSTEIN, E., 1968: *Künstchronik, 6,* 168.

24 HUBER, B., JAZEWITSCH, W. VON, 1956: *Tree-Ring Bulletin, 21,* 28.

25 HORN, W., 1970: in *Scientific Methods in Medieval Archaeology,* 80 (ed. R. Berger. Berkeley).

26 CHARLES, F. W. B., 1971: *TTJ Supplement,* 15.

27 BAUCH, J., 1968: *Künstchronik, 6,* 145.

28 BAUCH, J., 1970: *Mitteilungen Bundesforschungsanstalt für Först-und Holzwirtschaft* (Reinbeck), *77,* 43.

29 Private communication from Dr A. Lühning of the Schleswig-Holsteinisches Landesmuseum.

30 BECKER, VON B., GIERTZ-SIEBENLIST, V., 1970: *Flora, 159,* 310.

31 GIDDINGS, J. L., JR., 1941: *Tree-Ring Bulletin, 7* (part 2), 10. Also successive volumes of the same journal through to 1954.

32 BANNISTER, B., 1959: *Tree-Ring Dating of Archaeological Sites in the Chaco*

Canyon Region, New Mexico (MS, doctoral dissertation, University of Arizona).

33 OSWALT, W. H., 1949: *Tree-Ring Bulletin, 16* (part 1), 7.

34 OSWALT, W. H., 1951: *Tree-Ring Bulletin, 18* (part 1), 6.

35 HUBER, B., JAZEWITSCH, W. VON, 1958: *Flora, 146* (No. 3), 445.

36 BANNISTER, B., 1964: *VIIth International Congress of Anthropological and Ethnological Sciences* (Moscow).

37 KOHARA, J., 1958: *Kobunkazai no Kagaku, 15,* 12.

38 KOLCHIN, B. A., 1962: *Soviet Archaeology, 1,* 95.

39 BAUCH, J., ECKSTEIN, D., 1970: *Studies in Conservation, 15,* 45.

40 BAUCH, J., 1970: in *Mitteilungen Bundesforschungsanstalt für Forst-und Holzwirtschaft* (Reinbeck), 77, 43.

41 FLETCHER, J. M., TAPPER, M. C., WALKER, F. S., 1974: *Archaeometry, 16* (part I), 31.

42 TUDOR-CRAIG, P., 1973: *Richard III* (Exhibition, National Portrait Gallery, London).

43 FLETCHER, J. M., 1974: *Country Life* (March issue), 728.

44 ODDY, W. A., GEERSDAELE, P. C VAN, 1972: *Studies in Conservation, 17,* 30.

45 WADE-MARTINS, P., 1973: *Current Archaeology, 36,* 25.

46 FERGUSON, C. W., 1968: *Science, 159,* 839.

47 FERGUSON, C. W., 1970: in *Radiocarbon Variations and Absolute Chronology,* 237 (ed. I. U. Olsson. New York).

48 BERGER, R., 1970: in *The Impact of the Natural Sciences on Archaeology,* 23 (a joint symposium organized by The Royal Society and The British Academy). (Oxford.)

49 SUESS, H. E., 1970: in *Radiocarbon Variations and Absolute Chronology,* 303 (ed. I. U. Olsson. New York).

50 DAMON, P. E., LONG, A., WALLICK, E. I. 1972: *Proceedings 8th International Conference on Radiocarbon Dating, Lower Hutt City,* 45 (ed. T. A. Rafter, and T. Grant-Taylor. Royal Society, New Zealand).

51 RALPH, E. K., MICHAEL, H. N., HAN, M. C., 1973: *MASCA Newsletter, 9* (1), 1 (Applied Science Centre for Archaeology, The University Museum, University of Pennsylvania).

52 VRIES, HL. DE., 1958: *Koninklijke Nederlandse Akademie Wetensschappen, Proceedings, B6,* 94.

53 MILOJĆIĆ, V., 1961: *Germania, 39* (3), 434.

54 QUITTA, H., 1967: *Antiquity, XLI,* 263.

55 SACHS, A., 1970: in *The Impact of the Natural Sciences and Archaeology,* 19 (Oxford).

56 EDWARDS, I. E. S., 1970: in *The Impact of the Natural Sciences and Archaeology,* 11 (Oxford).

57 RENFREW, C., 1971: *Scientific American, 225,* 63.

58 RENFREW, C., CLARK, R. M., 1974: *Archaeometry, 16* (part I), 5.

59 MOOK, W. G., MUNAUT, A. V., WATERBOLK, H. T., 1972: *Proceedings, 8th International Conference on Radiocarbon Dating, Lower Hutt City,* 491 (ed. T. A. Rafter and T. Grant-Taylor. Royal Society, New Zealand).

60 FERGUSON, C. W., HUBER, B., SUESS, H. E., 1966: *Zeitschrift für Naturforschung,*
21a, 1173.

61 SUESS, H., STRAHM, C., 1970: *Antiquity, XLIV,* 91.

62 BAXTER, M. S., 1974: *Nature, 249,* 93 and following articles.

63 SMITH, A. G., BAILLIE, M. G. L., HILLAM, J., PILCHER, J. R., PEARSON, G. W.,
1972: *Proceedings, 8th International Conference on Radiocarbon Dating,*
Lower Hutt City, 92 (ed. T. A. Rafter and T. Grant-Taylor. Royal Society,
New Zealand).

3 RADIOCARBON DATING

1 LIBBY, W. F., 1946: *Physics Review, 69,* 671.

2a ENGELKEIMER, A. G., HAMMIL, W. H., INGHRAM, M. G., LIBBY, W. F., 1949:
Physical Review, 75, 1825 ($t_\frac{1}{2}$ = 5580 ± 45 yr).

 b JONES, W. M., 1949: *Physical Review, 76,* 885 ($t_\frac{1}{2}$ = 5589 ± 75 yr).

 c MILLER, W. W., BALLENTINE, R., BERNSTEIN, W., FRIEDMAN, L., NIER, A. O.,
EVANS, R. D., 1950: *Physical Review, 77,* 714. ($t_\frac{1}{2}$ = 5513 ± 165 yr).

3 BERGER, R., 1970: *Philosophical Transactions of the Royal Society* (London),
A269, 23.

4 LIBBY, W. F., 1955: *Radiocarbon Dating* (Chicago).

5 PARKER, R. A., 1950: *The Calendars of Ancient Egypt,* 63 (Chicago).

6 REVELLE, R., SUESS, H. E., 1957: *Tellus, 9,* 18.

7 SUESS, H. E., 1955: *Science, 122,* 415.

8 BAXTER, M. S., WALTON, A., 1970: *Proceedings at Royal Society* (London), *A318,*
213.

9 BAXTER, M. S., WALTON, A., 1971: *Proceedings at Royal Society* (London), *A321,*
105.

10 WALTON, A., BAXTER, M. S., CALLOW, W. J., BAKER, M. J., 1967: in *Radioactive*
Dating and Methods of Low-level Counting, 41 (Vienna: IAEA).

11 FEELY, H. W., 1960: *Science, 131,* 645.

12 WILLIAMS, P. M., OESCHGER, H., KINNEY, P., 1969: *Nature, 224,* 256.

13 L'ORANGE, R., ZIMEN, K. E., 1968: *Naturwissenschaften, 55,* 35.

14 TAUBER, H., 1967: *Radiocarbon, 9,* 246.

15 HARKNESS, D. D., WALTON, A., 1972: *Radiocarbon, 14,* 111.

16 WILLIAMS, P. M., MCGOWAN, J. A., STUIVER, M., 1970: *Nature, 227,* 375.

17 CRAIG, H., 1957: *Geochimica et cosmochimica Acta, 12,* 133. See also the detailed
discussion of fractionation effects by plants in: Troughton, J. H., 1972: in
Proceedings, 8th International Conference on Radiocarbon Dating, Lower Hutt
City, 421 (ed. T. A. Rafter, T. Grant-Taylor. Royal Society, New Zealand).

18 EMILIANI, C., 1966: *Journal of Geology, 74,* 109.

19 LIBBY, L. M., 1972: *Journal Geophysical Research, 77,* 4310.

20 UREY, H. C., 1947: *Journal of the Chemical Society,* 562.

21 FARMER, J. G., BAXTER, M. S., 1974: *Nature, 247,* 273.

22 SACKETT, W. M., ECKELMANN, W. R., BENDER, M. L., BÉ, A. W. H., 1965: *Science,*
148, 235.

23 ERICSON, J. E., BERGER, R., 1974: *Nature, 249,* 824.

24 CRAIG, H., 1961: *Radiocarbon, 3.*

25 FERGUSSON, G. J., 1955: *Nucleonics, 13*, 18.

26 BARKER, H., 1953: *Nature, 172*, 634.

27 BARKER, H., 1970: *Philosophical Transactions of the Royal Society* (London), *A269*, 37.

28 NOAKES, J. E., KIM, S. M., STIPP, J. J., 1965: *Proceedings, 6th International Conference on Radiocarbon and Tritium Dating*, 68.

29 LIBBY, W. F., 1970: *Philosophical Transactions of the Royal Society* (London), *A269*, 1.

30 DE VRIES, H. L., DE VRIES, A. E., HARRIS, A., 1958: *Science, 128*, 472.

31 EVIN, J., LONGIN, R., MARIEN, G., PACHIAUDI, CH., 1971: *Radiocarbon, 13*, 52.

32 LONGIN, R., 1971: *Nature, 230*, 241.

33 HUGHES, E. E., MANN, W. B., 1964: *International Journal of Applied Radiation Isotopes, 15*, 97.

34 CROWE, C., 1958: *Nature, 182*, 470.

35 MICHAEL, H. N., RALPH, E. K., 1972 in *Proceedings, 8th International Conference on Radiocarbon Dating, Lower Hutt City*, 28 (ed. T. A. Rafter, T. Grant-Taylor. Royal Society, New Zealand).

36 RALPH, E. K., MICHAEL, H. N., HAN, M. C., 1973: *MASCA Newsletter, 9*(1), 1 (Applied Science Centre for Archaeology, The University Museum, University of Pennsylvania).

37 RENFREW, C., 1971: *Scientific American, 225*, 63.

38 HOUTERMANS, J., 1966: *Zietschrift Physika, 193*, 1.

39 BUCHA, V., 1970: in *Radiocarbon Variations and Absolute Chronology*, 501 (*Nobel Symposium 12*, Uppsala, Sweden, ed. I. U. Olsson. Stockholm).

40 SUESS, H. E., 1970: in *Radiocarbon Variations and Absolute Chronology*, 595 (*Nobel Symposium 12*, Uppsala, Sweden, ed. I. U. Olsson. Stockholm).

41 SUESS, H. E., 1968: *Meteorological Monographs, 8*, 146.

42 LABEYRIE, J., DELIBRIAS, G., DUPLESSY, J. C., 1970: in *Radiocarbon Variations and Absolute Chronology*, 539. (*Nobel Symposium 12*, Uppsala, Sweden, ed. I. U. Olsson. Stockholm).

43 LINK, F., 1964: *Planetary and Space Sciences, 12*, 333.

44 LINGENFETTER, R. E., 1963: *Reviews in Geophysics, 1*, 35.

45 See, for example: CLARK, H. C., KENNETT, J. P., 1973: *Earth and Planetary Science Letters, 19*, 267 which reviews several earlier papers.

46 BARBETTI, M., MCELHINNY, M., 1972: *Nature, 239*, 327.

47 DANSGAARD, W., JOHNSEN, S. J., CLAUSEN, H. B., LANGWAY, C. C. JR., 1970: in *Radiocarbon Variations and Absolute Chronology*, 337. (*Nobel Symposium 12*, Uppsala, Sweden, ed. I. U. Olsson. Stockholm).

48 DANSGAARD, W., 1969: *Science, 166*, 499.

49 TAUBER, H., 1970: in *Radiocarbon Variations and Absolute Chronology*, 173 (*Nobel Symposium 12*, Uppsala, Sweden, ed. I. U. Olsson. Stockholm).

50 STUIVER, M., 1970: in *Radiocarbon Variations and Absolute Chronology*, 197. (*Nobel Symposium 12*, Uppsala, Sweden, ed. I. U. Olsson. Stockholm).

51 GODWIN, H., 1970: *Philosophical Transactions of the Royal Society* (London), *A269*, 57.

52 PIGGOTT, S., 1954: *The Neolithic cultures of the British Isles* (Cambridge).

53 GODWIN, H., WILLIS, E. H., 1964: *Radiocarbon, 6*, 116.

54 VOGEL, J. C., BEAUMONT, P. B., 1972: *Nature, 237*, 50.

55 BOSHIER, A., BEAUMONT, P., 1972: *Optima, 22*(1), 2.

56 British Museum (Natural History), *Catalogue of Fossil Hominids, Part II* (1971), 98.

57 OAKLEY, K. P., 1971: *Nature, 231*, 112.

58 ORR, P. C., BERGER, R., 1965: *Science, 148*, 1466.

59 SHAW, T., 1969: *Antiquity, XLIII*, 187.

60 WILLETT, F., 1971: *Journal of African History, XII*(3), 339. WILLETT, F., FLEMING, S. J., 1976: *Archaeometry, 18*, 141.

61 PROTSCH, R., BERGER, R., 1973: *Science, 179*, 235. TITE, M. S., 1972: *Methods of Physical Examination in Archaeology*, 183 (London).

62 PIGGOTT, S., 1965: *Ancient Europe*, 39 (Edinburgh).

63 See the contributions of W. HORN and R. BERGER in *Scientific Methods in Medieval Archaeology* (ed. R. Berger. California, 1970).

64 BERGER, R., EVANS, N., ABELL, J. M., RESNIK, M. A., 1972: *Nature, 235*, 160.

65 KEISCH, B., MILLER, H. H., 1972: *Nature, 240*, 491.

66 VAN DER MERWE, N. J., STUIVER, M., 1968: *Current Anthropology, 9*(1), 48.

67 FAGG, B. E. B., 1969: *World Archaeology, 1*(1), 41.

68 STUIVER, M., VAN DER MERWE, N. J., 1968: *Current Anthropology, 9*(1), 54.

69 VAN DER MERWE, N. J., SCULLY, R. T. K., 1971: *World Archaeology, 3*, 178.

70 COGHLAN, H. H., 1956: *Pitt Rivers Museum Occasional Papers on Technology, 8* (Oxford University).

71 THURBER, D. L., 1972: in *Calibration of Hominoid Evolution*, 1 (ed. W. W. Bishop, J. A. Miller. Edinburgh).

72 OLSON, E. A., BROECKER, W., 1958: *Transactions, New York Academy of Science, 20*, 593.

73 HO, T. Y., MARCUS, L. F., BERGER, R., 1969: *Science, 164*, 1051.

74 HOWARD, H., 1960: *Science, 131*, 712.

75 FLINT, R. F., 1971: *Glacial and Quaternary Geology*, 530 (New York).

76 HO, T. Y., 1965: *Proceedings of the National Academy of Sciences, 54*, 26.

77 BERGER, R., LIBBY, W. F., 1968: *Radiocarbon, 10* (2), 402.

78 LEMON, R. H. H., CHURCHER, C. S., 1961: *American Journal of Sciences, 259*, 410.

4 RADIOACTIVE DECAY TECHNIQUES

1 KRISHNASWAMY, S., LAL, D., MARTIN, J. M., MEYBECK, M., 1971: *Earth and Planetary Science Letters, 11*, 407.

2 KEISCH, B., FELLER, R. L., LEVINE, A. S., EDWARDS, R. R., 1967: *Science, 155*, 1238.

3 VOLCHOK, H. L., KULP, J. L., 1957: *Geochimica et cosmochimica Acta, 11*, 219.

4 BLACK, L. P., GALE, N. H., MOORBATH, S., PANKHURST, R. J., MCGREGOR, V. R., 1971: *Earth and Planetary Science Letters, 12*, 245.

5 DALRYMPLE, G. B., LANPHERE, M. A., 1969: *Potassium-argon dating: principles, techniques and applictions to geochronology* (San Francisco).

6 DEER, W. A., HOWIE, R. A., ZUSSMAN, J., 1966: *An Introduction to the Rock Forming Minerals*, Tables 18, 30 (London).

7 TURNER, G., 1971: *Earth and Planetary Science Letters, 10, 227.*

8 See, for example: FISHER, D. E., 1971: *Earth and Planetary Science Letters, 12, 321.*, FISHER, D. E., 1972: *Earth and Planetary Science Letters, 14, 255.*

9 RODDICK, J. C., FARRAR, E., 1971: *Earth and Planetary Science Letters, 12, 208.*

10 DALRYMPLE, G. B., 1969: *Earth and Planetary Science Letters, 6, 47.*

11 FITCH, F. J., 1972: in *Calibration of Hominoid Evolution*, 77 (ed. W. W. Bishop and J. A. Miller. Edinburgh).

12 GENTNER, W., LIPPOLT, H. J., 1969: in *Science in Archaeology*, 88 (ed. D. Brothwell and E. Higgs. London).

13 MANKINEN, E. A., DALRYMPLE, G. B., 1972: *Earth and Planetary Science Letters, 17, 89.*

14 KANEOKA, I., 1972: *Earth and Planetary Science Letters, 14, 216.*

15 PINSON, W. H., JR., 1960: *Annals of New York Academy of Sciences, 91, 221.*

16 EVERNDEN, J. F., CURTIS, G. H., 1965: *Current Anthropology, 6, 343.*

17 KIRSTEN, T., 1966: in *Potassium-argon dating* (ed. O. A. Schaeffer and J. Zahringer. New York).

18 GRASTY, R. L., MILLER, J. A., 1965: *Nature, 207, 1146.*

19 GRASTY, R. L., MILLER, J. A., 1966: *Earth and Planetary Science Letters, 1, 121.*

20 MITCHELL, J. G., 1972: *Earth and Planetary Science Letters, 14, 91.*

21 LANPHERE, M. A., DALRYMPLE, G. B., 1971: *Earth and Planetary Science Letters, 12, 359.*

22 EVERNDEN, J. F., SAVAGE, D. E., CURTIS, G. H., JAMES, G. T., 1964: *American Journal of Science, 262, 145.*

23 PILBEAM, D., 1972: in *Calibration of Hominoid Evolution*, 369 (ed. W. W. Bishop and J. A. Miller. Edinburgh).

24 WELLS, L. H., 1973: *Journal of Human Evolution, 2, 563.* See also, Pilbeam, D., 1969: *Nature, 224, 386* and Pilbeam, D., 1970: *Nature, 227, 747.*

25 ANDREWS, P., 1974: *Nature, 249, 188.*

26 BISHOP, W. W., MILLER, J. A., FITCH, F. J., 1969: *American Journal of Science, 267, 669*, and Andrews, P., 1971: *Nature, 249, 192.*

27 VAN COUVERING, J. A., MILLER, J. A., 1969: *Nature, 221, 628.*

28 BISHOP, W. W., 1972: in *Calibration of Hominoid Evolution*, 219 (ed. W. W. Bishop and J. A. Miller. Edinburgh).

29 HOWELL, F. C., 1972: in *Calibration of Hominoid Evolution*, 331 (ed. W. W. Bishop and J. A. Miller. Edinburgh).

30 PATTERSON, B., BEHRENSMEYER, A. K., SILL, W. A., 1970: *Nature, 226, 918.*

31 BROWN, F. H., 1972: in *Calibration of Hominoid Evolution*, 273 (ed. W. W. Bishop and J. A. Miller. Edinburgh).

32 FITCH, F. J., MILLER, J. A., 1970: *Nature, 226, 223.*

33 LEAKEY, R. E. F., 1973: *Nature, 242, 447.*

34 LEAKEY, R. E. F., 1971: *Nature, 231, 241.*

35 VONDRA, C. F., JOHNSON, G. D., BOWEN, B. E., BEHRENSMEYER, A. K., 1971: *Nature, 231*, 245.

36 MAGLIO, V. J., 1972: *Nature, 239*, 379.

37 BOWEN, B. E., VONDRA, C. F., 1973: *Nature, 242*, 391.

38 JOHNSON, G. D., 1974: *Nature, 247*, 520.

39 BROCK, A., ISAAC, G. LL., 1974: *Nature, 247*, 344.

40 LEAKEY, R. E. F., 1974: *Nature, 248*, 653.

41 LEAKEY, L. S. B., TOBIAS, P. V., NAPIER, J. R., 1964: *Nature, 202*, 5.

42 TOBIAS, P. V., 1967: *Olduvai Gorge, 2* (Cambridge).

43 LEAKEY, M. D., CLARKE, R. J., LEAKEY, L. S. B., 1971: *Nature, 232*, 308.

44 LEAKEY, M. D., 1967: in *Background to Evolution in Africa*, 417 (ed. W. W. Bishop and J. D. Clark. Chicago).

45 LEAKEY, M. D., 1971: *Nature, 232*, 380.

46 DAY, M. H., 1971: *Nature, 232*, 383.

47 ISAAC, G. LL., 1972: in *Calibration of Hominoid Evolution*, 381 (ed. W. W. Bishop and J. A. Miller. Edinburgh).

48 CURTIS, G. H., 1967: in *Background to Evolution in Africa*, 365 (ed. W. W. Bishop and J. D. Clark. Chicago).

49 ISAAC, G. LL., LEAKEY, R. E. F., BEHRENSMEYER, A. K., 1971: *Science, 173*, 1129.

50 LEAKEY, L. S. B., 1959: *Nature, 84*, 491.

51 ISAAC, G. LL., CURTIS, G. H., 1974: *Nature, 249*, 624.

52 COOKE, H. B. S., MAGLIO, V. J., 1972: in *Calibration of Hominoid Evolution*, 303 (ed. W. W. Bishop and J. A. Miller. Edinburgh).

53 BISHOP, W. W., CHAPMAN, G. R., HILL, A., MILLER, J. A., 1971: *Nature, 233*, 389.

54 See, for example, PILBEAM, D. R., SIMONS, E. L., 1971: *Nature, 229*, 408.

55 PILBEAM, D. R., 1970: *Nature, 225*, 516.

56 PILBEAM, D. R., 1969: *Nature, 222*, 1093.

57 MAGLIO, V. J., 1973: *Transactions of the American Philosophical Society, 63*(3), 1, see also BRAIN, C. K., ROBINSON, J. T., CLARKE, R. J., HOWELL, F. C., LEAKEY, M. D., 1970: *Nature, 225*, 1112.

58 COOKE, H. B. S., 1970: *Bulletin of Society for Vertebrate Paleontology, 90*, 2.

59 TOBIAS, P. V., 1973: *Nature, 246*, 79.

60 PARTRIDGE, T. C., 1973: *Nature, 246*, 75. See also the comments on this paper by DE SWARDT, A. M. J., 1974: *Nature, 250*, 683

61 JACOB, T., 1972: *Antiquity, XLVI*, 148.

62 JOLY, J. J., 1908: *Philosophical Magazine, 6*(16), 190.

63 SACKETT, W. M., POTRATZ, H. A., GOLDBERG, E. D., 1958: *Science, 128*, 204.

64 BERNAT, M., ALLEGRE, C. J., 1974: *Earth and Planetary Science Letters, 21*, 310.

65 KU, T. L., BROECKER, W. S., 1967: *Earth and Planetary Science Letters, 2*, 317.

66 ROSHOLT, J. N., EMILIANI, C., GEISS, J., KOCZY, F. F., WANGERSKY, P. J., 1961: *Journal of Geology, 69*, 162.

67 WOLLIN, G., ERICSON, D. B., RYAN, W. B. F., 1971: *Nature, 232*, 549.

68 WEHMILLER, J., HARE, P. E., 1971: *Science, 173*, 907.

69 BROECKER, W. S., BENDER, M. L., 1972: in *Calibration of Hominoid Evolution*, 19 (ed. W. W. Bishop and J. A. Miller. Edinburgh).

70 KU, T. L., 1968: *Journal of Geophysical Research, 73*, 2271.

71 SZABO, B. J., ROSHOLT, J. N., 1969: *Journal of Geophysical Research, 74*, 3253 and SZABO, B. J., VEDDER, J. G., 1971: *Earth and Planetary Science Letters, 11*, 283.

72 KAUFMAN, A., 1972: *Earth and Planetary Science Letters, 14*, 447.

73 GUSTAVSSON, J. E., HÖGBERG, S. A. C., 1972: *Boreas, 1*(4), 247.

74 HANSEN, R. O., BEGG, E. L., 1970: *Earth and Planetary Science Letters, 8*, 411.

75 HOWELL, F. C., COLE, G. H., KLEINDIENST, M. R., SZABO, B. J., OAKLEY, K. P., 1972: *Nature, 237*, 51.

76 LEAKEY, R. E. F., BUTZER, K. W., DAY, M. H., 1969: *Nature, 222*, 1137 and BUTZER, K. W., BROWN, F. H., THURBER, D. L., 1967: *Quaternaria, 11*, 15.

77 KLEIN, R. G., 1973: *Nature, 244*, 311.

78 KEISCH, B., FELLER, R. L., LEVINE, A. S., EDWARDS, R. R., 1967: *Science, 155*, 1238.

79 KEISCH, B., 1970: in *Application of Science in Examination of Works of Art*, 193 (ed. W. J. Young. Museum of Fine Arts, Boston).

80 ROUSSEAU, T., 1968: *Metropolitan Museum of Art Bulletin, XXVI*, 247.

5 THERMOLUMINESCENCE DATING

1 TURNER, R. C., RADLEY, J. M., MAYNEORD, W. V., 1958: *British Journal of Radiology, 31*, 397.

2 SUHR, N. H., INGAMELLS, C. D., 1966: *Analytical Chemistry, 36*, 730.

3 NORTHCLIFFE, L. C., SCHILLING, R. F., 1970: *Nuclear Data Tables, A7*, 233.

4 ICHIKAWA, Y., 1965: *Bulletin of the Institute for Chemical Research* (Kyoto University), *43*, 1.

5 FLEMING, S. J., 1966: *Archaeometry, 9*, 170.

6 AITKEN, M. J., TITE, M. S., FLEMING, S. J., 1967: in *Luminescence Dosimetry*, 490 (ed. F. H. Attix. USAEC, Washington D.C.).

7 ZIMMERMAN, D. W., 1972: *Radiation Effects, 14*, 81.

8 EVANS, R. D., 1955: *The Atomic Nucleus*, 511 (New York), and BELL, W. T., 1976: *Archaeometry, 18*(1), 107.

9 ALBURGER, D. E., 1951: *Physics Review, 81*, 888.

10 AITKEN, M. J., FLEMING, S. J., 1972: in *Topics in Radiation Dosimetry, Supplement 1*, 54 (ed. F. H. Attix. New York and London).

11 FLEMING, S. J., 1969: *The Acquisition of Radiothermoluminescence by Ancient Ceramics*, 253 (unpublished D.Phil. Thesis, Oxford University).

12 ZIMMERMAN, D. W., 1971: *Archaeometry, 13*, 29.

13 FLEMING, S. J., 1972: *Education in Chemistry, 9* (1), 9.

14 AITKEN, M. J., FLEMING, S. J., 1972: in *Topics in Radiation Dosimetry, Supplement 1*, 14 (ed. F. H. Attix. New York and London).

15 TITE, M. S., WAINE, J., 1962: *Archaeometry, 5*, 53.

16 FLEMING, S. J., 1968: in *Proceedings of the Second International Conference on Luminescence Dosimetry, Gatlinburg, Tennessee*, 266 (USAEC, Conf. 680920).

17 AITKEN, M. J., REID, J., TITE, M. S., FLEMING, S. J., 1967: in *Luminescence Dosimetry*, 236 (ed. F. H. Attix. USAEC, Washington, D.C.).

18 AITKEN, M. J., 1968: in *Proceedings of the Second International Conference on Luminescence Dosimetry, Gatlinburg, Tennessee*, 281 (USAEC, Conf. 680920).

19 FLEMING, S. J., 1970: *Archaeometry, 12*, 135.

20 BERGER, M. J., SELTZER, S. M., 1964: in *Studies in Penetration of Charged Particles in Matter*, 205 (ed. W. H. Barkas, M. J. Berger. *National Academy of Science/National Research Council Publiction, 1133*).

21 TANNER, A. B., 1964: in *The Natural Radiation Environment*, 161 (ed. J. A. S. Adams, W. M. Lowder. Chicago).

22 MEJDAHL, V., 1970: *Archaeometry, 12*, 149.

23 FLEMING, S. J., 1975: *Archaeometry, 17*(1), 122.

24 FLEMING, S. J., 1974: in *Application of Science to the Dating of Works of Art*, in press (ed. W. J. Young. Museum of Fine Arts, Boston).

25 WINTLE, A. G., 1973: *Nature, 245*, 143.

26 AITKEN, M. J., ALLDRED, J. C., 1972: *Archaeometry, 14*(2), 257.

27 FLEMING, S. J., STONEHAM, D. S., 1973: *Archaeometry, 15*(2), 229.

28 ZIMMERMAN, D. W., HUXTABLE, J., 1969: *Archaeometry, 11*, 105.

29 WINTLE, A. G., 1972: *Archaeometry, 14*(2), 257.

30 SAMPSON, E. H., FLEMING, S. J., BRAY, W., 1972: *Archaeometry, 14*(1), 119.

31 FAGG, B. E. B., FLEMING, S. J., 1970: *Archaeometry, 12*(1), 53.

32 SHAW, T., 1968: *Journal of the Historical Society of Nigeria, IV* (3), 453.

33 ZIMMERMAN, D. W., HUXTABLE, J., 1970: *Antiquity XLIV*, 304.

34 BRONSON, B., HAN, M., 1972: *Antiquity XLVI*, 322. For comments on this paper see LOOFS, H. H. E., 1974: *Antiquity, XLVIII*, 58.

35 GÖKSU, H. Y., FREMLIN, J. H., IRWIN, H. T., FRYXELL, R., 1974: *Science, 183*, 651.

36 ZIMMERMAN, D. W., HUXTABLE, J., 1971: *Archaeometry, 13*(1), 53.

37 AITKEN, M. J., MOOREY, P. R. S., UCKO, P. J., 1971: *Archaeometry, 13*(2), 89.

38 FLEMING, S. J., JUCKER, H., RIEDERER, J., 1971: *Archaeometry, 13*(2), 143.

39 FLEMING, S. J., 1974: *Archaeometry, 16*(1), 91.

40 FLEMING, S. J., 1973: *Medicine, Science and the Law, 14*(1), 11.

41 ZIMMERMAN, D. W., YUHAS, M. P., MEYERS, P., 1974: *Archaeometry, 16*(1), 19.

42 FLEMING, S. J., STONEHAM, D. S., 1973: *Archaeometry, 15*(2), 239.

6 FISSION TRACK DATING

1 SEGRÈ, E., 1952: *Physical Review, 86*, 21.

2 BONFIGLIOLI, G., FERRO, A., MOJONI, A., 1961: *Journal of Applied Physics, 32*, 2499.

3 BRILL, R. H., FLEISCHER, R. L., PRICE, P.B., WALKER, R. M., 1964: *Journal for Glass Studies, 6*, 151.

4 FLEISCHER, R. L., HART, H. R., 1970: *Report No.* 70-C-328, of The Research and Development Centre, General Electric, Schenectady, New York, *8*.

5 FLEISCHER, R. L., PRICE, P. B., WALKER, R. M., 1965: *Journal of Applied Physics, 36*, 3645.

6 UZGIRIS, E. E., FLEISCHER, R. L., 1971: *Nature, 234*, 28.

7 FLEISCHER, R. L., PRICE, P. B., 1963. *Journal of Applied Physics, 34*, 2903.

8 FLEISCHER, R. L., PRICE, P. B., SYMES, E. M., 1964: *American Mineralogist, 49*, 794.

9 PRICE, P. B., WALKER, R. M., 1963: *Journal of Geophysical Research, 68*, 4847.

10 NAESER, C. W., 1969: *Science, 165*, 388.

11 FLEISCHER, R. L., PRICE, P. B., 1964: *Geochemica et Cosmochimica Acta, 28*, 755 and 1705.

12 NAESER, C. W., 1967: *Geological Society of America, Bulletin, 78*, 1523.

13 DURRANI, S. A., KHAN, H. A., TAJ, M., RENFREW, C., 1971: *Nature, 233*, 242.

14 SIPPEL, R. F., GLOVER, E. D., 1964: *Science, 144*, 409.

15 NISHIMURA, S., 1971: *Nature, 230*, 242.

16 WATANABE, N., SUZUKI, M., 1969: *Nature, 222*, 1057.

17 NISHIMURA, S., SASAJIMA, S., TOKIEDA, K., 1973: *Proceedings, VI International Congress of Iranian Art and Archaeology*, in press.

18 AUMENTO, F., 1969: *Canadian Journal of Earth Sciences, 6*, 1431.

19 GENTNER, W., STORZER, D., WAGNER, G. A., 1969: *Naturwissenschaften, 56*, 255.

20 FLEISCHER, R. L., PRICE, P. B., 1964: *Journal of Geophysical Research, 69*, 331.

21 ZÄHRINGER, J., 1963: in *Radioactive Dating*, 283 (IAEC, Vienna).

22 MacDOUGALL, D., 1971: *Earth and Planetary Science Letters, 10*, 403.

23 FLEISCHER, R. L., PRICE, P. B., WALKER, R. M., LEAKEY, L. S. B., 1965: *Science, 148*, 72.

24 LEAKEY, L. S. B., EVERNDEN, J. F., CURTIS, G. H., 1961: *Nature, 191*, 478.

25 EDWARDS, G., MCLAUGHLIN, G., BARNES, V. E., 1964: *Geochimica et Cosmochimica Acta, 28*, 758.

26 FLEISCHER, R. L., PRICE, P. B., SYMES, E. M., MILLER, D. S., 1964: *Science, 143*, 349.

27 DAMON, P. E., ERICKSON, R. C., LIVINGSTON, D. E., 1962: *National Academy of Sciences, National Research Council, Publication 1075*, 113.

28 NAESER, C. W., FAUL, H., 1969: *Journal of Geophysical Research, 74*, 705.

29 HART, S. R., 1964: *Journal of Geology, 72*, 493.

30 FLEISCHER, R. L., PRICE, P. B., WALKER, R. M., 1964: *Journal of Geophysical Research, 69*, 4885.

31 ZARTMAN, R. E., 1963: *Nuclear Geophysics*, 43 (NAS-NRC, Publ. 1075, Washington, D.C.).

32 FAUL, H., STERN, T. W., THOMAS, H. H., ELMORE, P. B. D., 1963: *American Journal of Science, 261*, 1.

33 ALDRICH, L. T., WETHERILL, G. W., DAVIS, G. L. TILTON, G. R., 1958: *Transactions, American Geophysical Union, 39*, 1124.

34 GRAUERT, B., SEITZ, M. G., SOPTRAJANOVA, G., 1974: *Earth and Planetary Science Letters, 21*, 389.

35 NAESER, C. W., DODGE, F. C. W., 1969: *Geological Society of America Bulletin, 80*, 2201.

36 BERZINA, I. G., VOROB'EVA, I. V., GEGUZIN, YA. E., ZLOTOVA, I. M., 1967: *Soviet Physics, 11*, 1105.

37 STORZER, D., WAGNER, G. A., 1971: *Earth and Planetary Science Letters, 10*, 435.

38 BHANDARI, N., BHAT, S. G., LAL, D., RAJAGOPALAN, G., TAMHANE, A. S., VENKATAVARADAN, V. S., 1971: *Earth and Planetary Science Letters, 13*, 191.

39 LAKATOS, S., MILLER, D. S., 1972: *Earth and Planetary Science Letters, 14*, 128.

40 SEGRÈ, E., 1952: *Physical Review, 86*, 21.

41 PARKER, P., KURODA, P. K., 1956: *Journal of Chemical Physics, 25*, 5.

42 SPADAVECCHIA, A., HAHN, B., 1967: *Helvetia Physics Acta, 40*, 1063.

43 FLEISCHER, R. L., PRICE, P. B., 1964: *Physical Review, 133B*, 63.

44 KIRCHHEIMER, F., 1963: *Glastechnische Berichte, 36*, 488.

45 FLEISCHER, R. L., PRICE, P. B., WALKER, R. M., LEAKEY, L. S. B., 1965: *Nature, 205*, 1138.

46 DURRANI, S. A., KHAN, H. A., TAJ, M., RENFREW, C., 1971: *Nature, 233*, 242.

47 LEAKEY, L. S. B., 1959: *Nature, 84*, 491.

48 LEAKEY, L. S. B., LEAKEY, M. D., 1964: *Nature, 202*, 5.

49 LEAKEY, M. D., CLARKE, R. J., LEAKEY, L. S. B., 1971: *Nature, 232*, 308.

50 CURTIS, G. H., HAY, R. L., 1972: in *Calibration of Hominoid Evolution*, 289 (ed. W. W. Bishop and J. Miller. Scottish Academic Press for Wenner-Gren Foundation, New York).

51 LEAKEY, R. E. F., 1973: *Nature, 242*, 170.

52 FITCH, F. J., MILLER, J. A., 1974: in *Stratigraphy Palaeoecology and Evolution in the Lake Rudolf Basin*, in press (Wenner-Gren Foundation, New York).

53 HURFORD, A. J., 1974: *Nature, 249*, 236.

54 FITCH, F. J., MILLER, J. A., 1970: *Nature, 226*, 226.

7   OBSIDIAN HYDRATION RIM DATING

1 FRIEDMAN, I., 1968: *Science, 159*, 878 and Fig. 2.

2 MICHELS, J. W., 1971: in *Science and Archaeology*, 251 (ed. R. H. Brill. Cambridge, Mass.).

3 ROSS, C. S., SMITH, R. L., 1955: *American Mineralogist, 40*, 1071.

4 HURST, V. J., KELLY, A. R., 1961: *Science, 134*, 251.

5 GIBBON, D. L., MICHELS, J. W., 1967: *Proceedings, Electron Microscopy Society of America, 25*, 336.

6 LEE, R. R., LEICH, D. A., TOMBRELLO, T. A., ERICSON, J. E., FRIEDMAN, I., 1974: *Nature, 250*, 44.

7 FRIEDMAN, I., SMITH, R. L., 1960: *American Antiquity, 25*, 476.

8 FRIEDMAN, I., SMITH, R. L., LONG, W. D., 1966: *Geological Society of America, Bulletin, 77*, 323.

9 MEIGHAN, C. W., 1970: *Science, 170*, 99.

10 MEIGHAN, C. W., FOOTE, L. J., AIELLO, P. V., 1968: *Science, 160*, 1069. However there is strong criticism of this article expressed in: FRIEDMAN, I., EVANS, C., 1968: *Science, 162*, 813

11 MOULSON, A. J., ROBERTS, J. P., 1961: *Transactions, Faraday Society, 57*, 1208.

12 DRURY, T., ROBERTS, G. J., ROBERTS, J. P., 1962: in *Advances in Glass Technology*, 251 (New York).

13 SUZUKI, M., 1973: *Journal of the Faculty of Science* (University of Tokyo), section *V, IV* (3), 241.

14 See, for example: EMILIANI, C., 1966: *Journal of Geology*, *74*, 109, and EVANS, J. G., 1969: *World Archaeology*, 1(2), 170.

15 KATSUI, Y., KONDO, Y., 1965: *Japanese Journal of Geology and Geography*, *36*, 45.

16 Private communication from Professor J. W. Michels (February 1972).

17 CLARK, D. L., 1961: *Current Anthropology*, 2(2), 111.

18 Private communication from Dr D. L. Weide (August 21st, 1972).

19 CLARK, D. L., 1964: *Annual Report, Archaeological Survey*, UCLA, *6*, 143.

20 ERICSON, J. E., BERGER, R., 1974: in *Advances in Obsidian Glass Studies: Archaeological and Geochemical Perspectives* (ed. R. E. Taylor, New Jersey). Data was derived from a pre-print kindly supplied by the authors.

21 WEIDE, M. L., WEIDE, D. L., 1969: *Tebiwa*, *12*(2), 28.

22 SCHOLZE, H., 1966: in *Lectures on Glass Science and Technology* (New York).

23 HALLER, W., 1963: *Physics and Chemistry of Glasses*, *4*(6), 217.

24 ERICSON, J. E., MACKENZIE, J. D., BERGER, R., 1974: in *Advances in Obsidian Glass Studies: Archaeological and Geochemical Perspectives* (ed. R. E. Taylor, New Jersey). Pre-print kindly supplied by the authors.

25 ENDT, P. M., VAN DER LEUN, C., 1967: *Nuclear Physics*, *A105*, 1.

26 MORGENSTEIN, M., FELSHER, M., 1971: *Pacific Science*, *XXV* (3), 301.

27 EVANS, C., 1965: *Monograph of the School of American Research and the Kon-Tiki Museum*, *24*(2), Report 18 (ed. T. Heyerdahl, E. N. Ferdon Jr., Stockholm).

28 MICHELS, J. W., BEBRICH, C. A., 1971: in *Dating Techniques for the Archaeologist*, 164 (ed. H. N. Michael, E. K. Ralph. Cambridge, Mass.).

29 ERICSON, T. E., BERGER, R., 1974: *Nature*, *249*, 824.

30 SANDERS, W. T., MICHELS, J. W., 1969: *Occasional Papers in Anthropology*, 2 (The Pennsylvania State Univesity).

31 EVANS, C., MEGGARS, B. J., 1960: *American Antiquity*, *25*, 523.

32 Radiocarbon date, 10,450 ± 350 B.C. (GAK-949).

33 FLEMING, S. J., STONEHAM, D., 1973: *Archaeometry*, *15*(2), 229.

34 SUGIHARA, S., 1973: *Reports on Research by the Faculty of Literature*, Meiji University. *Archaeology*, *3*.

35 GREEN, R. C., 1962: *Newsletter, Dept. of Anthropology, University of Auckland*, *5*(1), 8.

36 AMBROSE, W., GREEN, R. C., 1962: *Newsletter, Dept. of Anthropology, University of Auckland*, *5*(4), 247.

37 AMBROSE, W., GREEN, R. C., 1972: *Nature*, *237*, 31.

38 SUZUKI, M., 1974: *Journal of the Faculty of Science* (University of Tokyo), section *V, IV* (4), 395.

8 ARCHAEOMAGNETIC DATING

1 STACEY, F. D., BANERJEE, S. K., 1974: *The Physical Principles of Rock Magnetism* (Amsterdam).

2 KAWAI, N., HIROOKA, K., TOKEIDA, K., 1967: *Earth and Planetary Science Letters*, *3*, 48.

3 HIDE, R., MALIN, S. C. R., 1970: *Nature, 225*, 605.

4 AITKEN, M. J., 1970: *Philosophical Transactions of The Royal Society* (London), *A269*, 77.

5 BULLARD, E. C., FREEDMAN, C., GELLMAN, H., NIXON, J., 1950: *Philosophical Transactions of The Royal Society* (London), *243*, 67.

6 AITKEN, M. J., WEAVER, G. H., 1964: *Journal of Geomagnetism and Geoelectricity, 17*, 393.

7 AITKEN, M. J., 1974: *Physics and Archaeology*, 52 (London).

8 WOLLIN, G., ERICSON, D. B., RYAN, W. B. F., 1971: *Earth and Planetary Science Letters, 12*, 175.

9 COX, A., 1969: *Science, 163*, 237.

10 BAUER, L. A., 1899: *Physical Review, 3*, 34.

11 WATANABE, N., 1971: *Journal of the Faculty of Science* (Univerity of Tokyo), section V, *IV* (1), 81.

12 HIROOKA, K., 1971: *Memoirs of the Faculty of Science* (Kyoto University), (Series of Geology and Mineralogy), *XXXVIII* (2), 167.

13 RUSAKOV, O. M., ZAGNIY, G. F., 1973: *Archaeometry, 15*(1), 153.

14 WEAVER, K. F., 1967: *National Geographic Magazine, 131*, 696.

15 THELLIER, E., 1966: *Nucleus, 7*, 1.

16 KAWAI, N., HIROOKA, K., NAKAJIMA, T., TOKIEDA, K., TOSI, M., 1972: *Nature, 236*, 223.

17 DU BOIS, R. L., 1969: *International Association of Geomagnetism and Aeronomy, General Scientific Assembly* (Madrid), *Paper III–19*.

18 BURLATSKAYA, S., NACHASOVA, J. E., NECHAEVA, T. B., RUSAKOV, O. M., ZAGNIY, G. F., TARHOV, E. N., TEHELIDZE, Z. A., 1970: *Archaeometry, 12*(1), 73.

19 KOVACHEVA–NOZHAROVA, M., 1968: *Comptes Rendus* (Bulgarian Academy of Sciences), *21*, 761.

20 BELSHÉ, J. C., COOK, K., COOK, R. M., 1963: *Annual Report of the British School at Athens, 58*, 8.

21 BARBETTI, M., MCELHINNY, M., 1972: *Nature, 239*, 327.

22 NÉEL, L., 1955: *Advances in Physics, 4*, 191.

23 DUNLOP, D. J., STACEY, F. D., GILLINGHAM, D. E. W., 1974: *Earth and Planetary Science Letters, 21*, 288. See also, SCHMIDT, V. A., 1973: *Earth and Planetary Science Letters, 20*, 440.

24 DUNLOP, D. J., 1973: *Journal of Geophysical Research, 78*, 7602.

25 HAROLD, M. R., 1960: *Archaeometry, 3*, 47.

26 TITE, M., 1972: *Methods of Physical Examination in Archaeology*, 143 and Plate 11 (London and New York).

27 AITKEN, M. J., HAWLEY, H. N., 1971: *Archaeometry, 13* (1), 83.

28 AITKEN, M. J., HAROLD, M. R., WEAVER, G. H., YOUNG, S. A., 1967: in *Methods of Palaeomagnetism*, 301 (ed. D. W. Collinson, K. M. Creer and S. K. Runcorn. Amsterdam).

29 FOSTER, J., 1966: *Earth and Planetary Science Letters, 1*, 463.

30 MOLYNEAUX, L., 1971: *Geophysics Journal of the Royal Astronomical Society*, *24*, 429.

31 THELLIER, E., THELLIER, O., 1951: *Comptes Rendus* (Academy of Sciences, Paris), *233*, 1476.

32 CROSSLEY, D. W., 1967: *Post-Medieval Archaeology*, *1*, 38.

33 HURST, J. G., 1966: *Archaeometry*, *9*,198.

34 WATANABE, N., 1972: *Andes 4, Excavations at Kotosh, Peru*, 315 (Tokyo).

35 BUCHA, V., 1971: in *Dating Techniques for the Archaeologist*, 57 (Cambridge, Mass.).

36 BUCHA, V., 1970: in *Radiocarbon Variations and Absolute Chronology*, 501 (ed. I. U. Olsson. Stockholm).

37 DU BOIS, R. L., WATANABE, N., 1965: *Journal of Geomagnetism and Geoelectricity*, *17*, 417.

38 NAGATA, T., ARAI, Y., MOMOSE, K., 1963: *Journal of Geophysical Research 68*, 5277: SASAJIMA, S., 1965: *Journal of Geomagnetism and Geoelectricity*, *17*, 413.

39 NAGATA, T., KOBAYASHI, K., SCHWARZ, E. J., 1965: *Journal of Geomagnetism and Geoelectricity*, *17*, 399.

40 KING, J. W., 1974: *Nature*, *247*, 131.

41 COX, A., 1969: *Science*, *163*, 237.

42 OPDYKE, N. D., 1972: *Reviews of Geophysics and Space Physics*, *10*, 213.

43 SMITH, J. D., FOSTER, J. H., 1969: *Science*, *163*, 565.

44 STACEY, F. D., 1969: *Physics of the Earth* (New York).

45 MCDOUGALL, I., WENSINK, H., 1966: *Earth and Planetary Science Letters*, *1*, 232.

46 GROMME, C. S., HAY, R. L., 1971: *Earth and Planetary Science Letters*, *10*, 179.

47 MCDOUGALL, I., WATKINS, N. D., 1973: *Earth and Planetary Science Letters*, *19*, 443.

48 MCDOUGALL, I., AZIZ-UR-RAHMAN, 1972: *Earth and Planetary Science Letters*, *14*, 367.

49 EMILIA, D. A., HEINRICHS, D. F., 1969: *Science*, *166*, 1267.

50 BONHOMMET, N., BABKINE, J., 1967: *Comptes Rendus* (Academy of Sciences, Paris), *264*, 92.
DENHAM, C. R., COX, A., 1971: *Earth and Planetary Science Letters*, *13*, 181.
CLARK, H. C., KENNETT, J. P., 1973: *Earth and Planetary Science Letters*, *19*, 267.

51 MÖRNER, N.-A., LANSER, J. P., HOSPERS, J., 1971: *Nature*, *234*, 173.

52 BARBETTI, M., MCELHINNY, M., 1972: *Nature*, *239*, 327.

53 RANSOM, C. J., 1973: *Nature*, *242*, 518.

54 OPDYKE, N. P., KENT, D. V., LOWRIE, W., 1973: *Earth and Planetary Science Letters*, *20*, 315.

55 HOUSE, M. R., 1971: in *Understanding the Earth*, 193 (Horsham, Sussex).

56 HAYS, J. D., 1971: *Geological Society of America Bulletin*, *82*, 2433.

57 HAYS, J. D., SAITO, J., OPDYKE, N. D., BURCKLE, L. H., 1969: *Geological Society of America Bulletin*, *80*, 1481.

58 OPDYKE, N. D., GLASS, B., HAYS, J. D., FOSTER, J., 1966: *Science*, *154*, 349.

59 UFFEN, R. J., 1963: *Nature*, *198*, 143.

60 HARRISON, C. G. A., 1968: *Nature, 217,* 46.

61 HAYS, J. D., OPDYKE, N. D., 1967: *Science, 158,* 1001.

62 CONLEY, C. C., 1969: in *Biological Effects of Magnetic Fields* (ed. M. F. Barnothy. New York).

63 GLASS, B. P., HEEZEN, B. C., 1967: *Scientific American, 217,* 32.

64 DURRANI, S. A., KHAN, H. A., 1971: *Nature, 232,* 320.

65 CHAPMAN, D. R., LARSON, K., 1963: *Journal of Geophysical Research, 68,* 4305.

66 KENNETT, J. P., WATKINS, N. D., 1970: *Nature, 227,* 930.

67 HEIRTZLER, J. R., 1968: *Scientific American, 219,* 60.
MANSHINA, L., SMYLIE, D. E., 1968: *Science, 161,* 1127.

68 FLECK, R. J., MERCER, J. H., NAIRN, A. E. M., PETERSON, D. N., 1972: *Earth and Planetary Science Letters, 16,* 15.

69 BROCK, A., ISAAC, G. LL., 1974: *Nature, 247,* 344.

9 CHEMICAL METHODS OF DATING BONE

1 MIDDLETON, J., 1844: *Proceedings of the Geological Society, 4,* 43.

2 OAKLEY, K. P., 1955: *British Museum (Natural History) Bulletin, Geology 2,* 254.

3 OAKLEY, K. P., 1963: in *The Scientist and Archaeology,* 111 (ed. E. Pyddocke. London).

4 BADA, J. L., 1972: *Earth and Planetary Science Letters, 15,* 223 and the references for section 9.2.

5 DEER, W. A., HOWIE, R. A., ZUSSMAN, J., 1966: *An Introduction to the Rock Forming Minerals,* 504 (London).

6 GLOVER, M. J., PHILLIPS, G. F., 1965: *Journal of Applied Chemistry, 15,* 570.

7 SINGER, L., ARMSTRONG, W. N., 1959: *Analytical Chemistry, 31,* 105.

8 HALL, R. J., 1960: *Analyst, 83,* 560.

9 TALVITIE, N. A., BREWER, L. W., 1960: *American Industrial Hygiene Association Journal, 21,* 287.

10 NIGGLI, E., OVERWEEL, C. J., VAN DER VLERK, I. M., 1953: *Proceedings of the Koninklijke Nederlandse Akademie van Wetensschappen, B56,* 538.

11 MEYERS, P., 1968: *Some Applications of Non-destructive Activation Analysis,* 63 (thesis, University of Amsterdam. Bronder-Offset, Rotterdam).

12 TANABE, G., WATANABE, N., 1968: *Journal of the Faculty of Science, University of Tokyo, Section V,* volume *111*(3), 199.

13 MCDONNELL, D., 1962: *Science, 136,* 241.

14 SEITZ, M. G., TAYLOR, R. E., 1974: *Archaeometry, 16*(2), 129.

15 JAWGROWSKI, Z., PENSKO, J., 1967: *Nature, 214,* 161.

16 SEITZ, M. G., 1972: *Carnegie Institution of Washington Yearbook, 71,* 557.

17 OAKLEY, K. P., GARDINER, E., 1968: *Revue Anthropologique,* 101.

18 OAKLEY, K. P., 1974: *Journal of Human Evolution, 3,* 257.

19 ASCENZI, A., 1969: in *Science in Archaeology,* 526 (ed. D. Brothwell and E. Higgs. London).

20 OAKLEY, K. P., 1969: in *Science in Archaeology,* 35 and Plates I and II (ed. D. Brothwell and E. Higgs. London).

21 ORTNER, D. J., VON ENDT, D. W., ROBINSON, M. S., 1972: *American Antiquity*, *37*, 514.

22 RANDALL, J. J., FRASER, R. D. B., JACKSON, S., MARTIN, A. V. W., NORTH, A. C. T., 1952: *Nature, 169*, 1029. See also Plate 1a of reference 20.

23 BUCK, D. D., 1975: *World Archaeology, 7*, 30.

24 RICHTER, K., 1958: *Eiszeitalter und Gegenwert, 9*, 18.

25 BERGER, R., PROTSCH, R., REYNOLDS, R., ROZAIRE, C., SACKETT, J. R., 1971: *Contributions of the University of California Archaeological Research Facility, 12*, 43.

26 HEINTZ, N., OAKLEY, K. P., 1969: *Comptes Rendus* (Academy of Sciences, Paris), *268*, 2873.

27 PARTRIDGE, T. C., 1973: *Nature, 246*, 75, and TOBIAS, P. V., 1973: *Nature, 246*, 79.

28 COON, C. S., 1966: *The Origin of Races* (New York).

29 OAKLEY, K. P., 1957: *Proceedings of the Third Pan-African Congress on Prehistory*, 76 (ed. J. D. Clark. London).

30 KLEIN, R. G., 1973: *Nature, 244*, 311.

31 OAKLEY, K. P., HOSKINS, C. R., 1950: *Nature, 165*, 336. See also the later analyses reported in WEINER, J. S., OAKLEY, K. P., LE GROS CLARK, W. E., 1953: *Bulletin of the British Museum (Natural History), Geology, 2*(3), 139.

32 OAKLEY, K. P., WEINER, J. S., 1955: *American Scientist, 43*(4), 573.

33 DE VRIES, H., OAKLEY, K. P., 1959: *Nature, 184*, 224.

34 *The Times*, 30 March, 1974.

35 PEACOCK, D. P. S., 1973: *Antiquity, XLVII*, 138.

36 HARE, P. E., 1969: in *Organic Geochemistry, Methods and Results*, 438 (ed. G. Eglinton and M. T. J. Murphy. New York).

37 VALLENTYNE, J. R., 1964: *Geochimica et Cosmochimica Acta, 28*, 157.

38 BADA, J. L., 1972: *Earth and Planetary Science Letters, 15*, 223.

39 BADA, J. L., PROTSCH, R., 1973: *Proceedings of the National Academy of Sciences, U.S.A., 70*, 1331.

40 BADA, J. L., KVENVOLDEN, K. A., PETERSON, E., 1973: *Nature, 245*, 308.

41 BADA, J. L., PROTSCH, R., SCHROEDER, R. A., 1973: *Nature, 241*, 394.

42 GLASS, B., ERICSON, D. B., HERZEN, B. C., OPDYKE, N. D., GLASS, J. A., 1967: *Nature, 216*, 437.

43 EMILIANI, C., SHACKLETON, N. J., 1974: *Science, 183*, 511.

44 WEST, R. G., 1968: *Pleistocene Geology and Biology*, 308 (London).

45 HENDY, C. H., WILSON, A. J., 1968: *Nature, 219*, 48.

46 BADA, J. L., SCHROEDER, R. A., PROTSCH, R., BERGER, R., 1974: *Proceedings of the National Academy of Sciences, U.S.A., 71*, 914.

47 HARE, P. E., 1974: *MASCA Newsletter, 10*(1), 4 (published by The University Museum, University of Pennsylvania).

48 SPADARO, J. A., BEEKER, R. O., BACHMAN, C. H., 1970: *Nature, 225*, 1134.

49 BRUMMEL, M., GERBECK, C. M., MONTGOMERY, R., 1969: *Analytical Biochemistry, 31*, 331.

50 FERDINAND, W., BARTLEY, W., COLE, W. J., BAILEY, E., 1973: *Comparative Biochemistry and Physiology, 44B*, 889.

51 BADA, J. L., 1972: *Journal of the American Chemical Society, 94*, 1371.

52 BADA, J. L., KVENVOLDEN, K. A., PETERSON, E., 1973: *Nature, 245*, 308.

53 BLAU, K., DARBRE, A., 1965: *Journal of Chromatography, 17*, 445.

54 BROWN, J. C., 1966: *CIBA Review, 3*, 1.

55 SIMON, K., 1956: *Naturwissenschaften, 43*, 353.

56 MACDONELL, H. L., 1961: *Nature, 189*, 302.

57 MCLAREN, L., MYERS, M. N., GIDDINGS, J. C., 1968: *Science, 159*, 197.

58 ORO, J., SKEWES, H. B., 1965: *Nature, 207*, 1042, HAMILTON, P. B., 1965: *Nature, 205*, 284.

10 NEW SCIENTIFIC TECHNIQUES APPLIED
    TO ART HISTORY

1 SIEVEKING, A., SIEVEKING, G., 1962: *The Caves of France and Northern Spain.*

2 EDWARDS, R., UCKO, P. J., 1973: *Nature, 246*, 274.

3 GETTENS, R. J., STOUT, G. L., 1966: *Painting Materials: A Short Encyclopaedia*, 149 (New York).

4 KUHN, H., 1970: in *Application of Science in Examination of Works of Art, II*, 199 (ed. W. J. Young. Museum of Fine Arts, Boston).

5 DE WILD, A. M., 1929: *The Scientific Examination of Pictures*, 28 (London).

6 TRILLICH, H., 1923: *Das Deutsche Farbenbuch, Parts I–III* (Munich).

7 ODDY, W. A., HUGHES, M. J., 1972: in *Royal Numismatic Society, Special Publication, 8*, 75 (ed. E. T. Hall, D. M. Metcalf. Oxford).

8 ODDY, W. A., BLACKSHAW, S. M., 1974: *Archaeometry, 16*(1), 81.

9 ORGAN, R. M., 1970: in *Application of Science in Examination of Works of Art, II*, 238 (ed. W. J. Young. Museum of Fine Arts, Boston).

10 COPE, L. H., 1972: in *Royal Numismatic Society, Special Publication 8*, 261 (ed. E. T. Hall, D. M. Metcalf. Oxford).

11 SCHUBINGER, A., WYTTENBACH, A., 1973: *Helvetica Chimica Acta, 56*(2), 648.

12 GETTENS, R. J., STOUT, G. L., 1966: *Painting Materials: A Short Encyclopaedia*, 174 (New York).

13 HOUTMAN, J. P. W., TURKSTRA, J., 1965: in *Radiochemical Methods of Analysis, Volume 1*, 85 (Conference Proceedings, Salzburg 1964. IAEA, Vienna).

14 HARLEY, R. D., 1970: *Artists' Pigments, 1600–1835*, 156 (London).

15 GETTENS, R. J., STOUT, G. L., 1966: *Painting Materials: A Short Encyclopaedia*, 176 (New York).

16 LUX, F., BRAUNSTEIN, L., 1966: *Zeitschrift für analytische Chemie, 221*, 235.

17 KUHN, H., 1966: *Studies in Conservation, 11*(4), 163.

18 LUX, F., BRAUNSTEIN, L., STRAUSS, R., 1968: in *Proceedings of the International Conference on Modern Trends in Activation Analysis*, 216 (US National Bureau of Standards).

19 See, for examples, PLESTERS, J., 1956: *Studies in Conservation, 2*, 110.

20 GETTENS, R. J., FELLER, R. L., CHASE, W. T., 1972: *Studies in Conservation, 17*(2), 45.

21 VAN SCHENDEL, A. F. E., 1972: *Studies in Conservation, 17*(2), 70.

22 Private communication from Professor J. P. W. Houtman.

23 KEISCH, B., 1972: *Secrets of the Past: Nuclear Energy Applications in Art and Archaeology*, 96 (in the *World of the Atom* series USAEC).

24 PLESTERS, J., 1966: *Studies in Conservation, 11*(2), 62.

25 KURZ, O., 1967: *Fakes*, 59 (New York).

26 KEISCH, B., 1970: *Studies in Conservation, 15*(1), 1.

27 SUTHERLAND, C. H. V., 1961: *Archaeometry, 4,* 56.

28 RAVETZ, A., 1963: *Archaeometry, 6,* 46.

29 ZUBER, K., 1965: in *Reports of Cekmece Nuclear Research Centre, Istanbul, 21.*

30 GORDUS, A. A., 1970: in *Application of Science in Examination of Works of Art, II*, 9 (ed. W. J. Young. Museum of Fine Arts, Boston).

31 KRAAY, C. M., EMELEUS, V. M., 1962: *The Composition of Greek Silver Coins Analysis by Neutron Activation* (Ashmolean Museum, Oxford).

32 DAS, H. A., ZONDERHUIS, J., 1964: *Archaeometry, 7,* 90.

33 MEYERS, P., 1972: in *Royal Numismatic Society, Special Publication 8*, 183 (ed. E. J. Hall, D. M. Metcalf. Oxford).

34 BACHARACH, J. L., GORDUS, A. A., 1968: *Journal of the Economic and Social History of the Orient, XI* (3), 298.

35 EMELEUS, V. M., 1958: *Archaeometry, 1,* 3.

36 See the Tables presented in *Royal Numismatic Society, Special Publication 8*, 96 (1972) (ed. E. T. Hall, D. M. Metcalf. Oxford).

37 MEYERS, P., 1968: *Some Applications of Non-Destructive Activation Analysis* (thesis, University of Amsterdam).
This work is summarized in MEYERS, P., 1969: *Archaeometry, 11,* 67.

38 WERNER, O., 1972: *Spektralanalytische und Metallurgische Untersuchungen and Indischen Bronzen*, 140 (Leiden).

39 BJORKMAN, J. K., 1973: *Meteoritics, 8,* 91 (*Publication 12* by the Centre for Meteorite Studies, Arizona State University).

40 GETTENS, R. J., CLARKE, R. S. JR., CHASE, W. T., 1971: *Occasional Papers, 4*(1) (Freer Gallery of Art, Washington D.C.).

41 CONDAMIN, J., PICON, M., 1972: in *Royal Numismatic Society, Special Publication 8*, 49 (ed. E. T. Hall, D. M. Metcalf. Oxford).

42 TYLECOTE, R. F., THOMSON, R., 1973: *Archaeometry, 15*(2), 193.

43 SCHWEIZER, F., 1972: in *Royal Numismatic Society, Special Publication 8*, 153 (ed. E. T. Hall, D. M. Metcalf. Oxford).

44 HALL, E. T., 1965: in *Application of Science in Works of Art, I*, 103 (ed. W. J. Young. Museum of Fine Arts, Boston).

45 HALL, E. T., SCHWEIZER, F., TOLLER, P. A., 1973: *Archaeometry, 15*(1), 53.

46 See, for example, ODDY, W. A., SCHWEIZER, 1972: in *Royal Numismatic Society, Special Publication 8*, 171 (ed. E. T. Hall, D. M. Metcalf. Oxford), and SCHWEIZER, F., FRIEDMAN, A. M., 1972: *Archaeometry, 14*(1), 103.

47 STOLOW, N., HANLAN, J. F., BOYER, R., 1969: *Studies in Conservation, 14*(4), 139.

48 CESAREO, R., FRAZZOLI, F. V., MANCINI, C., SCIUTI, S., MARABELLI, M., MORA, P., ROTONDI, P., URBANI, G., 1972: *Archaeometry, 14*(1), 65.

49 HAWKES, S. C., MERRICK, J. M., METCALF, D. M., 1966: *Archaeometry*, *9*, 98.

50 METCALF, D. M., MERRICK, J. M., HAMBLIN, L. K., 1968: *Minerva Numismatic Handbook*, *3*, 14.

51 METCALF, D. M., MERRICK, J. M., 1967: *Numismatic Chronicle*, 7, *VII*, 167 KENT, J. P. C., 1967: *Cunobelin XIII*, 24.

52 METCALF, D. M., SCHWEIZER, F., 1970: *Archaeometry*, *12*(2), 173.

53 BROWN, P. D. C., SCHWEIZER, F., 1973: *Archaeometry*, *15*(2), 175.

54 MCKERRELL, H., STEVENSON, R. B. K., 1972: in *Royal Numismatic Society, Special Publication 8*, 195 (ed. E. T. Hall, D. M. Metcalf. Oxford).

55 CESAREO, R., SCIUTI, S., MARABELLI, M., 1973: *Studies in Conservation*, *18*(2), 64.

56 GARNER, H., 1956: *Oriental Art*, *II*(2), 48.

57 YOUNG, S., 1956: *Oriental Art*, *II*(2), 43.

58 BANKS, M. S., MERRICK, J. M., 1967: *Archaeometry*, *10*, 101.

59 HARLEY, R. D., 1970: *Artists' Pigments*, *1600–1835*, 116 (London).

60 HARLEY, R. D., 1970: *Artists' Pigments*, *1600–1835*, 84 (London).

61 FARMER, J. G., BAXTER, M. S., 1974: *Nature*, *247*, 273.

62 DUCKWORTH, H. E., 1958: *Mass Spectroscopy* (Cambridge).

63 RUSSELL, R. D., FARQUHAR, R. M., 1960: *Lead Isotopes in Geology* (New York).

64 MCDOWALL, CH. A., 1963: *Mass Spectroscopy* (New York).

APPENDIX A

1 DE GEER, G., 1940: *Kungliga Svenska Vetenskapsakademiens Handlingar, Series 3*, *18*, 360.

2 FROMM, E., 1970: in *Radiocarbon Variations and Absolute Chronology*, 163 (ed. I. U. Olsson. Stockholm).

3 TAUBER, H., 1970: in *Radiocarbon Variations and Absolute Chronology*, 173 (ed. I. U. Olsson. Stockholm).

4 WENNER, C.-G., 1968: *Stockholm Contributions in Geology*, *XVIII*(3), 75.

5 ANTEVS, E., 1955: *Journal of Geology*, *63*, 495.

6 STUIVER, M., 1970: in *Radiocarbon Variations and Absolute Chronology*, 197 (ed. I. U. Olsson. Stockholm).

7 BRYANT, V. M., HOLZ, R. K., 1968: *Pennsylvania Geographer*, *6*, 11.

8 DIMBLEBY, G. W., 1969: in *Science in Archaeology*, 167 (ed. D. Brothwell and E. Higgs. London).

9 MARTIN, P. S., 1963: *The last 10,000 years: a fossil pollen record of the American Southwest* (Tucson, America).

10 INVERSEN, J., 1949: *Danmarks Geologiske Undersøgelse*, *4*(3), No. 6.

11 WEST, R. G., 1968: *Pleistocene geology and biology*, Table 24-C (London).

12 MERRYFIELD, D. L., 1974: *Nature*, *250*, 439.

13 TALLIS, J. H., SWITSUR, V. R., 1973: *Journal of Ecology*, *61*, 743.

14 MOORE, P. D., 1973: *Nature*, *241*, 350.

15 MITCHELL, G. F., 1956: *Proceedings, Royal Irish Academy*, *57B*, 185.

16 TURNER, J., 1965: *Proceedings, Royal Society*, *B161*, 343.

17 SCHÜTRUMPF, R., 1958: *Praehistorische Zeitschrift, 36,* 156.

18 SIMMONS, I. G., DIMBLEBY, G. W., 1974: *Journal of Archaeological Science, 1,* 291.

19 WATERBOLK, H. T., VAN ZEIST, W., 1967: *Palaeohistoria, 12,* 559.

20 DEEVEY, E. S., 1944: *American Antiquity, 10,* 135.

21 MARTIN, P. S., SCHOENWETTER, J., 1960: *Science, 132,* 33.
MEHRINGER, P. J., HAYNES, C. V., 1965: *American Antiquity, 30,* 168.

22 HILL, J. N., HEVLY, R. H., 1968: *American Antiquity, 33,* 200.

23 WRIGHT, H. E., 1972: in *The Minnesota Messenia Expedition: Reconstructing a Bronze Age Regional Environment,* 188 (ed. W. A. McDonald and G. R. Rapp. Minneapolis).

24 GREIG, J. R. A., TURNER, J., 1974: *Journal of Archaeological Science, 1,* 177.

25 EVANS, J. G., 1969: *World Archaeology, 1,* 170.

26 SPARKS, B. W., 1964: *Proceedings, Malacological Society of London, 36,* 7.

27 QUICK, H. E., 1952: *Proceedings, Malacological Society of London, 29,* 181.

28 LOZEK, V., 1965: *Geological Society of America, Special Paper 84,* 201.

29 KERNEY, M. P., 1968: *Symposium, Zoological Society of London, 22,* 273.

30 DIMBLEBY, G. W., EVANS, J. G., 1974: *Journal of Archaeological Science, 1,* 117.

31 EPSTEIN, S., BUCHSBAUM, R., LOWENSTAM, H. A., UREY, H. C., 1953: *Bulletin of the Geological Society of America, 64,* 1315.

32 UREY, H. C., LOWENSTAM, H. A., EPSTEIN, S., MCKINNEY, C. R., 1951: *Bulletin of the Geological Society of America, 62,* 399.

33 CRAIG, H., GORDON, L. I., 1965: in *Stable Isotopes in Oceanographic Studies and Palaeotemperatures* (ed. E. Tongiorgi).

34 DANSGAARD, W., TAUBER, H., 1970: in *Recent Developments in Mass Spectroscopy,* 640 (ed. K. Ogata, T. Hayakawa. Tokyo).
JACKSON, H. G., LIBBY, L. M., LUKENS, H. R., 1973: *Journal of Geophysical Research, 78,* 7145.
The neutron reactions involved are: (i) $^{16}O(n,p)^{16}N$ with a threshold neutron energy of 10·25 MeV, a cross-section, $\sigma_0 = 40$ millibarns, $t_{\frac{1}{2}} = 7\cdot15$ seconds and $E_\gamma = 6\cdot14$ MeV, and (ii) $^{18}O(n,\gamma)^{19}O$ formed by thermal neutron capture ($\sigma_0 = 0\cdot22$ millibarns), $t_{\frac{1}{2}} = 29\cdot0$ seconds and $E_\gamma = 1\cdot37$ MeV and 200 keV.

35 EMILIANI, C., SHACKLETON, N. J., 1974: *Science, 183,* 511.

36 SHACKLETON, N. J., WISEMAN, J. D. H., BUCKLEY, H. A., 1973: *Nature, 242,* 177.

37 DANSGAARD, W., 1964: *Tellus, 16,* 436.

38 DANSGAARD, W., JOHNSON, S. J., CLAUSEN, H. B., LANGWAY, C. C., 1970: in *Radiocarbon Variations and Absolute Chronology,* 337 (ed. I. U. Olsson. Stockholm).

39 WEST, R. G., 1956: *Philosophical Transactions, Royal Society, B239,* 265.
CASTELL, C. P., 1964: in *The Swanscombe Skull. A survey of research on a Pleistocene site* (ed. C. D. Ovey, Royal Anthropological Institute, Occasional Memoir 20).

APPENDIX B

1 FLEMING, S. J., 1973: *Archaeometry*, *15*(1), 13.

2 ZIMMERMAN, J., 1971: *Journal of Physical Chemistry: Solid State Physics*, *4*, 3265.

3 FLEMING, S. J., 1972: *Naturwissenschaften*, *59*, 145.

4 FLEMING, S. J., 1971: *Archaeometry*, *13*(1), 59.

   FLEMING, S. J., 1973: *Archaeometry*, *15*(1), 31.

   FLEMING, S. J., STONEHAM, D., 1973: *Archaeometry*, *15*(2), 239.

   FLEMING, S. J., 1975: *Authenticity in Art*, Chapter 3 (Institute of Physics, London).

5 FLEMING, S. J., 1971: in *Proceedings, The Third International Conference on Luminescence Dosimetry*, 895 (ed. V. Mejdahl. Danish AEC, Risø Report *249*).

Additional Bibliography

1 ASPECTS OF ARCHAEOLOGICAL CHRONOLOGY

BIDDLE, M., 1974: 'The archaeology of Winchester', *Scientific American 231*, 106.

BRYANT, V. M., JR., WILLIAMS-DEAN, G., 1975: 'The coprolites of man', *Scientific American 232*, 100.

CARLSON, J. B., 1975: 'Lodestone compass: Chinese or Olmec primacy?', *Science 189*, 153.

CLARK, J. D., STEMLER, A., 1975: 'Early domesticated sorghum from Central Sudan', *Nature 255*, 680.

CORVINUS, G., 1975: 'Palaeolithic remains at the Hadar in the Afar region', *Nature 256*, 468.

DANSGAARD, W., JOHNSEN, S. J., REEH, N., GUNDESTRUP, N., CLAUSEN, H. B., HAMMER, C. U., 1975: 'Climatic changes, Norsemen and modern man', *Nature 255*, 24.

DAVIS, K., 1974: 'The migrations of the human populations', *Scientific American 230*, 110.

HARLAND, W. B., 1975: 'The two geological time scales', *Nature 253*, 505.

KLEIN, R. G., 1974: 'Ice-age hunters of the Ukraine', *Scientific American 231*, 110.

LAUGHLIN, W. S., 1975: 'Aleuts: ecosystem, Holocene history and Siberian origin', *Science 189*, 507.

MEIGHAN, C. W., 1974: 'Prehistory of West Mexico', *Science 184*, 1254.

POTTER, P. E., 1974: 'Sedimentology: past, present and future', *Naturwissenschaften 61*, 461.

SIGLEO, A. C., 1975: 'Turquoise mine and artefact correlation for Snaketown site, Arizona', *Science 189*, 459.

2 DENDROCHRONOLOGY

FLETCHER, J. M., 1975: 'Relation of abnormal earlywood in oaks to dendrochronology and climatology', *Nature 254*, 506.

FREYER, H. D., WIESBERG, L., 1974: 'Dendrochronology and ^{13}C content in atmospheric CO_2', *Nature 252*, 690.

OTTAWAY, B., OTTAWAY, J. H., 1974: 'Irregularities in dendrochronological calibration', *Nature 250*, 407.

SCHIEGL, W. E., 1974: 'Climatic significance of deuterium abundance in growth rings of *Picea*', *Nature 251*, 582.

WILSON, A. T., GRINSTED, M. J., 1975: 'Palaeotemperatures from tree-rings and the D/H ratio of cellulose as a biochemical thermometer', *Nature 257*, 387.

3 RADIOCARBON DATING

BRAY, J. R., 1974: 'Volcanism and glaciation during the past 40 millennia', *Nature 252*, 679.

FAIRHALL, A. W., ERICKSON, J. L., 1975: 'Future impact of fossil CO_2 on the sea', *Nature 254*, 273.

LUEBBERS, R. A., 1975: 'Ancient boomerangs discovered in South Australia', *Nature 253*, 39.

OTTAWAY, B., 1973: 'Dispersion diagrams: a new approach to the display of carbon-14 dates', *Archaeometry 15*(1), 5.

POLACH, H. E., KRUEGER, H. A., 1972: in *Proceedings, 8th International Conference on Radiocarbon Dating, Lower Hutt City*, 718 (ed. T. A. Rafter, T. Grant-Taylor) (Royal Society, New Zealand).

STUIVER, M., WALDREN, W. H., 1975: '^{14}C carbonate dating and the age of post-Talayotic lime burials in Mallorca', *Nature 255*, 475.

4 RADIOACTIVE DECAY TECHNIQUES

BISHOP, W. W., PICKFORD, M. H. L., 1975: 'Geology, fauna and palaeoenvironments of the Ngorora Formation, Kenya Rift Valley', *Nature 254*, 185.

FITCH, F. J., FINDLATER, I. C., WATKINS, R. T., MILLER, J. A., 1974: 'Dating of the rock succession containing fossil hominids at East Rudolf, Kenya', *Nature 251*, 213.

FLEAGLE, J. G., SIMONS, E. L., CONROY, G. C., 1975: 'Ape limb bone from the Oligocene of Egypt', *Science 189*, 135.

HARRIS, J. M., WATKINS, R., 1974: 'New early Miocene vertebrate locality near Lake Rudolf, Kenya', *Nature 252*, 576.

HOWELL, F. C., WOOD, B. A., 1974: 'Early hominid ulna from the Omo Basin, Ethiopia', *Nature 249*, 174.

JONES, P. W., REX, D. C., 1974: 'New dates from the Ethiopian plateau volcanics', *Nature 252*, 218.

MELLOR, D. W., MUSSETT, A. E., 1975: 'Evidence for initial ^{36}Ar in volcanic rocks and some implications', *Earth and Planetary Science Letters 26*, 312.

PILBEAM, D., GOULD, S. J., 1974: 'Size and scaling in human evolution', *Science 186*, 892.

SHUKOLJUKOV, J., KIRSTEN, J., JESSBERGER, E. K., 1974: 'The Xe-Xe spectrum technique: a new dating method', *Earth and Planetary Science Letters 24*, 271.

SIEDNER, G., HOROWITZ, A., 1974: 'Radiometric ages of late Cainozoic basalts from northern Israel: chronostratigraphic implications', *Nature 250*, 23.

TEITSMA, A., CLARKE, W. B., ALLÈGRE, C. J., 1975: 'Spontaneous fission-neutron fission: a new technique for dating geological events', *Science 189*, 878.

VRBA, E. S., 1975: 'Some evidence of chronology and palaeoecology of Sterkfontein, Swartkrans and Kromdraai from fossil Bovidae', *Nature 254*, 301.

WENDORF, F., LAURY, R. L., ALBRITTON, C. C., SCHILD, R., HAYNES, C. V., DAMON,

P. E., SHAFIQULLAH, M., SCARBOROUGH, R., 1975: 'Dates for the Middle Stone Age of East Africa', *Science 187*, 740.

5   THERMOLUMINESCENCE DATING

AFORDAKOS, G., ALEXOPOULOS, K., MILIOTIS, D., 1974: 'Using artificial thermoluminescence to reassemble statues from fragments', *Nature 250*, 47.

FLEMING, S. J., 1975: 'Supralinearity corrections in fine-grain thermoluminescence dating: a re-appraisal', *Archaeometry 17*(1), 122.

WHITTLE, E. H., 1975: 'Thermoluminescent dating of Egyptian Predynastic pottery from Hemamieh and Qurna-Tarif', *Archaeometry 17*(1), 119.

WHITTLE, E. H., ARNAUD, J. M., 1975: 'Thermoluminescent dating of Neolithic and Chalcolithic pottery from sites in central Portugal', *Archaeometry 17*(1), 5.

6   FISSION TRACK DATING

BIGAZZI, G., BONADONNA, F., 1973: 'Fission track dating of the obsidian of Lipari Island (Italy)', *Nature 242*, 322.

DAVISON, C. C., 1974: 'NaOH etch of fission tracks in a soda-lime-silica glass', *Nature 247*, 103.

MACDOUGALL, D., PRICE, P. B., 1974: 'Attempt to date early South African hominids by using fission tracks in calcite', *Science 185*, 943.

MANTOVANI, M. S. M., 1974: 'Variations of characteristics of fission tracks in muscovite by thermal effects', *Earth and Planetary Science Letters 24*, 311.

MAYBURY, P. C., LIBBY, W. F., 1975: 'Non-etching optical detection of fission tracks using Teflon', *Nature 254*, 209.

REIMER, G. M., CARPENTER, B. S., 1974: 'Thorium determination in glasses using fission track technique', *Nature 247*, 101.

SEWARD, D., 1974: 'Age of New Zealand substages by fission track dating of glass sherds from tephra horizons', *Earth and Planetary Science Letters 24*, 242.

8   ARCHAEOMAGNETIC DATING

BINGHAM, D. K., EVANS, M. E., 1975: 'Precambrian geomagnetic field reversal', *Nature 253*, 332.

CHAPPEL, J., 1975: 'On possible relationships between Upper Quaternary glaciations, geomagnetism and vulcanism', *Earth and Planetary Science Letters, 26*, 370.

CREER, K. M., KOPPER, J. S., 1974: 'Palaeomagnetic dating of cave paintings in Tito Bustillo Cave, Asturias, Spain', *Science 186*, 348.

FREED, W. K., HEALY, N., 1974: 'Excursions of the Pleistocene geomagnetic field recorded in Gulf of Mexico sediments', *Earth and Planetary Science Letters 24*, 99.

HARRISON, C. G. A., PROSPERO, J. M., 1974: 'Reversals of the Earth's magnetic field and climatic changes', *Nature 250*, 563.

MORNER, N. A., LANSER, J. P., 1974: 'Gothenburg magnetic "flip"', *Nature 251*, 408.

SAWYER, J. S., 1974: 'Geomagnetism and the tropospheric circulation', *Nature* *252*, 368.

SKINNER, N. J., BHATT, N. V., HASTENRATH, S., 1974: 'Negative magnetic anomaly associated with Mount Kenya', *Nature 250*, 561.

TANGUY, J. C., 1975: 'Intensity of the geomagnetic field from recent Italian lavas using a new palaeointensity method', *Earth and Planetary Science Letters 27*, 314.

WATKINS, N. D., KESTER, D. R., KENNETT, J. P., 1974: 'Palaeomagnetism of the type Pliocene/Pleistocene boundary section at Santa Maria de Catanzaro, Italy and the problem of post-depositional precipitation of magnetic materials', *Earth and Planetary Science Letters 24*, 113.

9 CHEMICAL METHODS OF DATING BONE

BADA, J. L., DEEMS, L., 1975: 'Accuracy of dates beyond the ^{14}C dating limit using the aspartic acid racemisation reaction', *Nature 255*, 218.

KING, K., JR., 1974: 'Preserved amino acids from silicified protein in fossil Radiolaria', *Nature 252*, 690.

LEE, C., BADA, J. L., PETERSON, E., 1976: 'Amino acids in modern and fossil woods', *Nature 259*, 183.

OAKLEY, K. P., 1975: 'A re-consideration of the date of the Kanam Jaw', *Journal of Archaeological Science 2*, 151.

SZABO, B. J., COLLINS, D., 1975: 'Age of fossil bones from British interglacial sites', *Nature 255*, 680.

10 SCIENTIFIC TECHNIQUES APPLIED TO ART HISTORY

FLEMING, S. J., 1975: *Authenticity in Art: The Scientific Detection of Forgery* (The Institute of Physics, Bristol and London).

FLORKAWSKI, T., STOS, Z., 1975: 'Non-destructive radioisotope X-ray fluorescence analysis of old silver coins', *Archaeometry 17*(2), 165.

HEDGES, R. E. M., 1975: 'Mossbauer spectroscopy of Chinese glazed ceramics', *Nature 254*, 501.

HEDGES, R. E. M., MOOREY, P. R. S., 1975: 'Pre-Islamic ceramic glazes at Kish and Nineveh in Iraq', *Archaeometry 17*(1), 25.

LONGWORTH, G., WARREN, S. E., 1975: 'Mössbauer spectroscopy and Greek "Etruscan pottery",' *Nature 255*, 625.

MANFRA, L., MASI, U., TURI, B., 1975: 'Carbon and oxygen isotope ratios of marbles from some ancient quarries of western Anatolia and their archaeological significance', *Archaeometry 17*(2), 215.

PLESTERS-BROMMELLE, J., BROMMELLE, N. S., 1974: 'Science and works of art', *Nature 250*, 767.

APPENDICES

BARNARD, L. A., MACINTYRE, I. G., PIERCE, J. W., 1974: 'Possible environmental index in tropical reef corals', *Nature 252*, 219.

BISHOP, M. J., 1975: 'Earliest record of man's presence in Britain', *Nature 253*, 95.

BRADLEY, R., KEITH-LUCAS, M., 1975: 'Excavation and pollen analysis on a Bell Barrow at Ascot, Berkshire', *Journal of Archaeological Science 2*, 95.

BRYSON, R. A., 1974: 'A perspective on climate change', *Science 184*, 753.

BYRNE, R., MCANDREWS, J. H., 1975: 'Pre-Columbian purslane (*Portulaca oleracea* L.) in the New World', *Nature 253*, 726.

CERLING, T. E., BIGGS, D. L., VONDRA, C. F., 1975: 'Use of oxygen isotope ratios in correlation of tuffs, East Rudolf Basin, northern Kenya', *Earth and Planetary Science Letters 25*, 291.

DIMBLEBY, G. W., 1975: 'Archaeological evidence of environmental change', *Nature 256*, 265.

FRITZ, P., POPLAWSKI, S., 1974: '^{18}O and ^{13}C in the shells of freshwater molluscs and their environments', *Earth and Planetary Science Letters 24*, 91.

HSÜ, K. J., 1974: 'The Miocene dessication of the Mediterranean and its climatic and zoogeographical implications', *Naturwissenschaften 61*, 137.

KENWARD, H. K., 1975: 'The biological and archaeological implications of the beetle *Aglenus brunneus* (Gyllenhal) in ancient faunas', *Journal of Archaeological Science 2*, 63.

KENWARD, H. K., 1975: 'Pitfalls in the environmental interpretation of insect death assemblages', *Journal of Archaeological Science 2*, 85.

KERSHAW, A. P., 1974: 'A long continuous pollen sequence from north-eastern Australia', *Nature 251*, 222.

MARGOLIS, S. V., KROOPNICK, P. M., GOODNEY, D. E., DUDLEY, W. C., MAHONEY, M. E., 1975: 'Oxygen and carbon isotopes from calcareous nannofossils as palaeoceanographic indicators', *Science 189*, 555.

MERRYFIELD, D. L., MOORE, P. D., 1974: 'Prehistoric human activity and blanket peat initiation of Exmoor', *Nature 250*, 439.

MOORE, P. D., 1975: 'Origin of blanket mires', *Nature 256*, 267.

SRINIVASAN, M. S., KENNETT, J. P., 1974: 'Secondary calcification of the planktonic foraminifer *Neogloboquadrina pachyderma* as a climatic index', *Science 186*, 630.

THOMPSON, P., SCHWARCZ, H. P., FORD, D. C., 1974: 'Continental Pleistocene climatic variations from speleotherm age and isotope data', *Science 184*, 893.

WEBER, J. R., DIENES, P., WHITE, E. W., WEBER, P. H., 1975: 'Seasonal high and low density bands in reef coral skeletons', *Nature 255*, 697.

Index